The Ski Guide Manual

Advanced Techniques for the Backcountry

Rob Coppolillo

Foreword by Colin Zacharias,
with contributions by Colin Zacharias, Dr. Karl Birkeland, Sheldon Kerr, Marc Chauvin, Tom Murphy, Joe Stock, Ken Wylie, and more

Photography by
Matt Kennedy and Mahting Putelis

FALCONGUIDES®

GUILFORD, CONNECTICUT

FALCONGUIDES®

An imprint of The Rowman & Littlefield Publishing Group, Inc.
4501 Forbes Blvd., Ste. 200
Lanham, MD 20706
www.rowman.com

Falcon and FalconGuides are registered trademarks and Make Adventure Your Story is a trademark of The Rowman & Littlefield Publishing Group, Inc.

Distributed by NATIONAL BOOK NETWORK

Photos by Rob Coppolillo, Matt Kennedy, and Mahting Putelis

British Library Cataloguing in Publication Information Available

Library of Congress Cataloging-in-Publication Data

Names: Coppolillo, Rob, author.
Title: The ski guide manual / Rob Coppolillo ; Foreword by Colin Zacharias.
Description: Lanham, MD : FalconGuides, [2020] | Summary: "This updated, expert ski guide provides top-of-the-line insight for backcountry/off-piste skiers and guides. The Ski Guide Manual presents wisdom earned through decades of experience guiding and the result is a successful system of travel and risk management in the winter environment. The collective work of thousands of mountain guides has proven how to have the most fun and find the best snow, all while reducing risk of avalanche, cold, crevasses, and optimizing group dynamics"— Provided by publisher.
Identifiers: LCCN 2020010266 | ISBN 9781493043422 (trade paperback) | ISBN 9781493043439 (epub)
Subjects: LCSH: Skis and skiing—Handbooks, manuals, etc.
Classification: LCC GV854 .C5934 2020 | DDC 796.93—dc23
LC record available at https://lccn.loc.gov/2020010266

∞™ The paper used in this publication meets the minimum requirements of American National Standard for Information Sciences—Permanence of Paper for Printed Library Materials, ANSI/NISO Z39.48-1992.

Contents

Foreword

The first time I met Rob Coppolillo he was on a pair of skis. He'd come to Canada as an ambitious recreational skier and a writer. Years later, after he'd passed his guiding exams, we worked together, and these days I also know him as the successful coauthor of *The Mountain Guide Manual*. It makes sense to me that Rob would follow this trend with the completion of *The Ski Guide Manual*.

Rob is a good communicator. He was born with the motivation to reach out to every die-hard backcountry tourer and splitboarder (and rando racer!) who is keen to play in the high-stakes winter environment. As a guide and educator, Rob's mission has always been to help anyone enthusiastic make better decisions through the practiced mentorship of a ski guide.

A backcountry apprenticeship is a great way to gain knowledge, but it can be hard to attain. There is not that much of Rob Coppolillo in this world to go around. And we all recognize the tremendous benefit to vicarious learning. A manual is a great place for the neophyte to read and learn—and for the experienced to review and discuss. And why not? These are the lessons of your instructor in the comfort of your home.

The Ski Guide's chapters follow the schedule of a guiding day, starting with the trip plan and ending with the daily debrief. The topics present the guide's perspective on assessing hazard and evaluating risk, and help you choose the right tool and technique to manage the risk. It's basically a ski guide's primer.

As guides we mostly work alone and in small teams. We recognize the value of varied experience and individual perspective. Rob did his time as a mindful observer and apprentice in the guide training and avalanche education industries in Canada, Europe, and the United States. Consequently, Rob has a wide range of industry contacts, and the book's pages reflect this. Each chapter is full of experiences and stories from guides, forecasters, educators, and buddies.

There are fun and insightful quotes from his influencers, such as Doug Coombs, Marc Chauvin, Bruce Kay, and Dale Atkins. Rob is careful to include the expert's perspective.

Brief sidebars include the thoughts of Dr. Karl Birkeland, "The ECT in Context"; Ken Wylie, "Another Take on Intuition"; Joe

Stock's "Checklists Are Cool"; and Tom Murphy with his thoughts on AIARE's decision-making support tools. Several others have provided wise words on subjects that challenge our ability to learn or communicate, including Sheldon Kerr's article outlining a dozen key strategies to better team communication in a high-risk backcountry ski environment. Rob's longtime friend and Chamonix guide Dylan Taylor contributed to the "Technical Solutions" chapter; La Grave resident and IFMGA pal Joey Vallone contributed to the steep-ski techniques section.

Setting out to write a tome such as this, Coppolillo recognizes that you gotta know how before you can do. And while a book doesn't do it for everyone, one can at least reflect on the words of Dr. Birkeland. When describing the value of a snowpack test, he suggests that it's not only the results of the test that provide value but also that "doing the test will help you to slow down, cut through the distractions of the day, think about the snowpack, and connect and discuss the conditions with your partner(s)."

The same can be applied to this book. Slow down and read it. Cut through the distractions of the day and think about how you managed that terrain last time. And ask yourself whether a few of Rob's tools of the trade may have come in handy.

Colin Zacharias
Tofino, British Columbia, Canada
December 2019

Colin Zacharias EMILY GRADY

Colin Zacharias is a certified international mountain and ski guide (IFMGA) with several decades of experience in the avalanche industry. Like many winter professionals, Colin started with a ski area avalanche control operation, moved on to become the avalanche forecaster for the 1988 Winter Olympics, then spent a decade as a heliski guide. Colin is a former technical director for the Association of Canadian Mountain Guides (ACMG) certificate program at Thompson Rivers University. He has been the technical advisor for the American Institute for Avalanche Research and Education (AIARE) since 2004 and is a professional member of the ACMG, the Canadian Avalanche Association, and the American Avalanche Association. Based in a small town on the west coast of Vancouver Island with his wife, Colin is also an avid surfer.

For my mountain family, Marc Chauvin, Mikey Arnold, Tim Brown, Tom Wolfe, Colin Zacharias, Lee McNeely, Paul Rogers, Michelle Heerschop, Joey Thompson, Mahting Putelis, Matt Kennedy, Connie Sciolino, King Grant, Luca Boscardin, Tracy Martin, Joe Vallone—thanks to all of you for the help and friendship.

And for my given family, Cathy, Pete, Henry, Nina, Zio Rinaldo, Rebel, Luca, and Dommy—I lucked out with you all.

Introduction

Education: the path from cocky ignorance to miserable uncertainty.

—Mark Twain

Mastery over misery is no mystery. Time helps but much depends on what one does with time.

—Vincent Okay Nwachukwu

In nearly all cases, one single element lays the foundation for all our screw ups: we think we know what we are doing in an environment where "knowing" borders on the impossible.

—Bruce Kay

Welcome to the lifelong journey, our quixotic quest to attain the unattainable, perfect the imperfectible, and know the unknowable—the nonlinear, unmapped, and maddening road to becoming a True Mountain Jedi. Only a handful of practitioners achieve it, and they'd be the last ones to adopt this goofy moniker. But here it is, a few pages of distilled wisdom, yours for the taking on your path.

What follows is a wise and evidence-driven system for sliding into the backcountry with your friends and guests. It's a method for doing it more safely. It will make you smarter and more resourceful in the backcountry. And it's not mine. I stole almost everything you're about to read. Here is *The Ski Guide Manual*, an unabashed heist of ski and splitboard mastery from some of the best in the backcountry. I wrote it with an attitude of humility and daily attacks of imposter syndrome.

Imagine calling up Dr. Karl Birkeland, one of the developers of the Extended Column Test, and declaring that you're writing a chapter on snowpack. Or Mike Hattrup and telling him you're outlining a chapter on steep skiing. I knew from the get-go that without some outside help, I was unprepared to tell anybody else how to approach riding in the backcountry. I needed some coattails to ride.

Some days the uncertainty improves to manageable, rather than miserable. Fantastic corn skiing above the Barents Sea during a ski-and-sail mission in the Svalbard archipelago.
ROB COPPOLILLO

So, this is some stolen, outlaw, how-to manual on becoming a True Mountain Jedi? Now we're talking! Maybe, but I want to be clear: This is but one method for the journey. It might not even be the best method, but it's the best I know of and that's because, as I said, I poached the best ideas from a few of the best guides, academics, educators, and practitioners. The following wisdom is theirs; the errors, clumsy explanations, and out-of-focus photos are mine. Apologies in advance.

But herein you'll find some techniques, strategies, and methods drawing upon decades of research and practice. I completed my guide training with the American Mountain Guides Association (AMGA) in 2014 and studied under a few Canadians too. I've since had the good fortune to work alongside many Americans, Canadians north of the border, and a few Euros as well. My bias definitely runs toward "North American" methods, though, if I can differentiate between guiding approaches.

The System

Taken in total, from Trip Planning through the Debrief, I view this book as a system, method, or even an algorithm—a methodical, powerful app for gathering, interpreting, applying, error correcting, and implementing information, with the simple goal of enjoying a safer day in the mountains.

Much like this title's sister publication, *The Mountain Guide Manual (MGM)*, I draw on guiding techniques to help advanced recreationists improve their game and less-experienced mountain guides like me to learn the trade. Some of the techniques might seem aggressive or even risky for recreationists. Remember, humility and skepticism—if it doesn't feel right for you, seek some in-the-field instruction for context, practice in a non-consequential setting, or just ignore it. Again, this is but one system. It's certainly not *the* system.

Who's Reading This Thing, Anyway?

As you wade into the material, keep in mind that much like the *MGM*, this book builds upon knowledge you should already have digested and put into practice. A Level 1 avalanche course, several years' backcountry experience, crevasse-rescue knowledge, and probably some ample reading will have prepared you for tackling the information herein.

A preparatory reading list might include *Backcountry Skiing* by Martin Volken, Margaret Wheeler, and Scott Schell; Jimmy Oden's *Freeskiing*; and Bruce Tremper's *Staying Alive in Avalanche Terrain*. I further assume you're familiar with the most common snowpack tests and how to perform them.

If you find yourself a bit behind, no stress—focus on filling in some blanks with reading, and ask a more experienced buddy to help you over the coming weeks. Consider another avalanche course and inquire about your instructor's credentials and experience. Consider hiring a guide, especially for a hut-based avalanche course in a different snowpack. Strategies like these will jump-start your learning.

Systems Thinking

In researching and outlining the book, I happened upon Dr. Sydney Dekker's *The Field Guide for Understanding Human Error*. This title greatly influenced my understanding of debriefing and analyzing our near misses.

Dekker draws upon his expertise as a pilot and psychologist to, among many things, analyze accidents. He proposes in his *Field Guide* to view human error in a more panoramic, holistic way. Instead of identifying one person's error at a critical moment, he proposes taking a longer view and investigating why a more-than-likely smart, well-meaning person made a "dumb mistake." Rather than place blame with the individual, he urges investigators to connect the myriad subtle dots—the process—that led to an error or accident. One that might seem ridiculous in our oh-so-confident 20/20 hindsight.

Dekker's approach recalibrated my reading of accident analyses and, as I said, on debriefing too. I make mistakes every day I leave the trailhead; happily, most of them are relatively non-consequential, but nonetheless they're mistakes. Trying to view my, my guests', and my team's decisions and actions with more of Dekker's systems approach has not only helped me improve but also clarified some of the thinking here. Keep this approach in mind as you turn the pages—in particular, during the "Debrief" chapter.

Look at your backcountry days—from seasonal prep in the fall to the coolest tour you pull off all season—as a system or process or algorithm, start to finish. Evaluate your mistakes in that context. Showed up at the trailhead with dead batteries again? Sure, it's easy for my buddies to call me an imbecile when I do it, but I need to ask myself what's wrong with my system if I'm making "dumb mistakes." Maybe I need something as simple as a checklist for my mornings.

This book offers a system on its own, or one from which you can steal liberally. I did; why not you, too?

The Team and Your Guests

Throughout the book I will mention, at different times, "the team," or your "teammates," and "guests." I interchange the terms to simply include the people for whom we are responsible in the mountains. Obviously guiding people in the backcountry introduces other dynamics and expectations, not to mention a (potentially unproductive) hierarchy. Pay attention to this; more on it later in the "Team" and "Decision Making" chapters.

Consider the following system in the context of a team of committed skiers or splitboarders, all of them sharing two main goals: getting the goods and coming home safely. Some days most or all of the responsibility to attain these goals might fall on your shoulders (guiding); other times you'll be part of a team of equally skilled peers. Guiding introduces profit motive. International guiding? Centuries of shifting borders and cultural forces are at work, sometimes against you. Skiing with a low-functioning team will introduce other potentially pernicious motivations like ego, pride, avarice, and jealousy. It's a minefield, my friends!

Be conscious of these differing roles and responsibilities for your tours, and address them in your planning. Account for those days when you're responsible for the whole shooting match. Give yourself the bandwidth to succeed on those days by biting off a little less, perhaps, seeking expert advice, or putting in a bit more planning.

The team matters greatly. I draw on a varied roster of thinkers to try to uncover some strategies for building and nurturing an awesome team.

Structure and AIARE

This guide's chapters could've been arranged a few different ways, but ultimately it came down to what felt right. "Trip Planning," then "The Up," "The Down," and "The Debrief"; a day of backcountry touring. After that I visit some general ideas that underlie our touring, namely, "The Team" and "Decision Making." I try to tackle the specialized niches of "Steep Skiing," "Technical Solutions," and "Snowpack" at the end. I hope it feels approachable and logical.

You'll notice as you progress through the content, I refer to the American Institute for Avalanche Research and Education. AIARE offers proprietary professional- and recreational-level curricula. Some areas, like Colorado's Front Range, feature mostly AIARE courses; other pockets, like Salt Lake and Jackson, have more courses provided by organizations like the American Avalanche Institute (AAI). In Anchorage you can study with my friends at the Alaska Guide Collective.

I just happened to apprentice with a mountain guide who taught AIARE courses, so my avalanche education has been within that framework. I also helped edit/proof AIARE's new (as of 2019) recreational curriculum with one of my mentors, Colin Zacharias. I'm most familiar with AIARE's approach, and I like it.

This is not to say, as anyone at AIARE would echo, that the AIARE method is the only or best way. It's very good, but if you've trained with the great and wise Sarah Carpenter or Don Sharaf at AAI—count yourself lucky! Adapt your current knowledge, draw from the AIARE materials you'll discover here, and synthesize them into your own process.

Deliberate Practice and the Sidebars

Along the way, you will find two different types of called-out text. First, under the heading "Deliberate Practice," you'll find a few ideas for specific, focused practice on different techniques. I'll elaborate more on the characteristics of deliberate practice in a later section, but for now look for the text boxes and make a mental note to perhaps incorporate the exercises into your system.

As you read along, you will happen upon sidebars. Perk up—some of the smartest people in the business wrote these. These wise words are yours for the taking. Take a deep breath, wring out the sponge of your understanding, and absorb what they have to say. Thanks to all who contributed.

Helicopters, Cats, and Sleds

You won't find them here. First off, I have tail-guided for the merry band at Vail Powder Guides a handful of days—and that's it—so my "expertise" in mechanized guiding is, well, no expertise at all. That, combined with the highly specialized techniques found in the mechanized world, swayed me to simply not tackle the discipline. There are so few mechanized operations in the United States anyway, I'm not sure how useful a chapter on the topic would have been. Those Canadians do a great job of nurturing and training aspirants. They've got it wired.

Find yourself lucky enough to work in that world, and hopefully your operation will have a robust, thorough apprenticeship during which you'll learn the craft. (If they don't, heads up!)

Onward and a Nudge

And so now we get down to business, "Trip Planning." Dive into the process and let me know how it goes. Feedback from the *MGM* was mostly positive, so I hope this book's format works for you.

One consistent "concern" I've heard regarding the *MGM* and guide-candidates in the AMGA programs is that some of that material, while memorized, gets misapplied. It's one thing to learn *how* to lower a skier with a skinny, low-stretch cord and quite another to learn *when* to lower a skier on a skinny, low-stretch cord. Learning the hard skills are easy—performing a compression test, learning crevasse rescue, or executing a kick turn. The wisdom comes in knowing the right time and context.

I offer this as a nudge to remember that a book is two dimensions and necessarily limited. Take this knowledge and apply it slowly. Expect to make mistakes, and ask yourself in the moment, What would happen if I botch this? Leave yourself ample room for error. Keep consequences low for the time being. Someday, a few decades from now, you and I will know all this and more, and we will seamlessly transition between techniques and strategies, provoking silent awe from our guests and teammates.

Until then, do what I do. Double-check yourself, cultivate humility, and expect some pilot error along the way. Be cool when your teammates blow it, and learn from your own lowlights. I'm now 50 and it's worked for me so far. And the Jedi still let me hang around and poach their ideas from time to time.

Onward.

CHAPTER 1

Trip Planning

Where you ski should express everything you know about the snowpack.

—Colin Zacharias

Planning is bringing the future into the present so you can do something about it now.

—Alan Lakein

That's as simple as it gets—when planning our tour, we take all the information available to us and select a couple options for a fun, satisfying tour with friends. Just as we sit down the night before or morning of a tour, let's start the book with a look at trip planning.

A solid trip plan reduces hazards . . . and also delivers the best turns. Dr. Dominik Schneider proves the point outside Nelson, British Columbia.
MARTINS PUTELIS

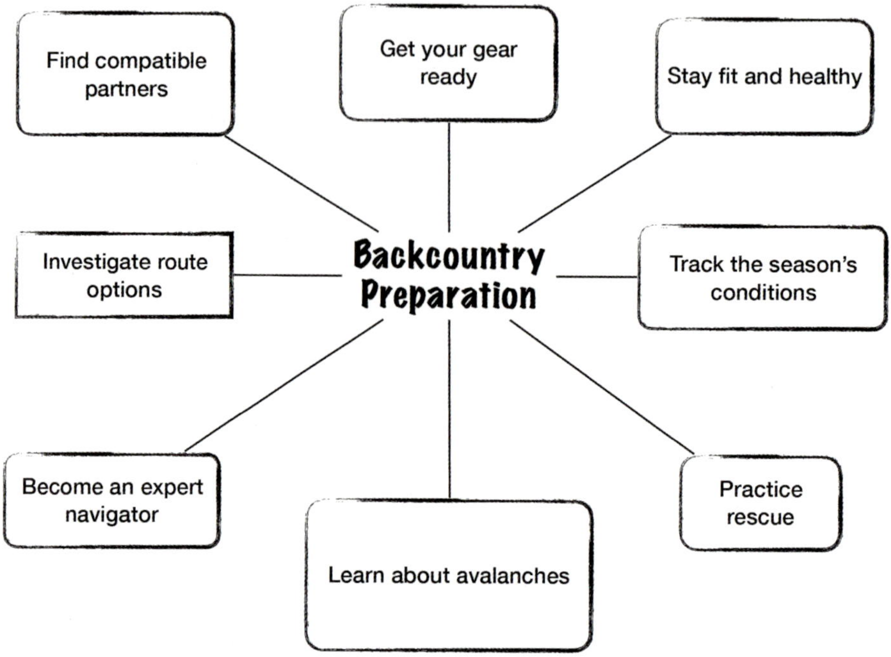

Going into the backcountry requires prep and planning. A checklist, process, or flowchart—however you conceive of it—helps mitigate risk, find the best skiing, and deliver safer, more enjoyable touring. This graphic captures the bird's-eye view of one process. COLIN ZACHARIAS

But why trip plan in the first place? Can't we just wing it? Our trip plan anticipates conditions and hazards. It prepares our team for what we expect to see in the field, rather than leaving us to merely react to conditions during the day. Think of the trip plan as a pre-event rehearsal. Do actors blow off a rehearsal and just "go for it" the night of the show? Of course not, and our trip plan offers solutions and mitigation strategies before we find ourselves exposed to hazards like avalanches, rock- and icefall, dangerous cold or hot weather, or the disconnect of an incompatible team.

We pre-bias and de-bias during our trip plan, elicit opinions, gather information, and come up with touring options that allow us to adapt during the day. This chapter offers one take on how to do it.

Backcountry Prep

Our trip plan really begins late summer and early fall, when we revisit our gear, begin working on ski fitness, incorporate new teammates, identify some season goals, and further develop our run atlas. Between your mountain biking, rock climbing, competitive

The Notebook

My mentors and I teach the AIARE Risk Management Framework during AIARE 1 and AIARE 2 courses. This process helps students approach backcountry touring and mainly focuses on the avalanche hazard. As mountain guides taking guests into the hills, we go beyond the AIARE approach. I'll refer to the AIARE fieldbook (or "blue book" as many students call it) and process throughout this book but also take deeper dives into other considerations, like decision making, de-biasing methods, more involved terrain strategies, backcountry skills like tracksetting, and team-management practices. The AIARE fieldbook will help you tour in the backcountry more safely. Look for ideas to complement it as you digest this book.

lawn-dart tournaments, a little work, perhaps some parenting, you should find the time to lay the foundation for a fantastic ski-and-ride season in the months leading up to it.

When the backcountry finally fills in, you want to be ready, mentally and physically. The easy part is getting the legs and lungs strong enough for the long days, believe it or not. Ask yourself, though: If you're willing to do your dead lifts, weighted hikes, and plyometrics, are you doing the same work mentally? Seasonal prep acts as gym time for your brain and decision-making skills.

The irony is, we often spend more time researching and buying a new set of skis than we do refining our skills for the upcoming winter. I'm guilty of it too! Be honest with yourself, though. Are you preparing as diligently mentally as you are physically? Is your head game as dialed-in as your new choice in steep skis? Do you practice your decision making? How? When? Hopefully, after reading this chapter you'll have some specific, actionable tasks to help your mental game.

One of the most enjoyable aspects of backcountry touring is the lifelong progression and learning it involves. I'll expand the idea of the daily debrief in a later chapter, but as we think about and get ready for the upcoming season, consider a debrief for your previous season(s). What went well last year? What were your successes from last year, or over the course of the year? And then be honest with yourself and your teammates: What could you improve moving into the future? Answer these questions and lay out a workable plan for the winter. These insights should help you identify areas for improvement for the fall.

A "Wicked" Environment

Backcountry touring brings us to stunning landscapes and braves tough weather, but this isn't the wicked environment researchers describe. Rather, a wicked environment involves any situation in which a decision maker faces multiple variables, each dependent upon the others. It is, by definition, unpredictable, nonlinear, and complex; it offers little to no feedback and, at times, even inaccurate feedback. By this researchers mean on some days the feedback you get isn't the feedback you *ought* to get.

Imagine a tour in which you ski thigh-deep untracked snow, lap after lap, under blue skies. You return to the lodge high on the experience, confident in how well you nailed it. What if, though, you got away with the tour simply due to luck? Perhaps the slopes you tore up were waiting to avalanche and you merely missed the "sweet spot" and didn't trigger one. Your feedback, though, indicated a great day and a rousing success. The feedback you should've gotten, however, was an avalanche and a big scare.

Bruce Kay, a longtime avalanche professional, uses the term "wicked environment"; Nobel Prize–winning psychologist Daniel Kahneman uses

In AIARE's blue fieldbook, the first component of the risk management framework is preparing for the upcoming season. This graphic from the book highlights the essential steps. COURTESY AIARE

the term "low-validity environment." Whichever you prefer, one of the critical criteria for this situation is a lack of feedback or even inaccurate feedback. We end up at the ski lodge brimming with confidence, when we should've slunk back quietly, knowing we need to do some serious rethinking about our process.

Professionals who study these environments explain that it is possible to make quality, safer decisions in a wicked environment by employing a "repeatable process." Trip planning is your repeatable process.

Trip planning is merely a method or algorithm by which you anticipate problems so that you can make better, safer decisions in a challenging environment. You then debrief to gain insights from your process and improve (more on the debrief in a subsequent chapter).

Keep in mind, all this proper planning will also set you up for better turns! Employing a repeatable process is your best strategy for a long, safer career in the backcountry . . . *and* getting the goods. This chapter (more accurately, this book) is one blueprint for the process—drawing on guide training and the avalanche industry in the United States and Canada. It is by no means the only one. It is one version but, keep in mind, a version time-tested by mountain guides and avalanche professionals over decades.

Stay Fit and Healthy

Keep it fun; that's the best advice for preseason training. I love Scott Johnston and Steve House's book *Training for the New Alpinism* if you're looking to really up your game. Their newer title, coauthored with none other than Kílian Jornet, *Training for the Uphill Athlete: A Manual for Mountain Runners and Ski Mountaineers*, should prove to be as authoritative. (It will be out by the time you read this.)

What I like about their approach is that it relies on decades of research and not the latest lingo or fads. Consider picking up either title and visiting their website, uphillathlete.com, if you'd like a more structured approach to the game. They focus on mountain fitness, not ski technique, but the foundation they provide will make you a better, stronger, safer skier.

However you choose to prepare physically for the new season, build in some variety, keep it fun, train with your teammates if you can—and don't neglect your weaknesses. If you're slaying 325-pound dead lifts, awesome. . . but what about your core strength and balance work? Love long, slow trail runs? Congrats . . . but what about explosive power, box jumps, weighted step-ups?

I don't mean to imply that you have to be training like a professional athlete to go backcountry skiing. You should, however, acknowledge that safer, more enjoyable backcountry riding requires more stamina and strength than lift-served skiing. Also consider the consequences of even a minor mishap. Can you help an injured partner to a safe area? What if he can't ski? What if you need to shoulder his pack for the remainder of a tour? Superior fitness will help you accomplish all of this and more. Don't go overboard, but challenge yourself to improve before the snow flies.

SKI AND RIDE LESSONS

Our movement skills should always be up for reevaluation. A truly expert instructor can quickly identify your weaknesses and room for improvement. Even during the off-season, unearth some video footage of yourself and send it to a knowledgeable instructor. Let her tear your technique apart, identify your areas for improvement, then prep you for the ski/ride drills you'll do on snow. She will probably give you some dry-land training too. These are the kinds of early season investments that will grow your skills by leaps and bounds in the new season.

This is by no means a book on ski movement or physical training, but those elements of your skiing shouldn't be neglected. Take advantage of the many worthwhile resources readily available.

Get Your Gear Ready

Even the most throwback, OG backcountry rider has to be a bit of a gearhead. From lighter, more functional bindings to the latest smartphone GPS app, newer technologies not only make touring more fun, they make it safer too. Starting with simple stuff like paper maps, let's progress through our list of appropriate gear for the season and then propose some exercises to improve their use. I assume you have solid fundamentals for many of these techniques, so if you find yourself second-guessing any of your competencies, get down to improving them.

OLD-SCHOOL MAPPING

Paper map, mirror compass. They still exist, and, *yes*, you should still master their uses. Digital mapping has upped the game, and it's relatively easy to have redundancy in the field with phones. But that said, a paper map still trumps digital tools in certain situations.

Have you ever tried running a smartphone in -25°C temps? How about on a long, flat glacier with zero visibility? It might sound like the phone is exactly what you want for these stressful situations, but removing gloves or constantly putting a phone in and out of a pocket is impractical, time-consuming, and, if it requires stopping, tedious for guests. Occasionally verifying one's position with a smartphone is a great help, but for moment-to-moment orienteering, having a quality mirror compass and paper map (ideally on waterproof, tearproof paper) keeps the flow going and provides a relatively trouble-free system.

Your compass should be a mirror compass, with a clinometer needle built in. This allows for precise resection (with the mirror) and more accurate slope-angle measurements. Don't balk at spending $100 on a quality model. You'll have it for years, and if you ever need to do heavy-duty orienteering, you'll be psyched to have a good model.

Add to your kit an altimeter watch. Models that verify your position periodically with a GPS signal are probably worth the money. You can include a heart-rate monitor and various features, but a reliable altimeter watch gives you another datum when using a topo map. It's quite easy to tell the direction you're traveling, or the direction a slope is facing, with a compass. Add to that an accurate elevation, and you can determine a more precise location quickly and easily.

If this sounds like gobbledygook, you need an orienteering refresher!

NEW-SCHOOL MAPPING

Smartphones have dramatically changed the game for navigation. With apps like CalTopo and Gaia

Phone versus GPS

I've mentioned smartphone apps and, generally speaking, the user interface of the phone apps is superior to dedicated GPS units. But keep in mind that the battery life on most phones is limited when compared with a true GPS. Some GPS models boast of "battery-saving modes" with capacities up to 40 hours. I certainly haven't tested every model out there, but in general, for hours of constant use, a GPS will outperform a smartphone.

Some still prefer the smartphone routine but remedy the battery issue by bringing a small battery "brick" into the field. Companies like Goal Zero, Mophie, and Anker all manufacture bricks and cases with capacities ranging from one additional charge to multiple charges. These add some weight to your pack or phone, and the external bricks require a charging cable—don't forget it at home.

In general, the displays on the dedicated GPS units pale in comparison to what our smartphones do, but for a remote trip or extended periods tracking or navigating on a GPS, it's worth considering a dedicated unit.

GPS, accurate, fast navigation is nearly brainless—and therein lies part of the problem. Guides advocate the use of these tools, and I certainly use them myself, *but* (and this is an emphatic "but") I remind myself—and you—to not let them lure us into trouble. I'll say it a few times over the course of the book: The blue dot is for getting out of trouble, not into it.

I don't mean to sound like a Luddite, but "easy" mapping has resulted in some people getting in way over their heads, and you don't want to become another stat in the annals of techno-carnage. Used in the proper context, though, smartphone/digital tools can make low-vis glacier travel, nighttime orienteering, and navigating in complex terrain much, much easier.

RESCUE TECHNOLOGIES

With a satellite signal comes not only GPS navigation but rescue capabilities as well. Seems like every season another tool hits the market, so keep your eyes peeled and up to date on the latest innovations.

Garmin's InReach options are probably the most common models at the moment, and you'll need to decide between a larger unit that also functions as a GPS or their "Mini," which is a dedicated rescue tool. The Mini weighs a scant 3.5 ounces (100g), and sends and receives text messages when paired with a phone app. For an "emergencies only" option, it's great. In addition to rescue capabilities, Garmin's larger InReach (the "Explorer+") has a larger display for use as a nav tool. Hit the SOS button to activate rescue services, or use it to record or follow a track, etc. Garmin relies on the Iridium satellite constellation for its GPS.

Bivystick offers another compact, lightweight unit (7 ounces; 200g) with texting, navigation via a paired smartphone, and an SOS option, but with a couple useful add-ons. It will also download three- and seven-day weather forecasts as well as recharge your smartphone as many as two times. Given most smartphone users carry a battery brick and an emergency device when applicable, the Bivystick might be a cool solution for you. Bivystick uses the Iridium network too.

SPOT offers yet another collection of tools, including the 7-ounce SPOT X, which sends and receives texts and offers SOS functions. You can also purchase GEOS rescue insurance as part of your SPOT plan. Note that SPOT's two-way messaging services exclude much of Asia and Australia.

Note: Verify this information before making a purchase. This is the most accurate information at the time of writing, but plans and technology change.

RADIOS

Radios act as rescue tools as well as excellent communication devices within your party. Particularly if you have several groups in the field, or if you have access to local SAR resources, a VHF radio might be your fastest resource for a rescue.

I'll mention radios elsewhere as a tool for group management, so make sure you use a VHF radio according to your local rules and regs. The public FRS channels are just that, public—so jump on, but don't be surprised when you've got cross traffic on your channel.

Acquiring repeater frequencies and the frequencies for local agencies can be challenging in certain areas. At least in the United States, land managers don't necessarily share their frequencies with guides, let alone the general public. Ask around and do some research. You'll need a VHF radio capable of operating on the ham radio bands to hit these repeaters.

At the very least, phone apps like Repeater Book and others will help you find nearby repeaters where you can relay a distress call. In an emergency you can transmit on any frequency you like. Again, these require a VHF radio operating on the applicable bands; FRS radios don't operate on the same frequencies.

Lightweight, streamlined, but large enough for even an overnight bivy, this guide pack has a removable back pad for versatility, a removable top lid, compression straps, and a tools pocket—all for just over 1 kilo. Custom-made by Alpine Threadworks, it compresses to next to nothing but will also carry a rope, crampons, ice tools, and a puffy jacket when it needs to.

MATT KENNEDY

THE PACK

Keep it simple. Well, as simple as possible . . . and at times that might not be that simple!

Let's start with the typical day tour. In the trip plan we scribble the following in our notebook: who's coming, what we're managing, where we're headed, and who has what gear—our rescue toboggan, communication device(s), a med kit, and a repair kit. Divided among the group, these items might add 0.5 kilo at best. Not much! Touring on a glacier, true ski-mountaineering, or unusual cold (or heat), and the gear list changes a bit.

Consider a lightweight, streamlined, durable, and versatile pack. Don't get sold on the latest-greatest ski-carry system or a pocket for every last item. Adding 2 kilos to your back for the duration of the season takes its toll on the joints and your engine. The more weight you add and the farther it is from your core, it becomes "swing weight," meaning mass that threatens to pull you off balance once it gets moving. This can be dangerous if you're riding in consequential terrain, where a slip or fall could be life threatening.

The terrain in which you're working will dictate pack size. With ample resources nearby (helicopters at an operation, other guides, European cell service, being nearer the frontcountry), you can probably get by with a 28-liter pack. The moment the weather closes in (no more helicopters), you're one ridgeline away from the road (no easy egress), or you plan to rock scramble a bit (harnesses, carabiners, and a rope), your pack begins to grow.

A simple pack with one main compartment gives us the most flexibility in packing. Despite what the sales kid will tell you at the gear shop, one large compartment swallows all your gear, allowing you to stash equipment however you see fit. More dividers, straps, and pockets begin to dictate where things need to go. Some guides even get away without a "tools pocket" on their packs; that is, dedicated pockets for their snow shovels and probes. If you're digging a lot, having a separate pocket for your shovel will keep snow out of your main compartment, but for fast day tours, it's totally fine to stash your shovel and probe in a main compartment.

To Helmet . . . or Not to Helmet?

As a rule, guides tell most guests to just wear a helmet. They're light, warm, and they will probably help rather than hurt you in the event of a crash or impact. The downside? More weight, more bulk, and yet another thing to deal with at transitions.

Some riders get away with wearing a helmet all day, but I see most folks remove a helmet for the up. So when buying a pack, consider how you'll carry the helmet. Many packs come with an integrated carry system. They're convenient but add weight. Some users simply carry a 3-foot section of bungee cord and improvise a carry system by threading the cord through the helmet's vent holes then tying the ends of the cord off. Be inventive—you might save yourself weight and streamline your pack.

When it's pounding snow, you'll enjoy having the helmet inside your pack on the up. Left on the outside, some snow inevitably sneaks into the inside of the helmet and then melts on your noggin on the down. Remember that simple ski pack we mentioned with a large, main compartment? Stuff some of your puffy jacket in the helmet and it'll sit right atop the rest of your gear inside the pack—perfect!

Most backcountry devotees perform their day missions with a 25- to 32-liter pack, with a simple tools pocket and ski- or snowboard-carry system. This size allows for food, water, a rescue toboggan, a puffy jacket, and enough space for small items like ski straps, sunscreen, goggles, and a spare pair of gloves.

As our tours and objectives grow, so does our pack. Now you're looking at 35- to 45-liter models, ones that will accommodate a rope, a bivy sack and sleeping bag, maybe boot crampons and ice tools too. If you're summiting 3,000- to 4,000-meter peaks in winter, now your belay jacket gets bigger. But rest assured, a more streamlined design will probably keep you happiest. The same one-big-compartment pack swallows a sleeping bag, pad, 60m rappel line, you name it.

Avoid using stuff sacks: A stuff sack turns your sleeping bag into a little oblong brick. If you leave your bag (or rescue toboggan or puffy jacket) loose, you can cram it into dead spaces and the corners of your pack. This avoids gear shifting and pulling you off balance while skiing, allows you to pack more gear, and helps keep your pack smaller.

Having a removable back pad improves your packing too. Most packs these days have sewn-in "fixed" foam in the back; it's comfortable, convenient, but less versatile. Being able to remove your pack's padding opens up options. The foam can be used as a leg or arm splint in a pinch. You can also use it as a sleeping pad or to insulate a patient in your rescue toboggan. Better yet, replace the foam in your pack with a full-length, lightweight inflatable air mattress. Manufacturers like Therma-a-Rest, CAMP, Exped, and Sea-to-Summit all make superlight backpacking mattresses. They sleep better, insulate better, and can become an air-cast in an emergency.

Overnight or multiday trips, or trips involving real climbing (steep ice and/or rock), require a pack big enough to handle the load but nimble enough for unimpeded movement. Easily said, but harder to actually find. As the pack grows in size and weight, your movement skills become compromised on the up and the down. Plan accordingly.

Long, less-supported traverses like the Rogers to Bugs or (get this) a once-in-a-lifetime mission like the Squamish-to-Skagway marathon that mother-and-daughter duo Tania and Martina Halik completed (2,300 kilometers over six months!) require a tremendous amount of planning. Your pack will be only one among many worries. In addition to a comfortable and voluminous backpack, you will need to plan food caches via airdrops as well as your cooking and sleeping systems. You might be hauling a sled. Your mental preparation will determine your success. Consider a psychiatrist and resources beyond this book for planning on this level.

TRANSCEIVERS

Avalanche beacons or transceivers constantly evolve. The major brands—Mammut, Backcountry Access (BCA), Ortovox, Pieps/Black Diamond, and

Avalanche Airbags

"Are avalanche airbags an essential piece of equipment?" Teach an avalanche awareness clinic at a gear shop, and this will be one of the first questions you get. Airbags are an interesting innovation and one you should consider.

Accident analysis and anecdotal evidence show that in certain situations they help an avalanche victim avoid complete burial, which significantly improves survival rates. Research presented in 2014 by Dr. Pascal Haegeli and others showed a reduction in mortality from 22 percent to 11 percent for avalanche victims wearing an avalanche airbag. The study's authors point out that the data sets used to generate this statistic and others are small at present, so in effect we should view these numbers knowing they will probably change as more robust data are available. By no means should you discount airbags' potential efficacy—just be skeptical of some of the more ambitious claims bandied about in marketing materials.

The Haegeli study also points out that the greatest shortcoming to airbags is the failure to deploy them. They wrote, "Overall non-inflation rate is 20%, 60% of which is attributed to deployment failure by the user." If you're wearing an airbag, at least practice the motion of deploying it. Some models even allow you to practice deployments now.

At present, no comprehensive data compares airbag survival rates in a place like Colorado, with trees up to 11,500 feet (compared to approximately 7,200 feet in Switzerland) and a relatively shallow snowpack (possibly more rocks to hit). As trauma rates are thought to be higher in places like Colorado, it stands to reason airbags will prove to be somewhat less effective too—but this is my own conjecture and not yet supported by a comprehensive study.

Sure, an airbag adds extra weight to your back, and terrain traps may limit their efficacy, but they can be very effective. If you decide an airbag is for you, incorporate it to your usual kit and wear it, no matter the terrain, danger rating, or time of year.

Arva—all make accurate, reliable models. If you're considering upgrading for the season, do it early and practice with the unit before heading out.

When choosing a transceiver, make sure you like the user interface. Some models have an LCD display with arrows and numbers; others have illuminated arrows, for example. There's no inherent advantage to different displays. Borrow a couple transceivers, see which one seems intuitive to you, and go with it. And then practice.

Gear Is Great, but Skills Are Better

With the appropriate gear at the ready, you need to make sure you're competent with all of it. Know your systems and gear, so you're not fiddling with it in the dark or with cold fingers, when it really matters. For first-timers, guides will often recommend putting skins on and off in the living room before venturing out. You're probably far ahead of that, but learning anything new in a relaxed, warm environment will be way easier than trying to search for the owner's manual online with one bar of service in the backcountry. Let's look at some skills to refresh as you prep for the upcoming season.

BECOME AN EXPERT NAVIGATOR

Awesome, you purchased a mirror compass and maps for your home zone. Waterproof paper lets you print durable maps on smaller sheets. With a home printer and a few bucks, you can print compact maps for your favorite tours in whatever format you like.

> ***DELIBERATE PRACTICE:*** Geocaching scavenger hunts challenge you to be efficient and accurate when applying the map to terrain, if you want to really dive down the rabbit hole. Sitting down with your crew and writing out a detailed tour plan with bearings (back bearings too), UTM or lat-long waypoints, and time estimates will keep your skills fresh.

Mapping and orienteering skills rust over time, so consider doing some exercises as part of your preseason practice.

A deep dive into orienteering falls outside our goals for this guide, and we expect most of you already have some familiarity with these skills. Refine and refresh them each season and you'll be ready if you need them.

NEW-SCHOOL MAPPING TECHNIQUES AND TOOLS

At the time of this writing, the website CalTopo (and its sibling, SARTopo) has a beta version of a phone app. If you haven't tried the CalTopo website, it's become the standard for many mountain guides, surveyors, and orienteers. Visit your app store and see how the finished product works.

Many other competent guides, skiers, hunters, and adventurers prefer apps like Gaia GPS, Backcountry Navigator, and FATMAP. There are pros and cons to each, so my advice is

Are You Better on Paper?

While the smartphone mapping apps offer more flash and a quicker result than paper, don't jump to the conclusion that you're better in the field with them. Compelling research shows that readers retain more accurate information and display higher reading comprehension when consuming paper content rather than digital. And when it comes to mapping, some research suggests a similar sway toward paper maps.

Paul Hurst (Royal School of Military Survey, Newbury, UK) and Paul Clough (Information School, University of Sheffield) conducted studies comparing orienteers' preferences and competence in mapping exercises with both paper and digital maps. They published their results in *The Journal of Information Science.*

In the study's abstract they write, "As geographic skill increases, there is a greater preference for paper maps; non-experts prefer online/digital maps. Also, paper is the preferred medium for planning and executing navigation on foot across all groups. Overall, results suggest that paper maps are here to stay for the foreseeable future and remain the preferred choice for some in the digital age."

Strangely enough, some of the cutting-edge research on this topic comes from direct-mail marketers. Looking at how consumers digest paper mail versus digital, researchers at Bangor University's Centre for Experimental Consumer Psychology discovered (via fMRI) that information presented on a physical card (rather than a screen) activated areas of the brain associated with spatial awareness and spatial memory networks; digital information failed to do the same.

Bottom line? Who knows how this will shake out, but it seems the best approach is to be comfortable in both media and have both at hand.

to choose your app and stick with it. Learn it well and apply its functions. If you constantly switch to the latest and greatest, you'll struggle to get truly fluent with any one method/app.

Digital tools give us highly accurate navigation options and the ability to share a track with a friend or colleague. Over time you'll find your app filled with colored lines, memories of great and some not-so-great tours. Label them and save them for future use. Add photos to particular waypoints along your route and you'll have an interactive run atlas in a couple seasons. Remember, though, conditions change, glaciers move, and what you pulled off on one day might not work the next. Use your saved tracks, but don't let them lead you into difficulty—or danger.

Likewise, many websites now exist where users share their tracks and waypoints. Camptocamp in France, for example, can be a fun and helpful resource, especially when onsighting. The .gpx files help orient you and streamline an approach or descent, but remember, that is just one party's experience or solution. Reference it, but stay vigilant; don't follow an anonymous line into more hazard.

Recall the point above regarding situational awareness and digital maps. See those zombified kids staring at screens at the shopping mall? Don't become one of them in the backcountry. You can't risk losing awareness of rockfall, a changing snowpack, terrain traps, seracs, polar bears, and/or rival locals hell-bent on poaching your line. Dangers are everywhere!

Practice Rescue

"Rescue," as a catch-all term for injuries, avalanches, and unforeseen mishaps, requires its own section. This is serious business, and you should prepare for the unexpected. Tour long enough and something will happen, even if it's just coming upon another, unprepared party. You need to perfect the use and application of transceiver, rescue toboggan, and other rescue equipment. Here are some guides' approaches to preseason practice.

Backcountry touring involves some hazard, no doubt. To put it in perspective, though, you are far more likely to die driving to and from the trailhead than you are touring. Phew! Feel better? Well, about the skiing at least?

Most people identify the first risk in backcountry riding as avalanches. In terms of fatalities, they're probably right, but most skiing injuries involve the lower leg. Luckily, if we hurt ourselves skiing or splitboarding, it will probably be relatively minor and something from which we can recover—provided we leave the trailhead prepared.

FIRST AID AND TRAUMA

Some basic preparations and knowledge will prevent a minor injury from becoming a serious situation. This might mean simply knowing how to close a wound or move a nonambulatory skier a few hundred meters.

Think seriously about taking at least a wilderness first-aid course (WFA). These prepare you to deal with common mishaps, illnesses, and injuries. Organizations like the Wilderness Medicine Institute (WMI) and others offer courses throughout the year, for relatively minimal cost.

Tour with a first-aid kit—a light, compact version ready for bleeds, pain, and minor trauma. Getting your group together involves knowing who needs what, so if you have a teammate who is deathly allergic to peanuts, insect

A sample leg-splint kit, suitable for a classic and common ski injury, a "tib-fib"—a fracture of the tibia and fibula (the two long bones below the knee) just above the top of the ski boot. Laid out below are two elastic Ace bandages (Nexcare Coban tape works very well for this too), 3 meters of 3mm cord (red/orange in the photos), two hook-and-loop closure cuffs (black "MEC" straps in the photos), a 1- to 2-meter adjustable strap (black loop), and finally just the leg of an inexpensive pair of rain or wind pants. This guide cut the leg (purple sleeve in the photo) from a used pair of wind pants for his kit. COLIN ZACHARIAS

Detail shot of the black, rolled-up strap used at the top of the splint system. You could also substitute the patient's or your belt for this piece of the system.
COLIN ZACHARIAS

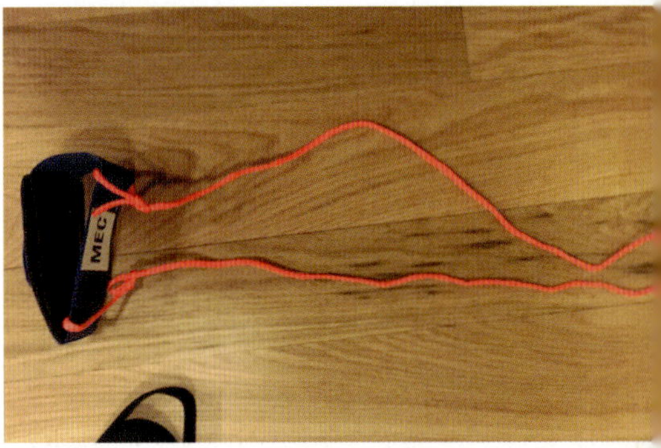

The guide ties a small loop on either end of the red 3mm cord. Through these loops he threads the hook-and-loop straps (labeled "MEC" in the photos). These straps will fasten around the hard boot cuff of the patient's ski boot and effectively secure the red cord to the patient's ski boot. The cord will then be used to gently pull and traction the patient's leg into alignment and (most likely) a more comfortable position. In subsequent photos, you will see the red cord tied/tensioned to the baskets of the patient's poles. COLIN ZACHARIAS

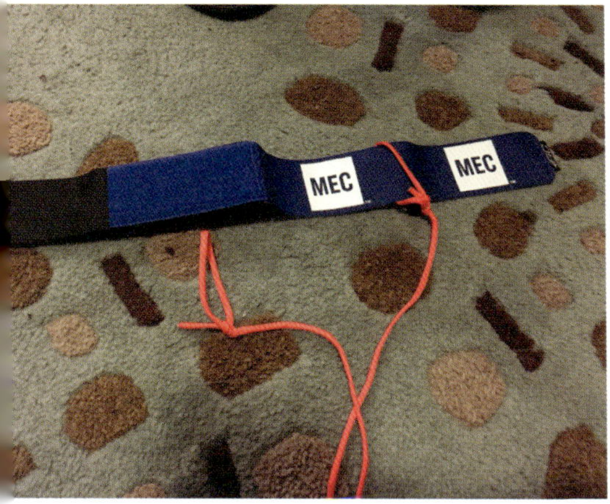

Detail of the hook-and-loop straps with cord attached. COLIN ZACHARIAS

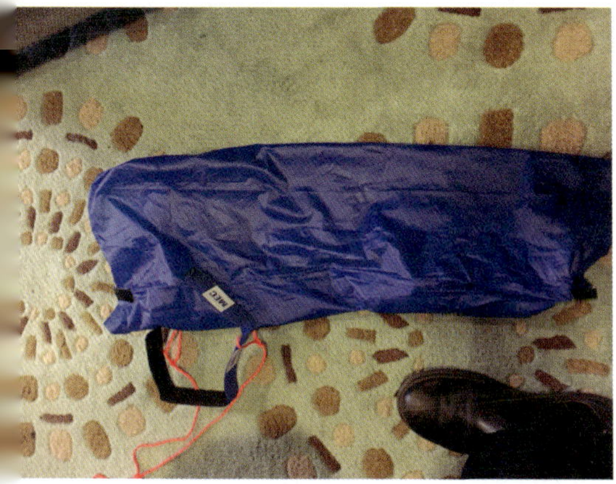

The leg sleeve laid out, with the cord-and-strap rig ready to attach around the patient's ski boot once his leg is set in the sleeve. The guide puts the patient's ski poles inside the leg sleeve, parallel to each other, and spreads them, creating a cradle or basket for the patient's leg. Ideally the guide pads this leg cradle so the patient does not feel pressure points from the ski poles. COLIN ZACHARIAS

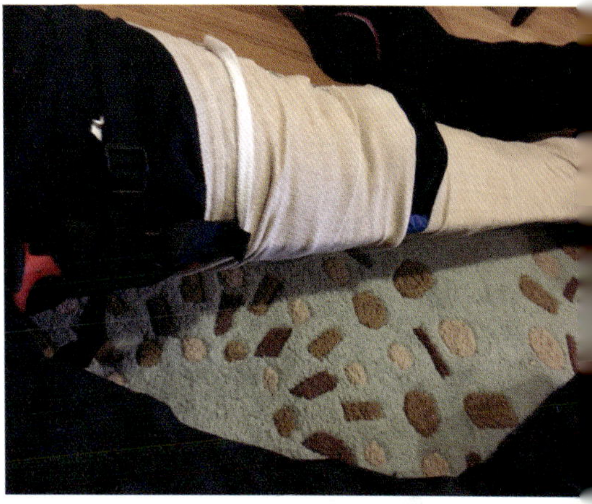

The guide and her helpers/teammates gently lay the patient's leg into the purple cradle. The ski poles run down the inside and outside of the patient's broken leg. The guide uses the long black strap to wrap the pole grips and patient's upper thigh so she can eventually tension the red cord around the spikes of the poles to gently(!) traction the leg in place. Caution here—too tight a wrap with the strap will result in discomfort, if not bruising and/or impeded circulation. At the other end of the splint, the team affixes the black hook-and-loop strap to the top of the patient's boot cuff and positions the red cord past the sole of the patient's ski boot, leaving it loose and ready to tension. Finally, by using the elastic bandages or Coban tape, the rescuers can firmly secure the entire cradle around the patient's leg, from top to bottom. COLIN ZACHARIAS

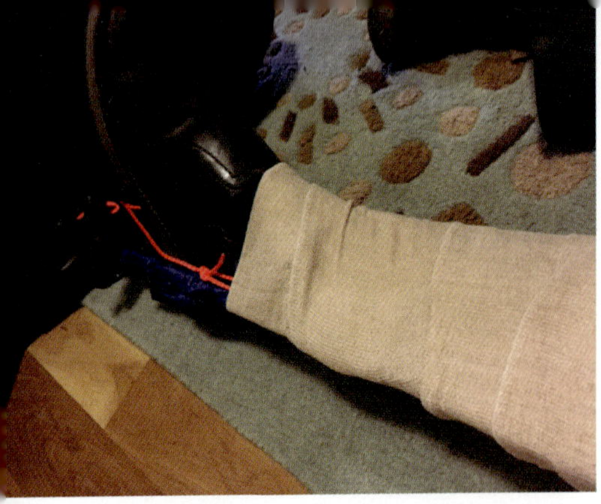

With the leg wrapped and pole grips secured to the upper leg, the guide can now grasp the red cord—which the rescuers gently laid out at the bottom of the splint system in the photo above—and tension and knot it around the baskets of the ski poles. This tractions the leg into place and protects it from being jostled or compressed if and when the rescuers move the patient. Again, padding the split around the leg will greatly improve patient comfort, and care should be given to check distal circulation in the foot if possible. COLIN ZACHARIAS

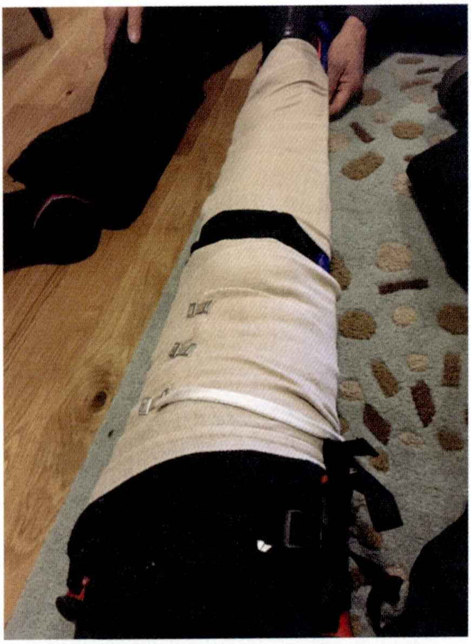

The finished product. As with any backcountry hazard, avoidance is key. You don't want to be in the position of extracting a nonambulatory patient. That said, it happens all too frequently. Pursuing wilderness medicine training will help prepare you for an unfortunate injury. Having versatile materials with you—bandages, a small knife, straps, and some cord—will help you deal with a variety of injuries. COLIN ZACHARIAS

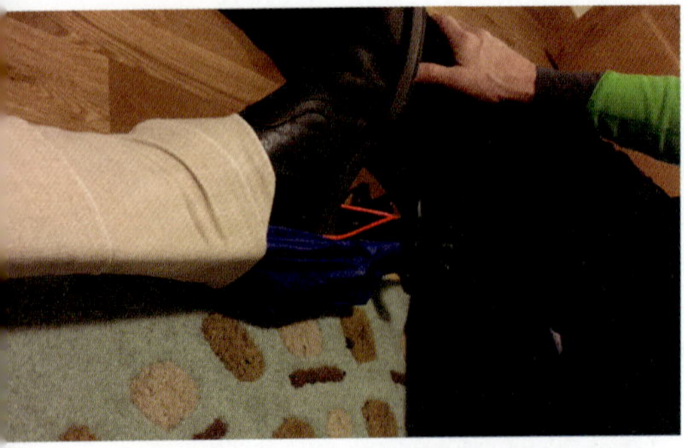

Another view of the patient's lower leg. The team has tensioned the red cord to the pole baskets or points, which pulls down on the patient's ski boot, helping to keep the leg in place and aligned during evac. COLIN ZACHARIAS

stings, or Justin Bieber, you need to know that, know how to treat it, and be ready. Write this information in your notebook and share it with your team!

As we mentioned earlier, most ski- and splitboard-touring injuries involve the lower leg. Your med kit should reflect this reality and include a system for splinting a broken leg or blown knee. A teammate rarely will break a femur, but it does happen; you should consider this possibility and be ready for it.

Prepare for common injuries and situations before the snow flies. Experiment with your leg splint in the comfort of your living room. Once you've assembled it a couple times, it's time to incorporate your rescue toboggan. Most human-powered mountain guides carry either the Brooks Range Eskimo (no longer in production, but you might find one online, used or new) or the Alpine Threadworks Ski Guides Tarp. Mechanized guides often prefer the Rescue Bubble, which is heavier than the above options but packages a patient more quickly.

DELIBERATE PRACTICE:
Take the time to build your sled around a patient several times. At first indoors, with warm fingers and all the time in the world. Model different situations—a patient who can tolerate some movement (imagine a blown knee without other injuries) and one with a back injury. Practice building the sled with and without skis. Testing by the ACMG suggests that a flexible air mattress below the patient tows better in winter/soft snow, while integrating skis pulls more easily on spring/firm snow and with an unstable injury.

Please note that neither I nor my contributing writer and mentor Colin Zacharias is a medical doctor. Adequate wilderness medicine training should be on your wish list for courses to complete, if you haven't already.

Once there's snow on the ground, but before the backcountry fills in, take your sled outdoors and test it out with a real body in there. Do it; in the event you have to move a patient, you will be ready.

AVALANCHE RESCUE

Any skill will rust without regular practice—decision making, kick turns, and, yes, your avalanche-rescue skills. Our approach, first and foremost, will always be avoidance of the avalanche hazard, but as with most adventures, you prepare for the worst and set yourself up for the best.

Most practitioners, it seems, give a nod toward rescue prep at some point during the season, but without recreating realistic scenarios. Searching for a shallowly buried transceiver will do a bit for your skills, but not nearly enough. Here are a few suggestions to help you better prepare for a successful rescue.

First off, take a bird's-eye view of your team's rescue response. Who has what gear? Who might be more skilled with individual components of a rescue? For example, if one of your team is a doctor or a nurse, she should be in charge of evaluating patients. If she's useless with a beacon, though, then identify that and focus on it early in the season. Likewise, if her teammates

Check Your Batteries

Believe it or not, there is quite a bit of variation in batteries, transceivers, and compatibility. My overarching advice is to check with your transceiver's owner's manual. It would be reckless to give advice here, as technologies and issues change so frequently; I strongly urge you to keep up to date on your transceiver's technology, capabilities, and limitations.

I will go so far as to say this: Make sure the batteries you install in your transceiver fit snugly into the compartment. If they rattle or move in the transceiver itself, it can result in your transceiver being shut off in an avalanche or search scenario.

My last point: Considerable confusion swirls around the types of batteries transceivers use. Consult your owner's manual and stick to the manufacturer's recommendation. A glitch in your transceiver could result in a tragic mishap.

can't even assist with treating blisters, perhaps it's time for them to do their wilderness first-aid training (or even a wilderness first responder, or WFR). You need a realistic appraisal of your team's skills and resources.

Before the snow flies, get together for a review of radios, satellite communication devices, and your rescue toboggan. Bring your ski notebooks, record relevant frequencies and information (local SAR, teammates' emergency contacts and numbers, etc.), and make sure everyone lends a voice to the process. You're building team cohesion and also making sure any new members of your crew share your goals and methods.

You can begin revisiting and refining your transceiver searches in the fall too. Again, this should not be your endgame for transceiver skills, but especially if you have a new unit, you can begin familiarizing yourself with it. You can use fallen leaves or soccer cones to "bury" transceivers and begin by doing single searches. Do you know the "special" features on your transceiver? How to enable and disable special modes? What types of batteries your unit takes?

Get your team together for a transceiver session and encourage everyone to bring his or her owner's manual. It's worth knowing what your teammates use in the field so that you can at least turn the unit on, off, in and out of search, etc. Every member should have a digital copy of their manual on their phone too; if you get an error code on your transceiver at a backcountry hut, you want to know what it means and how to fix it, if possible.

Assemble the team and begin with single searches, then add a second beacon. Again, this won't be realistic training, but you will get an idea of how your beacon behaves when it's equidistant between "victims" and how you might use the special functions on your unit, such as marking/flagging, "big picture," "scan," and the like. In a few hours you'll be set up for great training once you can actually bury and excavate transceivers later in the fall.

Once you have more than 50 centimeters of snow on the ground, you can begin to conduct slightly more realistic searches and complete rescue scenarios. Do your best to make them realistic. For example, track up the entire meadow you'll be searching in. Too often, students on avy courses "search" for beacons, but the tracks allow students to see roughly where the buried beacons lie as they travel down the "avalanche path." Don't make it easy on your partners when it's your turn to bury a transceiver. Use a 30 × 30-centimeter plank of wood to cover the buried beacons. This not only protects them from damage but also gives searchers a target that's big enough to hit but not so large that it's too easy.

If you use a fieldbook with a rescue checklist (you should!), go through it with your teammates as you effect a complete rescue. Strongly consider appointing a "leader" for each scenario and have her run it. Rotate positions; especially focus on any role in the rescue you deem a "weakness" of yours. Rinse and repeat.

The digging portion of the exercise will be nearly useless in shallow, soft snow, but do a few anyway. When you've executed several flawless, fast, efficient searches, find a 2-meter drift of snow and plunge your probe in 170 centimeters. (Recall that the average burial depth in rescues is somewhere around 120 centimeters. Recall further that we are anything but average, so we will perform an above-average shoveling drill!) Time your team, and dig until you expose the bottom of the probe.

You should do at least a couple of these realistic digs every year. First, it's sobering to see how long even a strong team takes to excavate a deeply buried victim; second, you've got to practice an efficient shoveling method. Various shoveling strategies exist, so experiment with them and see which technique works for you. (Search "conveyor belt" and "V method" to get ideas.) Remember to be one step downhill of the probe if the burial is 1 meter or less and two large steps downhill if excavating more than 1 meter.

THE RESCUE TOBOGGAN (SLED)

For another seasonal prep session, get together and assemble your rescue sled. Package a patient, splint his leg, and rig a towing system. A full sled kit shouldn't weigh more than a couple pounds, nor should it take up much more than the bottom of your pack.

Some guides use a foam pad in the sled; others use an inflatable air

Organize, Slow Down, and Speed Up

The International Committee on Alpine Rescue (ICAR) categorizes the phases of an avalanche rescue as organizing/allocating resources, a signal search, a coarse search, a fine search, and then pinpoint search. This flow helps you identify tasks for each step.

Searches, particularly ones involving a large number of well-meaning but impatient rescuers, go off the rails by not organizing and then allocating human power on the front end. Appoint a leader. Get a call out. Determine where to begin searching and in what pattern. This can happen in 30 seconds, and it needs to happen efficiently.

The team then searches for a signal, executing a disciplined search pattern as determined by the leader. Once a rescuer has a strong, regular signal, she can alert her companions to deviate from their patterns to follow the signal to the victim.

During this coarse search, don't plod along; searchers should be hauling butt, with the center arrow illuminated and numbers going down. Skis on or off? We get this question routinely in the AIARE 1. Do whatever's fastest, but if you remove skis early in the search, do not lose them! Consider plunging them upright in the snow or bundling them together securely atop a chunk of debris. You don't want to confuse additional rescuers, and you cannot risk losing your skis. You'll need them for your exit and/or to haul a patient in a sled.

Go quickly down to 20 meters and then slow down. If there's one mistake more experienced transceiver searchers make, it's moving too quickly from 20 to 10 meters. Various metaphors suggest the same thing: Go fast to 20, slow down to 10, and go very slow under 10 meters. Some instructors suggest the run-walk-crawl rule of thumb; others liken the process to an airliner flying cross country: Max speed across the continent, slow down to line up for landing, and then flaps down and slow for landing. Whatever method captures the idea for you, use it, but in general, go more slowly under 20 meters than you think—it will greatly increase your accuracy and therefore your chances of getting an early probe strike.

Fine searching just above the snow surface, but not right on it. The instructor is in the slow phase, not quite crawling but slow enough that he won't miss a direction change on the transceiver's display. Ideally a teammate would be probing just ahead of him, hoping to get an early strike.
BRETT WILHELM

At first you will feel as though you are wasting time. Bear with the work, though. At that 20 meter mark, walk approximately 1 to 2 meters per second, no more, and immediately adjust if you get an arrow indication to one side or the other. Keep your shoulders squared with the beacon held flat in front of you. The moment an indicator arrow tells you right or left, square your shoulders to get the middle arrow illuminated again. Continue.

Under 10 meters we slow down yet again and drop the beacon to a consistent height off the snow. By this I mean if the debris undulates and is chunky, keep the beacon just above the tallest piece of snow while you're searching. If you put the beacon just centimeters off the snow, you will have to constantly raise and lower it over irregularities in the snow surface. This will change your distances and your numbers will fluctuate, confusing the final meters of your search.

Once your direction arrows disappear, you are in the fine search. Some courses and methods may call this "bracketing." The point is, you should now be over your buried teammate and ready to determine a small area to probe—the pinpoint search.

Now, back up a sec. Expert teams can often avoid a fine search entirely by "probing on a line." Let's assume you're the lead transceiver searcher and you're under 5 or 6 meters. You have several teammates converging on your location because they realize you are closest to the victim. At this point they should see you crouching and slowing down, approaching your fine search.

As your teammates arrive to help, occasionally share your distance readings. The search leader can facilitate these steps, if she's dialed. She can direct one or two partners to deploy probe(s) and walk in front of you, eyeballing the line you followed in to the victim. This might be curved, remember. Your probers look at your line and anticipate where the victim might be. They begin probing along your line; if you've stayed slow and accurate under 20 meters, most of the time they'll get a probe strike before you ever need to fine search.

Successfully probing on a line negates the need for a fine search/bracketing, which saves you time. It will feel slow at first, but you'll soon discover having an earlier probe strike gets the team digging more quickly—and, as your realistic training above revealed, digging takes up most of your rescue time.

If you have sufficient numbers, the leader should direct teammates not probing to assemble shovels and get ready to dig in a systematic fashion. Even if you end up having to bracket or fine search, your shovelers can step downhill and begin digging in the general area. If you have readings below 1.2 meters, it's probably worth it to have shovelers begin their hard work just below where you're pinpoint searching. If they have to move 0.5 meter left or right, no problem, but the head start on digging will save you even more time.

A calm, collected leader should manage every step of this process, trying to maintain panoramic awareness. A few rehearsals in the fall and early winter will dramatically improve your rescues.

mattress. Still others expect to pad/insulate the patient with emptied backpacks. My main suggestion is to have a functional rescue toboggan that protects the patient from hypothermia, allows you to move the patient some distance, and can be securely lowered down a slope. Start experimenting with different configurations in the fall so that when the time comes to do a live exercise on snow, you know what works.

Just as a benchmark for training, keep in mind that ski guides for the ACMG and AMGA must pass a timed rescue drill to earn their certifications. The drill requires the guide to build her rescue sled, package a patient, lower the patient two rope lengths, pass a knot on one of the lowers, and then tow the patient across a meadow for a short distance—all while securing the patient (no risk of him falling out of the sled) and in less than 70 minutes. There's your standard; go beat it.

CRACK RESCUE

Those of us lucky enough to live and/or tour on glaciers need to refresh our crevasse-rescue skills too. Every season it seems like a new, skinny rope or superlight pulley comes out. Are they useful? Worth the cash? How about that confusing knot your buddy brought home from his two weeks in Slovenia? Now's the time to answer these questions. The rock gym, a park with a shady patch of ground, or somebody's basement can all work as venues to review systems.

> ***DELIBERATE PRACTICE:***
> If you find any of the exercises tedious, add a time component and race your teammates. Heckling is encouraged; don't hesitate to post your partners' worst mix-ups on social media (make sure to tag me when you do it). In short, keep it fun, get your team together, and get ready for snow.

Don't forget to include cliff rescue. Having a guest or teammate get cliffed out can be a 20-minute hassle or a life-threatening epic. Over the course of a few sessions, you can effectively refresh many of your essential skills for the season.

CELL COVERAGE

It's worth knowing where you can and cannot get a reliable cell signal. A cell call to 911 or, better yet, your local SAR agency will greatly speed rescue and medical services. As you assemble your group, ask who has a cell phone; if there's spotty coverage, make sure the person with the best coverage in that zone brings his or her phone. Different carriers have better coverage in different locations. Know whose phone works.

In Europe it's worth jotting down local rescue numbers, as well as the general emergency number: 112. Keep in mind that Switzerland uses 144 for ambulances, 117 for police, 118 for the fire department, and 1414 or 1415 for

Recharging That Battery Brick

More and more of us carry power-hungry gadgets in the backcountry, including our smartphones. That means carrying supplemental batteries. Numerous companies make models ranging from single-charge units weighing mere ounces to car-battery-size pigs that can last a week at the hut.

We trust you won't be touring with the heavier ones, but regardless, any time you are recharging your phone, headlamp, or any other lithium-ion battery, do not do so if the battery temperature is below 0°C. Imagine that you return from a frigid ski tour with a discharged phone and immediately recharge it. Doing so can ruin the phone battery's capacity, as well as make it more prone to failure and fire later. Heads up!

Rega, the helicopter rescue service. Cell coverage in Europe is generally much better in the mountains than it is in the United States and Canada, and an emergency call usually summons the helicopter in minutes rather than hours. Don't blindly rely on the phone, though—some areas are still cell-free, and in inclement weather, the helo might not fly.

For your home touring areas, it's worth recording in your notebook local SAR numbers, hospitals, and any other relevant info. When visiting a new zone, particularly somewhere without robust medical and rescue infrastructure, a few minutes online can at least get you info on hospitals, SAR providers, taxis, huts, etc.

Having reliable cell coverage means you can leave the satellite communication device at home, in addition to the radio, unless you want it for intraparty comms.

20 and 50

With all this talk of electronics, remember that your transceiver does not want any interference. When transmitting, try to keep anything electronic 20 centimeters away; in the event of searching, 50 centimeters away. Remember, that's *anything* switched on that's electronic: smartphone, battery-powered gloves, GPS watch, VHF radio.

A REPAIR KIT FOR EVERY OCCASION

Assemble as versatile a repair kit as you can, with as many items that do as many things as possible. Make it super light and compact; otherwise you won't carry it. It's a bit of an impossible mission, right? A repair kit that will fix any problem but weighs just a few grams. The holy grail!

Some thoughts: Carry washers, nuts, bolts, and screws that fit the hardware on your specific boots, bindings, skis, and other gear. If a teammate has unique boot buckles or a rare binding, make sure he has the necessary hardware to fix it. A "pole splint" for a broken ski pole is a must, even for day tours. On multiday or secluded backcountry trips, you might consider carrying a full toe- and heelpiece for your bindings.

Ski straps, bailing wire, duct tape, a smallish multi-tool, one-shot ampules of instant-glue, and zip ties fix an enormous array of gear and problems. Often an in-field repair only has to function long enough to get you to a trailhead or back to a hut. There you can devise a more permanent fix—the ski shop if you're headed to the frontcountry, or perhaps two-part epoxy, ski straps, and a couple hours by the stove at the hut. It's amazing what a bunch of motivated backcountry tourers can do with a good repair kit. Don't pack the kitchen sink, but for about a pound or two, I bet you can put together a good kit.

BACKCOUNTRY PREP TAKEAWAYS

It sounds like a lot, but just get your crew together for a couple afternoons and evenings during the fall, and spend some time refreshing the skills you can. Once your winter snowpack begins to build, take the skills outdoors and perform them in more realistic scenarios. Just a few hours of invested time in the fall will make any mishap far more manageable in the backcountry. And besides—you like hanging with your team, right? Get them together.

Track the Season's Conditions

Finally, the snow piles up and the high-altitude resorts in the States open around Halloween—it's coming! Even before your local forecast center begins issuing advisories, you can begin tracking the season's conditions. How much snow, what happened between storms, where did the first storms persist, and where did they melt? Questions like these should be topics of conversation with your team from the first snowfalls of the year through the end.

HOW TO TRACK?

It seems like no two practitioners track the season's conditions in the same way. In the pre-digital age, forecasters used to lay out the entire season on one long sheet, tracking precipitation amounts, wind speeds and directions, storm durations, and incorporating pit information and test results. They were detailed, laborious, beautiful documents. I certainly don't expect you to go to such lengths.

Techier types might use a spreadsheet, which allows them to record each storm event, and even color-code notes corresponding to the danger during and after a storm. Others might jot notes in the back of their daily trip notebook. Some of you may just read your local bulletin religiously, including the forecasters' blogs, but I encourage you to put a little more effort into taking formal notes—it forces you to really distill what's important and get intimate with what's happening in your zone.

TRENDS AND CONDITIONS

Even the most casual backcountry rider tracks conditions. Ask a weekend warrior if he's getting out this Saturday and he might say, "It's all time out there, I wouldn't miss it!" Obviously he's tracking conditions . . . perhaps not in the same detail as you, but he's paying some attention. What I'm looking for is not only riding quality but also history, trends, and overall conditions.

In the simplest terms, we ask what sort of season we're having. Lots of snow? Very little? Warm, rainy, windy, epic? If you can put a word to the season, ask yourself, Why? If the answer to your question is "epic," then have specific, data-driven reasons it's epic. Snowfall amounts? Fewer persistent problems? Tons of sun?

You should certainly record unusual events in your spreadsheet

A Scale versus a Rating

Ever notice that professional forecasters talk about the "North American Danger Scale" and not the "rating"? You recognize that this is the five-level danger scale by which forecasters assign the danger on a given day. Seems obvious, but let's consider their language for a sec.

A rating would be a fixed thing, a set value of the danger that day. Forecasters assign that danger a spot on the *scale*, which implies a continuum between "Low" (green) to "Extreme" (black). Rather than five simple labels, the danger exists on a scale along these five levels. After four days at "High," then two days at "Considerable," and finally a day of "Moderate," you might be wise to recognize that trend and see that day's "Moderate" as closer to "Considerable" than it is to "Low." It's on a sliding scale, not a simple rating.

Keep this in mind the next time you check the bulletin, and remember that's it's a scale and not a simple rating.

or notebook—not only what's going down but also what the implications might be for later in the season. A buried rain crust in November could become your deep slab problem in February. Noting these events, layers, and trends in your process tunes you in to making better decisions down the road and not missing something subtle.

Tracking conditions will go into every day's trip plan. You'll be best prepared to understand the avalanche problems, know what's working to avoid them, and make better decisions.

Learn about Avalanches

I'll use words like "lifelong" and "progress" throughout the book, and learning about avalanches gives you the opportunity to acquire more knowledge. No one person on the planet knows everything there is to know about avalanches. It's a young science, and intelligent people across the world are adding to our body of knowledge every season. Join the discovery and endeavor to learn more about the science and practice of avalanches on an ongoing basis.

State, regional, and international avalanche workshops provide the opportunity to interact with other practitioners and learn from experts we might not normally have access to. They're a great starting point to revisit your avalanche knowledge in the preseason. Visit your local forecast center or avalanche nonprofit to see when your closest workshop might be. Keep your eyes peeled, too, for the International Snow Science Workshop (ISSW). It rotates venues every two years in the autumn, typically alternating between Europe and North America, but not always. And it's usually held in fantastic locations like Davos, Switzerland; Bozeman, Montana; and Innsbruck, Austria. Good time for a climbing or mountain biking trip.

Beyond that, revisit your previous seasons and ask yourself what conditions were less familiar and comfortable to you. Which problems gave you the most uncertainty in your trip planning? Identify glaring gaps in your knowledge and address them. Books like Bruce Tremper's *Staying Alive in Avalanche Terrain* provide the fundamentals. Doug Latimer's excellent e-book, *Avalanche! The Guide's Guide to Safer Travel in the Mountains*, takes a more detailed look at avalanches, sharing multimedia information that goes deep into the Canadian recreational (AST) curriculum and beyond.

There are ample web-based resources, too, but buyer beware: Check that what you're reading or watching is from a reputable source like the Canadian Avalanche Association (CAA), the National Avalanche Center (NAC), one of your regional forecast centers, or another professional organization. Some manufacturers produce content online with their sponsored athletes, but if you're hearing wild claims or kooky information, verify it elsewhere. Selling stuff and genuinely educating the public sometimes go hand in hand, but not always. Be discerning.

When you feel you're ready to go beyond recreational sources, consider taking a professional avalanche course. You'll need to apply and have a résumé ready to make the leap. Check with the CAA in Canada and American organizations like AIARE in Jackson, the Silverton Avalanche School, the Alaska Avalanche School, Colorado Mountain College, and the National Avalanche School. As the professional program matures in the United States, more providers may come online, but these are the sole professional-level providers at the time of this writing.

Also consider contacting certified mountain guides in your area, particularly ones who specialize in education and/or who have been forecasters. There are a few. Shop around, and ask for credentials and experience. Discuss with them exactly what you're looking for and come up with a curriculum of sorts to help you make a jump in your skill set.

Find Compatible Partners

You will spend the whole season making life-or-death decisions (as well as decisions like where to get doughnuts in the morning) with your team, so now is the time to assemble an ideal squad. Much more on this in "The Team."

The first obvious criterion is risk tolerance. Does your buddy have the same tolerance for risk as you? If she's looking to repeat Kílian Jornet routes next winter while you're content to master the stem christie, you're not going to find a lot of overlap in your goals. Zero judgment on skiing "you fall, you die" terrain, but if one of your team is into it while the rest of you are not, you are building conflict and uncertainty into your team and season. Now is the time to gauge your compatibility with a new teammate.

Decision making and one's mindset in the backcountry can be make-or-break traits in teammates. If you prefer to discuss options, decide by consensus, allow everyone in the group a veto if he or she is uncomfortable, and enjoy your end-of-day debrief but your buddy is a "decide-on-the-fly" guy, it's not going to work. It's perfectly fine to have dear friends with whom you don't ski. Great person, just a different approach to the hazard and practice? No worries, but now is the time to determine that, not midway up a slope on a high-hazard day.

Often just the suggestion of getting together to perfect transceiver skills or review literature on a particular avalanche problem or practice assembling a rescue toboggan will reveal who's on the same page as you and who is not.

Revisit your team from last year, and be honest about what went well and what did not. Can your team discuss disagreements or mistakes without assigning blame and/or arguing? Is your team more committed to being accurate than being "right"? It's an amazing thing when the team "clicks"—and potentially dangerous when it doesn't. Study and analyze avalanche accidents. You'll quickly see how often it's a team breakdown that contributes to them.

In his white paper "Human Factors in Avalanche Accidents," Dale Atkins, past president of the American Avalanche Association, attributed human factors as the primary cause of the accidents he studied in the 1990s.

He writes, "Human factors are the cause of most avalanche accidents involving avalanche-aware people. Staying alive is not as simple as being able to recognize avalanche hazards. The problem is seldom a lack of information regarding terrain, weather, and snowpack. The problem is how that information is processed."

The problem, in a sentence, is ineptitude not ignorance—a failure to use and apply information rather than a lack of it. Your team and its process are your two best defenses against an avalanche accident. Put together a group of smart, open-minded, committed, process-driven individuals, and then spend the time required to transform that group into a cohesive team.

Investigate Trip Options

By late fall you're jonesing for some real snowfall and the legs should be getting stronger. I hope you put in the time to refine your rusty skills from last year and perhaps address some gaps in your knowledge. You want to be ready when the backcountry finally turns on, so have some trips ready to go.

What do we mean by "ready to go"? The pages of a guidebook earmarked? A loose dream of "sending the Sara-gnar Supercouloir" this spring? Many guides try to have a "run atlas" built not only for their home spots but also for anywhere they plan to visit. With virtual guidebooks, online trip reports, and friends on social media, it's pretty easy to get a ton of info up front, before you step out of your Lamborghini SUV and into your sticks. Let's share some planning thoughts.

THE RUN ATLAS

A run atlas can be photos, notes, a spreadsheet listing particular tours, or any combination of these and other relevant elements. Ideally, you're putting together different tours suited to different teams, different conditions, and different goals. For example, you get low-low-low avalanche danger midseason, your best teammates are available and stoked, and the snow conditions are ripe for a steep ski—perhaps in the back of your run atlas you have several tours appropriate only when the stars align. Low danger, A-list crew, good snow? That sounds like aligned stars to me, and now you're prepped to get some.

Likewise, you'll have some tours for low-vis days, days on which you're touring with totally inexperienced partners, days when you're testing new gear, days with persistent-slab problems. The run atlas not only sets you up with information on approaches, descents, and other relevant beta but also helps to de-bias your decision making by defining what tours are appropriate when. You're less likely to "talk yourself into it" on a high-hazard

Critical Considerations

You might tag each of your runs or touring zones with specific characteristics, like "high-hazard days" or "half-day tours." Some more ideas:

- **High freeze level.** Days when the freeze level comes up and you're avoiding rain and/or wet snow in the valleys.
- **High hazard days.** Some tours only go on low-danger days, while you can pull off others in almost any conditions. Have trips cataloged for trickier avalanche conditions.
- **Less fit friends and teammates.**
- **Late-season tours** for longer days/better conditions.
- **Specific weather conditions.** High wind, intense solar, low vis; certain tours will keep you more comfortable under different conditions. For example, keep your secret tree stashes for the days you're cowering from the wind.
- **Storm track.** Storms coming from a particular direction often favor certain portions of a range, drainage, or aspect. Prepare for it and you're more likely to get the goods.
- **Team.** Don't discount team dynamics or underestimate the effect of an unknown, newer member. For a "stars must align" tour, you need your reliable, predictable teammates. Don't drag the cousin from Regina out for a look at a Greg Hill line on Cheops!

We're matching tours to the conditions appropriate for them. Those conditions range from teammates to avalanche conditions to weather events to just how you're feeling overall.

day if the tour is cataloged under "safe conditions only," etc.

So how do we compile a run atlas? For the past several seasons, I've had the good luck to run an AIARE 2 avalanche course at a backcountry lodge south of Nelson, British Columbia, with one of my mentors, Colin Zacharias. You've been looking at his charts already in this book. During each of those courses, we and the students shot photos daily then spent time each evening annotating the images with as little as a name and as much as arrows indicating entrances to runs, sketchy spots, etc. After several

What Gives Us the Confidence to Carry Out This Plan?

This is the final question in the AIARE Trip Plan (from the AIARE fieldbook, 2019). It's a final safety check that asks you to bring uncertainty into the discussion and make it part of the daily decision.

Assessing Sources of Uncertainty

No matter how skilled, experienced, or local you are, there is always a measure of the unknown when anticipating and managing mountain hazards. Uncertainty is intrinsic to the mountain decision. Risk is by definition "the effect of uncertainty on objectives" (from ISO 31000), and it's our job to identify and manage the risk and optimize the objective. Our job as mountain and ski guides and avalanche forecasters is to ask ourselves, "What do we know?" and, more importantly, "What don't we know?" During the morning guide meeting, we discuss our confidence and come up with an operational plan to gather information that helps to reduce knowledge-source uncertainty. Most importantly, we ensure decisions are evidence based and do not evolve from one or more assumptions.

Easier said than done.

Assessing Your Confidence

More Confident

Familiar with the team?
Is our risk tolerance compatible?
Familiar with the terrain or the proposed route?
Familiar with the conditions?
Familiar with the weather pattern?
Familiar with the snowpack?
Is the local information reliable?
Do we have enough information to support our decision?
Do we have a plan to stop, gather info, and reassess?
Are we skilled enough at identifying the current problem from field observations?
Are we fit enough to have a healthy reserve at day's end?
Is the objective realistic? Does it match the team and the conditions?

Less Confident

Applying a Margin of Safety

Even if we are good, we still make mistakes. The plan is always to be more right than wrong, give ourselves time to decide, and have time to error correct. Most importantly, we apply a *margin of safety* that allows for error. We define this as *additional caution that matches our measure of uncertainty* (from *Technical Aspects of Snow Avalanche Risk Management*, published by the Canadian Avalanche Association, 2016, section 3.4.3, 15).

Often this plays out when we choose more conservative terrain. If we are worried about avalanches, we choose safer terrain until we gather relevant information and have a reason to step it out. When in new terrain, plan a shorter excursion and allow extra time to explore and find elegant ways to navigate around hazards and through the terrain. In spring, when you aren't sure how quickly the snowpack deteriorates with daytime radiation and warming, plan to exit the sunny aspects sooner rather than later.

- Keep it simple.
- Identify uncertainty.
- Communicate your level of confidence.
- Apply a margin of safety.

Now you will have the confidence to carry out your plan.

—Colin Zacharias

seasons doing this, we've amassed high-quality, detailed photos showing much of the tenure. Not only does it help us on subsequent courses, but if we're working with a new guide, we can simply hand over a digital file and give her a ton of info with which to prep.

High-traffic venues like Rogers Pass have their own run atlas they'll share (even digitally), and an established backcountry hut like Sorcerer Lodge has an enormous three-ring binder of images compiled over decades. Guides there use the images during morning meetings and snap photos on their phones before heading into the field.

In short, a run atlas gives you more information for planning (and even terrain management in the field). Sort images into folders, or dump them into notes in a note-taking app, like Evernote, on your computer. Add images of your trip-planning pages from your notebook, random notes from your tours, etc. And because you're tracking the season's conditions, you'll have a great idea which tours should be on the table for any given day.

Putting It Together

And now the p-tex meets the pow. It's time to put it all together and plan a tour. Our homework sets us up to make smarter decisions when planning. You already have some sense in your head about what tours to do in what conditions, but hopefully your run atlas helps rule out an inappropriate decision due to "mad pow disease" or any of our other potential biases. For example, the first big snow of the year isn't the time to huck pillows.

In the big picture, you and your team have a sense of what the season's doing (and not doing!) and what current conditions are. With this context, now you gather the gang (literally or, more likely, virtually) and integrate all of your information and observations, select a mindset, and plan a tour.

In a perfect world, we wake up at a cozy hut in the backcountry, with the coffee ready and 50 centimeters of blower overnight. You and your gang stroll down to a spacious table, notebooks in hand, the weather report and avalanche bulletin readily available on the Wi-Fi, and no rush to get out the door.

Right. For most of us, that's one or two weeks out of the year. A full-time ski guide gets a version of that much of her winter, but with way more stress and pressure. After all, she's been paid to keep people safe, and she'll have to make some serious decisions on her own throughout the day. The point is, however you and your team get together, make the best of it, be

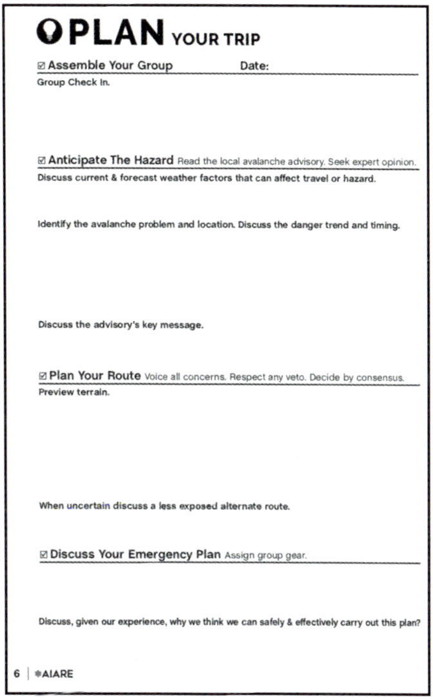
PLAN YOUR TRIP

☑ Assemble Your Group Date:
Group Check In.

☑ Anticipate The Hazard Read the local avalanche advisory. Seek expert opinion.
Discuss current & forecast weather factors that can affect travel or hazard.

Identify the avalanche problem and location. Discuss the danger trend and timing.

Discuss the advisory's key message.

☑ Plan Your Route Voice all concerns. Respect any veto. Decide by consensus.
Preview terrain.

When uncertain discuss a less exposed alternate route.

☑ Discuss Your Emergency Plan Assign group gear.

Discuss, given our experience, why we think we can safely & effectively carry out this plan?

6 | AIARE

The AIARE trip planning page, featured in its fieldbook. Each teammate fills it in, compiling and synthesizing data. It functions as both a checklist and a process or algorithm in and of itself—using prompts like "Identify the avalanche problem and location." Not having an answer gives the team immediate feedback that it needs more information and to revisit its planning process.

COURTESY AIARE

efficient, and, most of all, get it done—this is your chance to perform your repeatable process, catch an oversight, correct an error before you're in the field, and get the best touring possible.

We'll call your team meeting, group gathering, virtual chat, or early-morning rendezvous a "guide meeting" as a catch-all term. Even if you're not a working guide, what you're doing should be more similar to a professional meeting at Canadian Mountain Holidays than dissimilar. Take it seriously, do the work, prepare well. The activity we all love is life-or-death serious. And decades of experience from risk managers, heli operators, mountain guides, and academics confirm that a guide meeting is one of the best ways to mitigate risk and manage our wicked environment.

The Guide Meeting

Kids, work, distance, time—all these things threaten to derail your guide meeting. I get it, and I don't discount the many competing forces in our lives. That said, even a 10-minute chat will help you significantly lower your hazard and de-bias your trip planning. The science is unequivocal—all of us fall prey to biases and heuristics, and the more tired/dehydrated/distracted/stressed/stoked we are, the more likely we are to make a compromised, emotional, or rash decision. The guide meeting helps protect us against a poor decision in the field, but only if you and your team buy in and get it done before leaving the trailhead.

Distilled to a simple checklist, your guide meeting is an effort to identify hazards and the strategies/practices

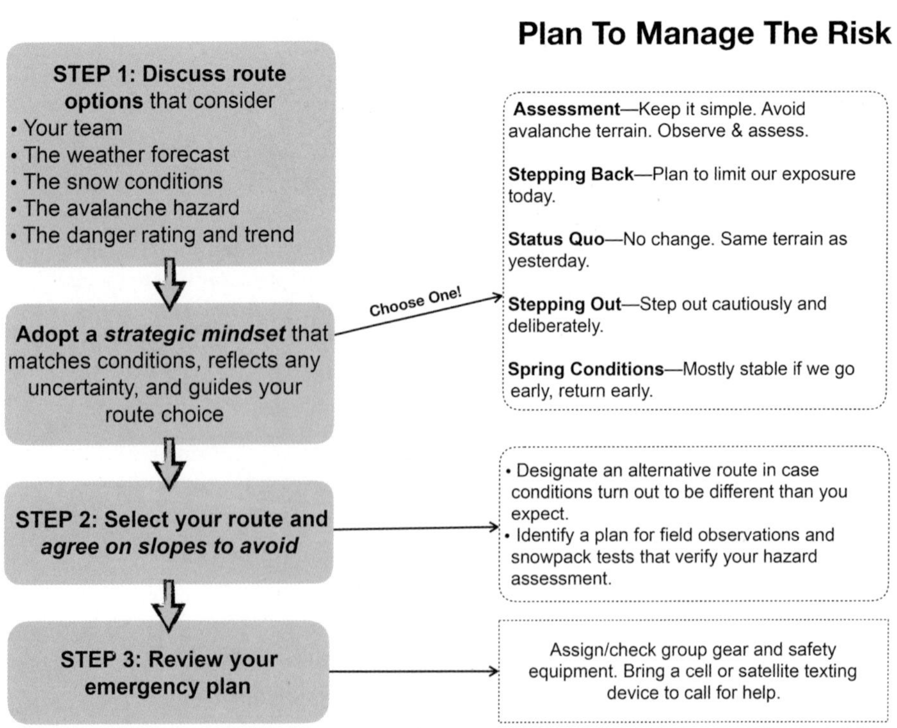

COLIN ZACHARIAS

Your Team

By now you've noticed the terms "team" and "teammates." I don't use those terms lightly. Whether we're guiding with guests or riding with a bunch of friends, the vibe needs to be of a cohesive team rather than a group. Ask yourself: Are you skiing with a team or merely a group?

Former professional poker player Annie Duke pursued a PhD in cognitive psychology at the University of Pennsylvania before her world-championship poker career, and she's now a renowned "decision strategist." She and other thinkers recognize a functioning team as an extremely powerful tool in short-circuiting bias and making better decisions. Duke suggests any team remind itself, "What we care about is being accurate, not being proven right."

Consider bringing that language into your team. Being right is about arguments and ego; being accurate is about evidence and reality. I bet you know which approach is better in the backcountry!

you'll use to avoid them. Your meeting should:

- List who's coming and evaluate whether the group is compatible.
- Identify the specific problems you'll face on the day (avalanche and otherwise).
- Decide where you're going and evaluate if that zone/run is appropriate, given the day's conditions; establish an alternative tour so you have two desirable options.
- Identify uncertainty and blind spots, and strategies to address them, gather more information, etc.
- Determine how the team will travel in the terrain and at different times. As a group? Roped together? One at a time?
- Discuss rescue options and strategies. Who has what gear? Communications? First aid? Special considerations within the team or due to venue?

First off, consider dividing up your duties. One teammate can gather comprehensive weather information, another can summarize several days of the avalanche bulletin, while still another can work on the team and its gear list. If the group arrives at the meeting (or gets on a conference call, etc.) with this information compiled, it will speed your session up. Rotate roles so that everyone keeps the variety of skills fresh. Each teammate should have a notebook, ideally in a similar format so you're all repeating a similar process.

WEATHER

Find a weather process that works for you. You'll first need weather observations—what has been happening over the season, then the past 72 hours, and finally last night. Temperatures (freeze level most importantly), wind directions and speeds, cloud cover, and of course precipitation (type and amount) all factor into your decision making.

Start by amassing information via local weather stations. In Colorado, for example, there are dozens of these peppered throughout the state. The Colorado Avalanche Information Center (CAIC) links to many but not all of these. Explore similar systems in your home zone, if they exist. In the United States you can find many of these through your state's water/natural resources division.

Eventually you will learn which weather stations are most representative of wind speeds/directions while others give a more accurate indication of how much snow fell from the sky, how much it settled, etc. Ridgetop stations give a good indication of overall wind direction; a more sheltered station will hold all the snow that fell overnight.

Some weather stations offer a complete set of data, while others might only give you precipitation totals and temp. Depending on who maintains the station, it might come on- and offline throughout the year. Do some digging and figure it out. Webcams can be helpful too.

In spring, stream flows also will be useful information. Through monitoring the amount of runoff (measured in "cfs," cubic feet per second, in the United States; "cms," cubic meters per second, in Canada), you can see how well the snowpack is or is not draining—helpful for timing a wet slab cycle and considering glide cracks.

After just a few weeks you should have a fast, efficient process for gathering accurate conditions on the ground. Now you'll need to get an idea of your forecast. While different sites offer interpretations and products, there are in reality just a handful of weather models forecasting in North America. Don't get sold on some guy's high-ticket "prediction"! Avalanche centers like the Utah Avalanche Center and Avalanche Canada offer forecasts and products as good as anyone's—and for free.

Note that you can obtain a regional forecast as well as a "spot forecast." Spot forecasts vary from location to location, but these are often computer-generated forecasts down to as little as a 2-kilometer grid. You can access them in a variety of ways and on different services, so experiment to find the interface you like. Consider saving a graphical representation of the weather (called a meteogram) as a PDF and then sharing it with your crew (between phones via Bluetooth, or you can text).

If you've taken on the weather component of your guide meeting, arrive with current conditions and an idea of what's going to happen during the day or week. Have a succinct, clear synopsis ready for your team.

Backcountry trips, expeditions, and traverses require more planning for your weather information. You can receive a text with weather information on a satellite communication device. The United States' National Oceanographic and Atmospheric Administration (NOAA) issues forecasts from 1,000 stations, and with a VHF radio you can receive transmissions (between 162.400 and 162.550). Canada also broadcasts on these same frequencies, in both English and French, but from 230 stations. This can be a great help for a remote trip.

By the time you're ready to present the weather to the team, you'll probably already have an idea about how it's going to influence avalanche hazard and your tour. Save your personal predictions for the discussion—let team members digest the information on their own first and make notes before diving into interpretations. This not only avoids group-think and the expert halo but also keeps the meeting moving.

AVALANCHE CONDITIONS

Wise teams take a deep dive into this portion of the trip planning, going far beyond just the danger rating on the day. As English-speaking avalanche centers transitioned to presenting advisories through the lens of avalanche problems (around 2011), recreationists had an easier time discussing avalanche hazard in a broader, more consistent context.

Most English-language avy centers now present a written summary of conditions, the character(s) of predicted avalanches, some sense of where we might find them, the likelihood of our triggering them, and the size they could be—overall, you have a sense of the avalanche problems you're facing. In addition to this, there's also an overall danger rating by number and color. Some centers also issue a "bottom line," a one- to two-sentence distillation of all the above information. This makes your job as a trip planner easier than ever, provided you truly digest the information.

We take all of the above and extract the main information: What's the problem, and is it improving or worsening? Where is the problem, and what terrain do I need to avoid?

At press time the professional avalanche community is revisiting how the general public uses and applies avalanche advisories. Formal results have yet to be published, but what the community agrees on is that using incomplete bits of the bulletin invites problems. The public bulletin compiles field and weather observations from pros and recreationists in addition to avalanche observations. For most of us leaving the trailhead, the bulletin acts as our best defense against surprises and accidents.

As an advanced recreationist or mountain guide, we expect that you already read and understand your local bulletin and its format. Many centers also feature a blog from the forecasters—excellent reading—and you should drill down into these posts. They often reveal what snowpack tests

Donate to Your Avalanche Center!

Need we say more? Forecaster centers need our support, and we rely on them daily. Donate a few bucks, volunteer, or e-mail them to ask how you might help at an event.

the forecasters are using and why, what trends they're seeing, and other invaluable information. Use all of it!

Don't forget to look at the weekly trend of the danger too—knowing whether the hazard is generally worsening or improving is great information. Have a clear sense of what's going on around you. Consult friends and experts too if you've been out. If you know a patroller or mountain guide in your zone, don't hesitate to fire off a text. Chances are you will receive a terse reply, but those few words might just save your hide.

WAIT, MIND-WHAT?

A few paragraphs ago we used the vague and sometimes mysterious term "mindset." Mindset simply refers to a set of beliefs and behaviors that govern how an individual or group approaches the world or a task. For the high-end recreationist and ski guide, let's customize the concept to a "terrain-use mindset."

Our terrain-use mindset provides a set of protocols and behaviors that govern our touring on the day. Once we've assembled our group, gathered our information and observations, and identified hazards, we identify our terrain-use mindset and let it help govern our choices of where we tour, what slopes we will ski, and how we plan to travel. It also helps us decide where we will not tour. It is an adopted bias of sorts; some might call it a pre-bias. It defines our approach and mindset toward the terrain.

Scholars modify and define "mindset" differently, but let's stick to the general definition above for our discussion.

Imagine your team of five skiers. Two teammates have a "the summit

A good trip plan sets you up for the best skiing . . . just ask this joker in the plaid pants. Selkirk Lodge, British Columbia. MATT KENNEDY

or death" mindset, while another two trend toward the "I love skiing, but it's not worth risking an injury" mindset. All sorts of conflicts, disconnects, and problems jump to mind, right? What's your objective on the day? What sounds like a fun tour? What conditions would make you turn back? With conflicting mindsets, you can see it might be impossible to even plan a tour, let alone pull it off in the field!

Herein lies one of the strengths of a guide meeting: identifying potential problems in a dispassionate setting. An effective guide meeting, performed in an environment of honesty and respect, will reveal problems, mistakes, and oversights before you're in the field. Any "desire-driven" activity immediately introduces a bias to that activity. Ski touring, surfing, car shopping—everybody loves to do something.

For most of us, that something is backcountry touring. We share a solid case of mad pow disease: We all want to ride deep, light snow on interesting terrain. Modern neuroscience and psychology says that because of this bias toward skiing the goods, our brains tilt that direction and we unconsciously put a finger on the scale of any decision between "safe enough to ski?" and "should we bail?" Knowing this, in an effort to remove some of that mad pow bias, we do our guide meeting before we're looking down 1,000 meters of untracked snow.

We choose a mindset on the day, which helps us go one step further—pre-biasing ourselves. Different mindsets give us different sets of rules and behaviors for each day touring. Professional ski-touring operations use the term "strategic mindset"; they literally select a mindset from a list, and that mindset colors the guides' and pilots' actions on the day.

Chances are you already have at least a vague sense of applying mindset. When you leave the trailhead or hut, are you feeling on the defensive (on a high-danger day, for example) or are you and your team stoked for conditions and ticking a big line (low danger just after a big snowfall)? Those are mindsets, but the question needs to be: What is our mindset, given the conditions? Does everyone have that same mindset? How did we arrive at it? Can we stick to it during our tour?

In your guide meeting, once you've gone over weather and avalanche conditions, the group then selects a mindset on the day, incorporating all the information you have (including on the team). I suggest creating several terrain-use mindsets, such as "avoid avalanche terrain," "step out carefully," "step back," "status quo," and "go early, return early." You notice in the Guide Meeting chart above that Colin Zacharias poses these as questions in an effort to prompt a discussion and self-reflection. Presented with a decision in the field, like avoiding a particular slope, for example, we ask ourselves, Are we "avoiding avalanche terrain"?

Consider pausing to let each member select a mindset on the day, before deciding as a team. This prevents less-experienced teammates from deferring to senior members and their judgments. At decision points, let each teammate revisit the mindset and ask him/herself: "Are we sticking to our plan? Does this decision fit our terrain-use mindset on the day?" Then discuss as a team.

As Dr. Daniel Kahneman writes in his bestseller *Thinking, Fast and Slow*, "The proper way to elicit information from a group is not by starting with a public discussion but by confidentially collecting each person's judgment."

What we are doing is harnessing a cognitive bias to work for us—in effect, we are employing anchor bias. A terrain mindset anchors our behaviors and decisions to some "rules of engagement" on the day, all in a dry, comfortable setting, away from wind, cold, sun, powder, and that oh-so-perfect-looking slope beneath your skis—before we're subject to emotions, fatigue, group stoke, or pressure from other skiers.

TERRAIN CODING

We are down to deciding where to ski and ride—right on! All we're doing is anticipating what our hazards might be, deciding on how to avoid and mitigate those hazards, and amping up the fun meter.

You and your teammates can now discuss route options in the context of the day's avalanche hazards, group dynamics, and weather. As you develop your run atlas, this becomes easier and easier. We apply our terrain-use mindset to those choices. If we select a "step out carefully" mindset, then perhaps it opens up longer tours, more vert, or more complex terrain. Conversely, a "step back" mindset reminds us to dial back exposure to avalanche terrain. We consider lower-angle terrain, terrain

Terrain, Terrain, Terrain

In real estate they say, location, location, location. For backcountry touring, it's terrain, terrain, terrain. We can't control the weather, the snowpack, or the avalanche hazard on the day, but you and your team can control where you tour—the terrain. And terrain comes at different scales. You might get to choose the range in which you ski (the Rockies or drive over to Rogers Pass?). You can almost always choose one drainage over another, and you most definitely have control over a slope-scale piece of terrain. (Are we comfortable skiing this slope?) And once on that run, terrain can even be at the feature-scale: just a single convex roll on the slope. You can always control terrain—work it and use it to your advantage.

Stacked tracks keep skiers away from more hazardous terrain on either side of fantastic skiing. Selkirk Lodge, British Columbia.
MATT KENNEDY

without overhead hazard, terrain with fewer trigger points, and avoid any run that sounds similar to the terrain the bulletin might have warned us about.

At this juncture in the meeting, you may code terrain as "open," "closed," or "open if . . ." Professionals in the mechanized industry coined the term "terrain coding" to describe this process. However you conceive of it, it's a good idea to determine what terrain is closed on the day. Again, this is an exercise better done indoors, with the facts at hand, without the allure of untracked blower-ific snow downhill of your ski tips. You might code the terrain as closed by description: slope angle, elevation band, and slope shape. If you know the terrain in which you'll be riding, you might list full drainages or named runs as closed on the day.

Likewise, you categorize some runs as open, or open with caveats of sorts. For example, you might suggest to the team, "If we get to the top of the Huckgnar Couloir and there's no wind effect, we can consider skiing it." These caveats should be specific and verifiable. Beware of saying, "Yo, if it feels good, we'll charge it!" Too vague and too open to modification in the field! These parameters and caveats get listed clearly in your notebooks.

What has worked best in the mechanized industry in Canada is closing and opening terrain on the day, and the agreement is—and this is inviolable—that it stays that way for the day. No opening terrain on the fly. You might close terrain due to worsening conditions or unexpected conditions, but there's certainly no opening a run that was listed as closed in the meeting. This de-biasing strategy protects against impulsive, on-the-fly decisions.

We choose a couple options for awesome tours from our open terrain. Notice you don't choose a "great" tour and a "second choice" tour. If you make your second option obviously less appealing than your first, guess which one you'll lean toward? You

The Danger of the Blue Dot

The advances in smartphone and GPS technologies have made backcountry navigation much easier for most of us. The ubiquity of the smartphone and the dramatic improvements in user interface has made navigating by smartphone the standard for everyone from casual hikers to professional adventurers, but this comes with a downside.

The "blue dot" shows one's location on an imperfect, incomplete representation of the earth's surface. During avalanche courses, we often get the question: "Why don't the forecast centers issue a digital bulletin, with the avalanche problems mapped in the terrain by aspect, elevation, and slope angle?"

As one wise practitioner opined, "You can't get avalanche forecasters to agree on much, but the one thing they all agree on is that we will never issue a digital map of the avalanche bulletin."

Why, you ask. Avy professionals worry that as soon as a skier can open his phone app and see his blue dot, he risks ceding his decision making to the phone. The blue dot is a navigation tool far more than a decision-making tool.

Forecasters worry that if the blue dot falls outside the forecasted problem area, riders might think it's "game on, we're safe." Problem is, no phone app can account for how the wind swirls below a rocky ridgeline or how an unusually formed cornice influences the wind downslope or if a slope has slid earlier in the season. The blue dot does an excellent job telling you where you are; it can't identify local conditions or account for different avalanche problems. Only you and your teammates can do that.

The blue dot is a great navigation tool, but it is extremely limited. Don't overestimate what the blue dot can do.

know it's true! You're weak and prone to indulging yourself—exactly like me. Decision-making science strongly supports this. By giving yourselves two fun options, you're more likely to truly evaluate those options in the field rather than pretend you have options, when in actuality you're just going to ski your "plan A."

THE ROUTE

Once you've closed and opened terrain, selected a mindset, and discussed options, you need to reach consensus

Consensus?

Why not say "reached agreement" instead of "consensus"? Consensus implies a decision everyone has come to and can live with. This differs slightly from agreement in the sense that you might have a guide meeting and, at first, two teammates don't feel that a particular run should be open on the day. After a long, evidence-driven discussion, though, they recognize that perhaps that run is less hazardous than they thought and you arrive at a consensus that you can safely carry out that plan. Consensus. We arrive at consensus after discussions, debates, and information sharing rather than just asking, "Do you agree?" Strive for consensus in your decisions. If you can't reach it, that's telling you something about the option, the process, or the team.

on your terrain and routes. In this day and age, at least digital maps if not a full .gpx track of your potential routes should be in your phone/GPS device. One nice advantage of a smartphone is the ability to share tracks and run atlas photos via Bluetooth or texting. Share with your team to provide redundancy and to allow for multiple verifications of info in the field.

For low-vis days or more complicated routes, writing out salient information helps. It can be everything from just critical details, like where to cross a river, to a full-blown tour plan that includes time estimates, coordinates, elevations, and beyond. If you don't know how to do this . . . you know what I'm going to say.

Make sure you have two phones with maps and you've reached consensus on the decisions.

The Emergency Plan

As part of our trip plan, we prepare for the worst. An accident, an illness, broken gear, a navigation mistake—you name it, we need to have at least a few tools at our disposal to manage a problem.

During the guide meeting, divide up the group gear to ensure that no one person gets stuck with the full list—med kit, repair kit, rescue sled, bivy sack, communication device(s). Note who has what, in writing. It's a simple, quick process, but one that will reveal "Oops, I forgot my headlamp!"

The farther afield you'll be going, the more you need to really focus on this step. A bush flight into the Brooks Range in Alaska is a way different deal than dialing 112 in the Vallée Blanche. Recognize that, and take what you need.

CHAPTER 2

The Up

Craftsmanship names an enduring, basic human impulse, the desire to do a job well for its own sake.

—Richard Sennett, *The Craftsman*

There are several ways to perform almost any act—an efficient, workable, artistic way and a careless, indifferent, sloppy way. Care and artistry are worth the trouble. They can be a satisfaction to the practitioner and a joy to all beholders.

—Helen Nearing

Skiing and riding in the backcountry require a lot of time walking uphill—setting a skintrack or kicking steps up a couloir or along a knife-edged ridge. We need to have the skill mastered, even if we spend much of our time in "sidecountry" or heli- or catskiing. Doing a masterful job on the up allows us to reduce exposure to avalanche terrain, gather information about the snow, and find the best ski conditions. Laying down an elegant, enjoyable uptrack gives us the satisfaction that we are offering our teammates or guests the most efficient way up the hill. It is our signature. And moving well in the mountains is its own reward!

Group management in hazardous terrain is one of the challenging subtleties in the ski discipline. When we take friends rock climbing, we're literally tied to them for much of the day. They can't wander off; the rope limits how much trouble they can get into and "leads" them along the route. With the exception of a roped ascent in complex, crevassed terrain, as soon as we're ascending on skis, we lose the rope's connection. Setting a track that your group wants to follow, and is natural to follow, keeps your team together. Few instructions may be required. Other times we give a couple verbal instructions to increase space between skiers or ensure that we do not delay under a short section of increased exposure.

Our uptrack, modeling, pacing, and discussions manage our group; this in turn helps us mitigate fatigue, anxiety, and risk. It requires forethought, excellent planning and prep, and articulate communication to make all this happen.

Students leading a tour outside Nelson, British Columbia, on an AIARE 2 avalanche course. An efficient, lower-angle (12- to 15-degree) skintrack lets the group tour all day without excessive fatigue. Notice that the guide, last in line, stands upright and takes a short stride, his heelpiece rarely going farther than the toepiece on the opposite ski. This conserves energy on the day and on the week. The student in the front takes a longer stride, which at first feels more efficient but eventually tires a skier out. MAHTING PUTELIS

Context

Skiers and snowboarders accustomed to staying on piste often regard the up as misery defined. It's understandable; imagine having to tour on heavy gear, dressed for a cold day of lift-served riding, with limited tour function in your boots and bindings. You'd hate it too!

Our job as guides or mentors is to show newer backcountry riders that going up doesn't have to mean suffering. We have to model everything the up can be—a demonstration of our proficiency in the mountains, a means to gather and discuss observations within the team, and a method of tapping out a huge day without crushing our guests. By appropriately pacing the group, maintaining a consistent, lower-angle skintrack, and taking short, even strides, we coax our clients into bigger days than they would dream of doing on their own and show teammates how to cover thousands of meters of up over the course of a day or week in the hills.

Guides setting track on an early morning below Loft Peak, British Columbia. Vents open, dressed lightly, short strides, and a gradual skintrack—this is how you tick a 1,400-meter day without trashing yourself or your guests. HENRY COPPOLILLO

Once people have a few quiet, comfortable, untracked tours under their belts, they quickly discover the joy and reward of a long climb on an efficient skintrack, followed by the unequaled stoke of laying tracks down 1,000 meters of pristine pow. You know those runs—almost any amount of suffering is worth it!

Risk Management

Use terrain to reduce your risk. Not only does this mean minimizing exposure to avalanche hazard, rockfall, seracs, cornice fall, and even other riders, but a mellow, efficient skintrack saves the team's energy. Tired riders make worse decisions and have less "gas in the tank" for emergencies. Saving energy on a single-day tour, not to mention a weeklong holiday, keeps everyone safer and happier.

Sharpening a keen eye for navigating through challenging terrain and reducing exposure requires a few seasons. This needs to become a solid skill, both in the field and during the planning phase of a tour. Strategic tracksetting also can save kilometers

Making the up enjoyable for guests and friends keeps the day fun and rewarding. Thoughtful terrain selection and tracksetting go beyond that, though. By carefully considering your uptrack, you can accomplish many tasks at once. ROB COPPOLILLO

of wasted effort and distance. Imagine basing a week of touring at a popular backcountry lodge. In the first few days, when the legs are fresh, a smart team can establish a few "essential" uptracks that will help access a variety of terrain and can be reused during the daily back-and-forth. This can be a blessing during the 1.5-hour return leg to the hut after a leg-shattering 10-kilometer day—provided of course the weather gods don't fill in the track every night with 30 centimeters of fresh snow. In that case—you won't mind.

The slower uphill pace gives the team a chance to check in, discuss options, and keep an overall "feel" for how the day is going. Less-experienced riders might let their guard down on the up, having focused their attention on hazards expected on the steeper, more complex terrain of the downhill run. Modeling a vigilant attitude when ascending a slope is essential for guests and our less-experienced friends. A relaxed, conversational pace and track angle lets everyone add their voice to the decision-making process and conversation.

Track Angle—The Endless Debate

How steep to go, that is the question. Lifetimes have been spent debating the merits of a steeper skintrack, the use of heel risers, the benefits of a low-angle uptrack. I'll make some suggestions, but I also concede I'll never settle the debate once and for all. Do what you will! Fair warning to ski guide candidates: Set consistently steep tracks and you may find yourself, er, . . . repeating your exam.

Heel risers come in a variety of shapes, depending on your uphill travel mode. All of them function similarly—they elevate a rider's heel and lessen strain on the calf muscle. There's nothing inherently wrong with them. They can keep a guest more comfortable on a steeper uphill section. I only caution you not to use them as a bandage over poor tracksetting. Some guests feel wobbly on them, and asking a less-competent tourer to kick turn with the risers up sets the skier up for a fall.

Some chargers prefer to throw up the risers and "just get it over with." Fair enough, as long as it doesn't result in dead legs by lunchtime, or by midweek on the Haute Route. If you and your posse thrive on an 18- to 20-degree track, have at it.

As mountain guides, we often take first-timers or deskbound riders into the backcountry. The combination of a level 12- to 14-degree skintrack (meaning feet flat and side by side, not angled on the slope), a short stride, and an easy pace takes much of the pain out of a long climb for a less-fit guest. "Avoid 'em when you can; use them when you have to" is most guides' preferred use of heel risers on steeper tracks.

Observations

Reducing exposure to avalanche hazard is primary to our uphill terrain selection—assuming soft snow conditions. If we can navigate around the hazards and gather relevant observations, then it's win-win. Previewing terrain helps us get the goods and avoid low-quality riding conditions.

Planning to take a slightly longer or steeper uptrack might seem tedious in the moment, but if it gives you a good look at upcoming terrain or a potential descent, then it might just be worth it. Consider taking photos from a distance; once you're up against a feature or in dense trees, you'll be psyched to have a reference photo from a better vantage point.

The Local Perspective

We've all toured in a new area and been presented with an existing skintrack that we want to modify or avoid altogether. So, do we set our own? There are no set rules in the backcountry (for better or for worse), but one thing to keep in mind is the locals' perspectives and ethics. Will you draw the ire of the locals if you reestablish the skintrack? Do you care? Consider that the locals might have the track there for a very good reason—anything from preserving pow to avoiding a subtle hazard.

I won't take sides, but at least ask yourself, *Am I upsetting the local tradition?* Put in your own version of a safe, efficient uptrack, but try to at least consider the locals!

General Techniques

Making uphill progress isn't rocket surgery, but there are some tricks to improve comfort and efficiency. Let's discuss gaining vert with both skis and splitboard and then consider booting.

Skis and Splits

Ski and split technology continues to evolve. It seems that alpine touring (occasionally referred to as "randonnée") gear gets lighter and more efficient every season. Ferocious competition among brands too numerous to mention keeps product innovation at warp speed.

Telemark, the original mode of transport, has lost some popularity. Tele boots, for example, have dwindled to just a handful of manufacturers. There are a few boutique brands out there making releasable, relatively efficient tele bindings, though, so if that's your thing, keep your kit updated with the latest, safest gear.

Perhaps the most interesting developments in the past few seasons have been the inventive splitboarders who've developed techniques for "split-skiing" when the terrain calls for it.

SKINNING STRATEGIES

No matter your travel system, climbing skins function similarly between disciplines, and effective skinning techniques apply equally.

"Tall and proud" is how you'll hear the tourer's uphill stance and stride described—standing up, with the hips forward and a proud posture. This body position helps keep the skins adhered to the snow and minimize backward sliding. As soon as a rider begins struggling, he often bends at the waist and reaches uphill

Splitboard Wisdom from the Up-and-Comer

by Benja Glatz

Binding Platforms

Spark R&D

This small company based out of Bozeman, Montana, has quickly gained traction with their easy-to-use systems that are considered a workhorse in the field. While these bindings lack the bells and whistles of other brands, they are almost indestructible. Due to the nature of a sliding puck system, they rarely ice up, and the lack of moving parts creates a trustworthy system in all conditions. The puck options are Voile plastic or Spark aluminum/plastic pucks. Both are dependable. It is important to make sure to get the canted pucks to alleviate pressure on your knees.

Phantom Splitboard Bindings

John Keffler is quite literally a rocket scientist converted to shredder-evolutionist. Phantom engineering is second to none in its visionary systems. Phantom bindings use the latest materials and construction to create lightweight and highly technical kits.

While they fit significantly tighter than their Spark R&D counterparts, the Phantoms also come with a "con." Phantoms have notorious icing issues in the field. Most users tend to figure out their system for deicing and can alleviate this issue pretty handily. The Phantom design allows a little bit of play within the bails of the bindings in order to create the feel of a soft-boot binding.

Technical Toes

"Tech-toes" certainly make up the most universal piece of the technical splitboard binding system. That said, every system has its own pros and cons. I have personally broken almost every toepiece on the market due to the nature of "split-skiing" without a heelpiece. The integrity of the bindings and the forces on the various parts all have limits. Most of the new models are specifically created for uphill travel and light split-ski use.

Spark R&D and Phantom Splitboard Bindings have collaborated to make the first American tech-toe designed for splitboard use. Created specifically for uphill use, these toes do not come with a heelpiece. The arms feature stronger aluminum with reinforced pins and multiple locking settings for the lever. They feature the three-hole pattern of splitboards, creating a universal fit without any adaptor plates.

Benja's splitboard setup
BENJA GLATZ

France's Plum Splitboard has created a similar version to their American counterparts'.

Another option pairs a Spark R&D adaptor plate with any tech-toe you desire. The advantage here—that you can easily use any technical toe on the market—appeals to some riders. Four extra screws and an adaptor plate do add some vulnerability to the system, though. I have found the Dynafit Speed toes with the adaptor plate to be the strongest option, but they are also the heaviest.

Voile and Phantom both make two heelpiece options, with the Phantom Rocket Riser by far the superior product at present. It's light, indestructible, and offers the ability to lock your heel down with a ski strap.

Boots

Hard boots offer better edge control on steep skintracks, a technical fit for boot crampons, durability and strength for kicking steps in firm snow conditions, and of course significantly better feedback while riding due to the overall stiffness of the boot.

The hard boot has taken the splitboard mountaineering and guiding community by storm. Most splitboarders have historically coveted the Dynafit TLT6. Easily modified (check out the WildSnow blog [wildsnow.com] or

Benja Glatz COURTESY BENJA GLATZ

Phantom modification kits), it's also a strong and durable boot that has been put through the test by many high-end splitboard mountaineers.

Some new boots on the market have also started to inch their way into the mainstream. The Atomic Backland has been subject to the Phantom franken-boot wizards. They have created a new heel lever that is supposed to mimic the feel of a soft boot but still have the technical feedback of a hard boot. Other options include the Scarpa F1 and Alien, Arcteryx Procline, Dynafit Speedfit, and the Fischer Travers series, just to name a few.

The scent of winter moisture, the forged and determined miles, the elevation gains amid the solitude—these shared experiences are why I guide, and the lived moments are why I am a backcountry traveler. I'm a splitboarder based in Jackson Hole, Wyoming, an AMGA aspirant rock and alpine guide, and an assistant ski guide.

with the poles—thereby guaranteeing his skins will slip backward. Exertion level goes through the roof; frustration builds. We've all heard a less-experienced teammate say, "These skins are terrible!" Might be right, but often it's a body position issue and not some mysterious failure in skin technology.

So, first and foremost, remind our friends and guests to stand tall. With proper body position comes balance and stability, but don't forget the low-angle skintrack. Coaching our friends to take shorter, relaxed strides (don't let them push their foot forward too much, which wastes energy and unbalances them) with their boot buckles loosened will save energy on longer tours. Double-checking your teammates' boots to make sure they're in walk mode isn't a bad idea either.

A team of adventurous skiers leaves the sea ice and heads into the mountains in Svalbard, Norway. These skiers stand upright, hands on the grips of their poles, leaning into their strides and staying balanced over their skis. TOM WOLFE

King Grant, former AIARE and AMGA board member, decides to "choke up" on his uphill pole, allowing him to stay upright and take in the ho-hum view on his way to the east summit of Vekkerofjellet, Svalbard. ROB COPPOLILLO

You've seen it a million times—the newer backcountry skier overdressed in a base layer, a fleece, and then a hard shell. Within minutes he's broiling; another 5 minutes in the skintrack, he's shedding layers, re-layering, you name it. Help your friends dress appropriately by endorsing a "minimalist" sartorial approach to their riding: only as much clothing as they need to stay warm and protected on the up—not an ounce more! Leg vents, a lighter base layer, and a wind shell are usually all they need on the body. A cap (or a toque if you're north of the border) and a wide, lightweight, stretchy, multipurpose headband (often called a "buff," named for the Spanish brand that popularized the piece of gear), especially when paired with a light hood on a base layer, can keep you warm most of the season.

Now that your touring companions are dressed appropriately and standing tall, make sure to help them manage their position as the slope steepens or during awkward sections. In most situations, tourers can keep their hands comfortably on the grips of their poles, reaching only slightly

Pack askew, hunched over, with the center of gravity starting to move forward—this technique will tire a skier out and result in slipping on his skins. Shortening his stride will also spare his quads for the down. If he can push the hips forward, stand upright, and relax, he'll save energy and have stronger legs for skiing. ROB COPPOLILLO

Strong and efficient: Nearly 1,600 meters (more than 5,000 feet!) above the trailhead, these two skiers and their guide top out on Youngs Peak, Rogers Pass, British Columbia. With a mellow skintrack and good technique, the legs are fresh for a phenomenal run back to the car. ROB COPPOLILLO

The Smötli

Every ski guide and backcountry master should know the term "*smötli*," a Swiss-German term for the undisturbed column of snow left between your feet when tracksetting. The *smötli* indicates you've created a wide enough skintrack that everyone behind you can comfortably slide along in a stable hip-width stance that accommodates both the bowlegged and knock-kneed. It was popularized in the United States by Swiss-German guides like Freddy Grossniklaus and Martin Volken, who report that it's slang from Grindelwald. Now you know.

As teammates follow their leader, their feet compact the smötli, creating a flat, wide skintrack that's comfortable for everyone. Sapphire Col, Rogers Pass, British Columbia. ROB COPPOLILLO

forward as they stride. This preserves the balanced position and keeps them relaxed and exertion low.

On steeper sections or traversing a steeper slope, model how to "choke up" on the uphill pole, or shorten it if it's adjustable. During a traverse especially, this position might help them maintain an upright body position. Different riders and guides have preferences for these techniques, so keep them in your toolbox; if you notice a teammate having difficulties, suggest one or the other.

For guides and more experienced teammates, you might also consider "spotting" or "bracing" on a tricky section of the uphill track. Stabbing your poles just below the downhill ski edge can give the nervous person just enough support to negotiate a turn or hold an edge on a steep, icy section of the track. Standing above the struggling skier, you can also grab her pack's loop or offer your ski pole as a brace. You can't fully take her weight, but it might allow her to stand upright, relax, and survive a tricky section.

Often, though, these awkward sections can best be avoided by expert tracksetting and occasional trickery (more below). Try your best, especially when guiding, to set a skintrack that keeps everyone comfortable and moving along—this is how you get a 15-kilometer-plus, 1,600-meter vertical day out of a less-fit guest. She'll slide along the skintrack, check her watch at the end of the day, and say, "Wow, I've never done a day this big before." It's our job as guides to "levitate" guests through a big day, as if they're comfortably chatting on an escalator, and help them go bigger than they thought they could—all the while keeping them smiling. No small feat!

TERRAIN

Like so much of touring, terrain selection will set you and your guests/team up for a successful uptrack. Sharp

Trimming the Skins

Trimming skins demands some focus and attention. Too wide and you won't have your edges exposed, making traverses more difficult. Wider skins are heavier and don't glide as well. Choices, choices! In certain terrain you can get away with a slightly narrower skin, but beware: the more base showing, the less grip you'll get. If you go shorter and narrower on the trim, your technique will need to be even more dialed.

Splitboarders benefit from wide, grippy skins, but on traverses the wider profile of a split snowboard can become unwieldy when tracksetting in rough terrain—especially in firm snow. (Wide powder skis around 125 millimeters underfoot present the same problem!) Remember that when touring in a mixed group, what is easy for the narrower skis might be slippery and awkward for the split or the wide powder-planked members of the group. No matter the gear, fully exposed edges will make for more control on a scoured, firm snow surface.

reading of a topo map starts the process; augmenting this with Google Earth, terrain imagery, and perhaps guidebooks will give you an excellent idea of the best terrain for the up.

We strive for a cruisy skintrack that climbs at a consistent rate and look for terrain with features and bumps that facilitate comfortable turns. When previewing terrain photos, maps, and guidebooks, look for possible lines that minimize avalanche exposure, avoid dense forest, and avoid cliffy areas, crevassed glacier convexities, and mountain slopes pitched at 25-plus degrees. Search out broad ridges, benched and bumpy terrain with protruding features that provide a look ahead to the next section of your uptrack. Eventually, though, even the best laid plans go awry; we run into dead ends, and the terrain simply won't accommodate our high hopes of the easy skintrack. Now you really start working for it.

> ***DELIBERATE PRACTICE:***
> On your "game" days, do your best to choose easy terrain for the up. When you've got the time or the skiing isn't so hot, challenge yourself and teammates by selecting trickier terrain for the up. Dense forest, complicated terrain, or steeper-than-usual slopes all present challenges. Master them, but then avoid them once you have the skills. Keep it safe, provide one another feedback, and don't incur additional hazard—but these are skills worth having.

SKI CRAMPONS

On firm snow, we often have difficulty placing our whole ski flat on the snow surface. This means two things: When our ski is on edge, the climbing skin is no longer in full contact; we slip, and it's hard on our ankles when we try to lay the ski down on a sidehill to gain more purchase. One solution is that we can opt for a ski crampon. Merely a sheet of aluminum or steel that mounts (usually) to a ski's or split's binding, ski crampons have teeth on either side of the ski and provide "bite" into the snow, like a boot crampon. Paired with a skin, they provide exceptional grip on the up.

Seems like 90 percent of the time, our ski crampons stay in the pack. When you need them, though, you want them. Refrozen uptracks, steep icy trails in the trees, firm spring snow conditions, or frozen conditions after a midwinter thaw are all times when travel can be eased with the application of ski crampons. In these conditions the combination of skins and crampons can keep you on the up instead of struggling, slipping, or, worse yet, kicking steps for a couple of thousand feet through crusty snow when you could otherwise be skinning in the old track.

Many guests like to hang their ski crampons on the outside of their packs. While handy, you need to balance the likelihood of using versus losing them. One particularly spooky practice I've seen is clipping them to the waist belt of the pack—an awkward fall could result in shredding one's abdomen.

A nice trick to store ski crampons, or anything sharp for that matter, is to take an old stuff sack, just big enough for the 'pons, turn it inside out, and then lay strips of duct tape on the interior surface. Once you've lined it, inside-out it again so the duct tape is inside and prevents the ski crampons' sharp edges from slicing the stuff sack and your pack's contents.

FORGOT THE SKI CRAMPONS? BLEW 'EM OFF?

Eventually you'll be on a tour where you plain forgot, or mistakenly decided not to bring, ski crampons. All is not lost.

You've got to have a quick, honest discussion with yourself and/or the team and make sure you're not forcing it and taking on too much hazard. Ensure that the team is aware of the difference between a potential slip and a slide-for-life. An embarrassing fall down a slope is one thing; a long, sliding fall with rocks, trees, cliffs, or crevasses present could end in a devastating injury, even death. It's happened—be honest with yourself about the conditions.

If it feels manageable, and for a short section of firm track, you can always pull out the shovel and chop in a reasonable track for your followers. This presumes you're able to either do so with skis on (careful!) or you can do it in boots. We're assuming you do not have boot crampons, so make sure you have some foot penetration and that you're safe while chopping a track.

To conclude, ski crampons are light and, with some smart packing, barely take up any space. If you're undecided, bring 'em. But when you use them, remember they have a dark side. Be honest, and assess the slide potential before committing to exposed terrain. You might be safer walking up in a solid boot track, or be roped up to prevent a slip from turning into a slide-for-life. You'd rather back off and learn from the mistake than end up with an injury—or worse.

Soft Snow versus Firm Snow—Things to Keep in Mind

We need to keep in mind that our techniques and strategies differ a bit in firm and soft snow conditions. Taking a slightly different progression between techniques will help keep you and your team more comfortable, more efficient, and safer on uptracks, so let's dive into firm snow tracksetting.

Firm Snow Considerations

As soon as we find ourselves on firm snow, we need to think about keeping our skins as flat as possible so that we maximize contact and grip on the snow surface. On lower-angle terrain, no problem, but as soon as we're forced to turn across the slope, we find ourselves up on an edge. This works for shorter stretches, but it's trickier

Short Sections of Firm Snow

We've all put on the ski crampons, just to realize a few meters later that we could've done without. This is a tricky calculation, because wasting time putting them on/off slows down our day. If we accidentally forgo them and then find ourselves on exposed, icy terrain, it can be a real hazard.

The guide removes his ski to stomp and kick a workable track for guests, heading toward the Solitaire Glacier, above the Burnie Glacier Chalet in Canada. PETE COPPOLILLO

All this is to say, do your best and err on the side of having crampons on if you're worried about a long, sliding fall—especially with less-experienced teammates and guests.

For short sections, though, where it's obvious that stopping to put on ski crampons would be overkill, consider this simple trick: The guide or person in the lead removes her uphill ski, puts both poles in the downhill hand, and uses the ski in the uphill hand for support. She then slides across the firm section, kicking in a track with her foot. She then coaches her teammates or guests to use the kicked-in track on their *downhill* skis/boards. After the few meters of firmness, she puts her ski back on and off to the races. Quick and easy.

Transition into Ski Crampons before You Need Them!

Your expert tracksetting takes you onto a steeper, bulletproof slope and you increase the angle, coaching your teammates to bump up their risers and keep the skins flat. Awesome, it's working . . . until it's not. If the skins start to slip, you're by definition on a firm slope. A long slide is a drag, if not an outright danger. Before you and your posse find yourselves sketched out above a long slope ending in cliffs, consider cracking out the ski crampons.

Knowing when to put on the ski spikes is challenging. Err on the side of putting them on too soon rather than hoping folks can transition mid-slope. Don't rule out sliding beneath a wobbly teammate or guest and helping him with the transition. Hopefully in your trip planning, you identified firm, steeper snow as a possibility, so maybe your crew already has crampons hanging on their pack straps or harnesses.

If you can practice putting on your ski crampons without removing your skis, go for it. Do it in a low-stress situation, though—not when you realize you should've had them on for the last 250 meters. Again, if someone seems in danger of falling or losing a ski, slide beneath him, remove his ski crampons for him, and help him get into them. First and foremost, avoid this situation, but if you've blown it and gone too far without ski crampons, *stop and correct the issue immediately—and don't be afraid to help your guests!*

Phew! OK, deep breath and lower the stress. So now you and your group have the ski spikes on and you're ready to rock. First thing, lower your track angle again. Time and again you'll see folks taking too steep a track and getting surprised when their ski crampons slide backward. Remind folks that ski crampons help traversing, not going straight up. Lower your track angle, and let the teeth provide traction and stability. Getting on the ski crampons allows you to lower the angle again and hopefully surmount the slope without drama. But if you find things getting dicey again . . .

travel, less efficient, and, for certain riders, problematic.

TRAVERSING ON HARD SNOW

Consider how traversing a bulletproof slope would feel on 116-millimeter-underfoot powder skis. Welcome to the reality of sidehilling on a splitboard! Wider skis or a split means real pressure and leverage on your knees and hips when traversing. Instead of sliding the feet along casually, you're up on edge and using plenty of energy to stand a wide ski on only 2 to 3 millimeters of its edge. In addition, there's very little skin in contact with the snow. Not only are you more likely to slip in these conditions, you'll eventually start feeling the torsional pressure on your joints as you work to keep the ski or split up on edge. Take it from a dude with older joints—this matters!

I mentioned trying to keep the uptrack angle between 12 and 14 or 15 degrees for comfort and efficiency. As you feel your track steepening, you'll naturally want to begin traversing the slope a bit, but if it's firm conditions, you're in a pickle. Traversing without being able to set a flat track for your teammates (because there's no ski penetration on firm snow) requires having them put the skis and boards up on edge. For a short section, not a problem, but for a long traverse, you need to change tactics.

Rather than keep the angle low, consider going steeper and bumping up the heel risers. Risers do give less-experienced riders a sense of being on stilettos, so a little coaching might be in order. That said, the sensation of sidehilling on a firm slope with little traction is probably worse, so don't rule out going steep. Those of us on wider skis, and just about anybody on a split, will need to keep a steeper uptrack in mind as a viable option on firm snow.

BOOTS (AND BOOT CRAMPONS)

Sometimes there's no avoiding strapping the skis on the pack and heading up. Once the ski crampons–and-skins combo no longer feels efficient or safe, you're on foot. Don't immediately assume that you'll have crampons on, though. Step-kicking can work, and you might even have the ice ax out to chop a step here and there.

Again, try your best to anticipate the best means of travel and adopt it before you're in a sketchy spot. A quick recon mission by the leader might yield enough information to make the right call. If the team can't decide between booting with or without crampons, perhaps a quick sprint up the hill by one of the group will give you an idea.

If you're on the fence or your best efforts at step-kicking yield little security, put on the boot crampons. You'd rather manage the hassle and hazard of boot crampons than risk a long, sliding fall by not having them on. Help anybody who needs it, remembering that you've got skis on your pack now. If you do and you bend forward to help a teammate with her transition, don't

The team confronts a short section of firm snow, but with just enough boot penetration and a lower-consequence slope below, they can boot the last section to the col without crampons. Spitsbergen, Svalbard, Norway.
ROB COPPOLILLO

knock her unconscious with your skis! It has happened.

Boot spikes may solve one problem (traction), but don't forget that they create others. Ski-touring apparel is frequently more "Euro fit" than baggier, freeride clothing; whatever the case, make sure your and your guests' pant legs are as trim as possible. Park-style pants tend to be baggiest of all, so if you've got a jibber along, consider folding over her pant legs and securing them with a ski strap. Even the best of us occasionally snag a pant leg with a crampon, so heads up—you don't want to provoke a fall because you put on crampons to avoid one in the first place.

One more detail, as long as we're talking about pointy, sharp stuff: If you're stepping into boot crampons, you probably should have an ice ax out. Conditions that firm mean you're managing a sliding/falling hazard—most ice axes are designed for that.

DELIBERATE PRACTICE: Climbing firm snow in crampons is a breeze, but how about walking on rock or scrambling? Use your old, trashed crampons to practice moving efficiently and securely on rock while wearing ski boots and crampons. It's awkward! Toprope a snow-covered outcrop or scramble on low-consequence terrain next time the skiing is terrible.

THE ROPE!

Once the snow surface becomes "bulletproof," you need to ask yourself if you and the team are up to the task. Maybe so; maybe everyone accepts the responsibility of traveling in "no-fall" terrain. Great! However, if you have clients or teammates who are inexperienced or don't even perceive the hazard, you need to recognize this and adjust accordingly. Should you even be there? Can you coach/model for them? Do you need to deploy the rope?

Guides commonly reserve the rope for navigating crevasse fields and shorter technical sections during belays and lowers. Using the rope to manage fall hazard while skiing requires expert execution. While the rope may solve some problems, it can also be a Band-Aid used to cover over a poor terrain choice. Should you be elsewhere? Did you mistime your outing? Can you really offer security with the rope, or is it just psychological? Remember too that deploying the rope takes time; with less-experienced folks who might have skis on the pack and spikes on the feet, things can get fumbly and awkward pretty quickly.

Aluminum versus Steel

Techy tools come in all shapes and sizes these days, not to mention materials. Reputable brands like CAMP/Cassin, Black Diamond, Grivel, and Petzl craft ice axes and boot crampons in aluminum, lightweight steel, and burlier steel. The debate rages about which tool for what day in what kind of snow and ice. Choose carefully, young Jedi!

While the superlight aluminum (and even carbon-fiber) tools and crampons feel great on the pack, remember that if you're pounding a picket, chopping a step, or kicking/swinging into water ice, they feel much less secure and take more work. On névé, superlight tools can work very well, but if you find yourself on harder ice or climbing much rock, they can be a liability. Choose carefully.

Prepping the Night Before

Imagine finishing a long ski tour and returning to base camp, the trailhead, or (lucky you) a comfortable backcountry hut. Phew! You just want to pull off the boots, kick back, and debrief the day. You earned it!

Wait a sec, though—your first climb tomorrow is west facing and has been in the sun all afternoon. By tomorrow morning, it will have refrozen, offering you and the team no traction, no edge penetration, no easy travel. Maybe, just maybe, it's worth putting in an uptrack or booter this afternoon/evening while you have softer, forgiving conditions. We know; you've been imagining the sublime delight of a cold pilsner all afternoon, and now we're suggesting you put in another hour of work? Madness! Ask yourself, though, if it's safer/easier to put in the track now . . . or tomorrow morn, with cold legs and bulletproof snow.

But all these cautionary considerations aside, the rope can be a real solution across a glacier riddled with crevasses. Also, it can help manage short, steep, firm sections approaching a saddle or a narrow, exposed ridge en route to a summit. Teaching short-roping in a book is way beyond my means, but for mountain guides, it can be a realistic option. It requires constant vigilance and years of training, though. For recreational teams of peers, belaying pitches of firm, steep snow can be helpful; just make sure you are actually increasing security and not merely tying everyone together and simul-soloing.

Dive into the chapter on roped techniques for some ideas of using the rope to mitigate hazard.

Soft Snow

Soft snow gives you more options and more forgiving tracksetting conditions, but it still demands some specific techniques. Guests and newer skiers will feel less of a sense of a sliding hazard, which helps dial down the stress. Softer—hopefully new!—snow presents challenges, though, so let's discuss some strategies. We'll progress from laying a track across even, simple terrain to crafting turns to, yes, even booting in deep snow.

EFFICIENCY

Soft, boot-top pow presents some of the easiest tracksetting we encounter. We still need to keep our ascent efficient, though. One exercise to see if you can maintain an even trajectory and pace is to cross a snow-covered lake; when you reach the far side, see if your line is dead straight or a wobbly mess. Strive to keep your tracksetting uniform and consistent, whether it's on flat ground or a climb.

As you begin climbing, challenge yourself in the same way, always checking to see if your line is elegant, efficient, and logical. There is a great sense of mastery in arriving at a col with relaxed guests and looking back to see a lithe, beautiful track coming up from the valley. Strive for perfection—you and your teammates will enjoy it

A relaxed and happy skier walks casually through a turn on a frigid morning above Selkirk Lodge, British Columbia. MATT KENNEDY

ROUNDED "WALKING" TURNS

As we begin ascending steeper terrain, we will inevitably need to make some turns to avoid steeper portions of the slope, circumvent tree islands, or just keep our track at a comfortable angle. Our first strategy should be gradual, rounded turns, ones in which our followers can maintain their rhythm, pacing, and effort level. This will prove to be most restful and efficient for the team.

Too often practitioners default immediately to some sort of kick turn. Do a little test the next time you watch someone perform a kick turn. Just glance at your watch and notice how many seconds it takes to negotiate the turn, not to mention what his perceived rate of exertion is. For a first-timer, it will be a difficult, tedious, and slow maneuver. For the best skimo racer, perhaps it will be only 1 or 2 seconds. For the average rider, it will be slower and require more effort than a rounded, gradual turn.

"AVA" OR "STEP" TURNS

Just beyond the rounded, walking turn, we use an "AVA" or "step" turn to keep our angle mellow. Some use the letters "AVA" to remind us of the shape our skis make when executing the turn; others simply use "step turn." Whatever your preference, the turn is the first specialized technique we use on steeper terrain.

The AVA turn has been covered elsewhere extensively, but to review: The counterintuitive thing about the technique is that we initiate the turn with our outside/downhill leg. By that we mean, as you're climbing and about to turn toward the left, you first step from a parallel position out with the right leg into an "A." This puts you

The leader enters the turn and steps out with his left ski into a shallow "A" while looking uphill at the next leg of his track. MATT KENNEDY

Now he steps out and slightly downhill into a "V." He can demo to his follower what he's doing. By coaching his follower to initiate the V portion of his turn from slightly above the established track, it ensures that the follower steps into a secure, braced position. This improves confidence and security on firmer snow. MATT KENNEDY

The leader ends his turn in a relaxed, low-angle track, skis parallel. When guiding or teaching, you can first model the turn then coach your follower or guest with a couple simple verbal cues. Try to make it look easy! MATT KENNEDY

The follower steps out left into a shallow "A" while trying to maintain an upright posture. Eventually, once the technique is mastered, he should be able to keep the hips forward and head up. MATT KENNEDY

Stepping slightly down and into a "V," the follower should feel relatively secure and balanced. This sets him up for an easy step into parallel and keeps his effort down. Saving time and energy with AVA turns keeps the legs fresh for the down. MATT KENNEDY

Stoked! Smiling, relaxed, and without losing momentum, this guy is ready for a long, efficient tour. MATT KENNEDY

into a secure stance, with little chance of sliding backward/downhill. You then step with the left leg to form a "V." We repeat the steps A-V-A until our skis are headed across the slope at an appropriate angle for the next leg of our uptrack.

A couple pointers: It helps to flatten our skintrack to almost perpendicular across the fall line of the slope before stepping out and into the "A." Followers should skin until their feet are slightly above the track exiting the turn; that way they can step down and into a secure "V" in the track. To recap: Followers skin until their feet are approximately 20 centimeters above/past the next leg of the track, step out with the outside leg into an "A" (the tip of the "A" faces uphill), then back and down with the other leg into a secure "V." If the turn requires another step into an "A," they step into an "A" before stepping into another "V," and so on.

If the shovel of one's ski or split becomes stuck in the snow, remember to stand up straight (do not bend at the waist to extricate the ski!), and simply bend at the knee, moving the offending foot slightly behind the other leg. With a tech binding, the weight of the heelpiece on the ski naturally drops the tail of the ski, and the skier will be able to pivot into the next "A" or "V" and continue. With a split or frame binding (like a Duke or older Fritschi), the rider might need to snap his bent leg a bit to get the tail to drop and pivot the tip of the ski around.

NATURAL FEATURES

Tree wells, benches, and even wind-sculpted features like sastrugi can all help you avoid a kick turn. In the absence of appropriate terrain for an AVA turn, keep an eye out for any little low-angle spot on which you could sneak in a turn.

Often just downhill of a tree is enough of a platform for you to carve out a turn. The tip of your split or ski might swish through a few small branches, but our experience has been that a turn on the downhill edge of a tree well usually spares us a kick turn.

If the stance is at all insecure or tight, consider incorporating the "veg belay." Approach the tree as you would, leveling off the track right as you arrive at the downhill side of the tree well. Put both poles in your uphill hand, then reach across your body with your downhill hand and grab a thick, live branch at chest level. Hold on and lean back, walking your feet around in small steps until you're ready to continue the skintrack out the other direction. Bam! Another kick turn avoided. Your guests will thank you!

SHOVELING

Many a mountain guide has spent the day shoveling out platforms for guests. It's hard work, but it speeds up the group, saves guests' energy, and provides a much better uptrack if you plan to reuse it during the day or week. If you're working alone, shoveling turns can be sweaty business, but there are times when it's the smartest call.

Imagine a firm slope, one on which most teams will elect to make a kick turn. It's day four of a long ski week, and the guests have tired legs. Chances are some of the guests might be on their risers if it's steep enough for kick turns. Tired bodies, risers, and kick turns? That's a recipe for somebody to take a long, sliding fall, potentially knocking other guests off their feet as well; not good. Hopefully you and your co-guide(s) decided to shovel out a beautiful platform earlier in the week in this very spot. Maybe it's a high-traffic area, or just the main route back to the hut. Whatever the case, having put in the extra 5 minutes to dig on day one will now save you coaching/spotting/stressing on day four. Good job!

Whoever does the digging, you're trying to sculpt out just enough of a platform that the team can walk through the turn rather than have to perform a kick turn. Often guests will say, "Oh, you don't have to do that for me." In truth, the guide does it for herself; it gives her peace of mind to know that guests will casually walk through a turn rather than risk getting into trouble or wasting energy. Consider shoveling out turns an investment in your own mental well-being.

The leader or guide will need her shovel out. If it's a series of turns that need to be shoveled, she can put away the poles for this portion of the uptrack. If there are long intervals between shoveling, she can also slide the shovel between the small of her back and pack. She slides into the turn and then removes a few shovels of snow from the eventual platform. She can also throw in a quick kick turn herself so that she's facing the direction of her next leg and then sculpt out just enough of a platform to allow her guests to walk through the turn. She might also shovel a platform sufficient for a more secure kick turn—whatever seems appropriate based on conditions, guests, and the situation at hand. A few of these in a row will get the blood moving, but the guests will appreciate the effort—and, she hopes, tip accordingly!

As you expertly craft platforms for your guests, ask yourself: Could you do an adequate job with your boots? Sometimes the snow surface permits you to use just skis, boots, even poles to accomplish the same job.

KICK TURNS

Kick turns are the black magic of the touring universe. You must know the secrets, but you should use them sparingly. Beware!

Joking aside, a fluid, relaxed kick turn is a great thing. When confronted with a steep track, it poses no additional hazard and a manageable effort. The trick becomes practicing and mastering all the kick turns but then putting them on the shelf until you really need them. Features like the Col de Valpelline on the classic Haute Route, for example, are almost always zigzagged with a steep skintrack requiring secure kick turns. If it has endured a few days of freeze-thaw, it'll be slick—many a guide has chosen to boot this section with guests rather than risk a slip and a fall back to the flats below.

The downhill kick turn should be in your toolbox. A steep slope can feel intimidating for the less-practiced rider, and for many resort skiers, a downhill kick turn is second nature. With a ton of new snow (oh, yeah!), confined quarters (timber or a couloir), or in bulletproof conditions, the downhill kick turn might be the savior. A savvy teammate or guide can also get above the person turning and hold his haul loop on his backpack, offering a reassuring "spot."

Prep your team, prep your guests, master the kick turn yourself. As with any of these techniques, you can give a spot from below (brace someone's skis from below with your poles) or above. Coaching with clear, patient instructions helps, as does effectively modeling the turns. And don't forget to tell guests to lower their risers before blasting out a perfect turn. Whatever you do, just don't let me see you laying down kick turns everywhere you go. Please?

The Downhill Kick Turn

Kick turns have been comprehensively detailed in the Volken-Wheeler-Schell book, so review them there. We include them here to remind folks that there are several distinct versions, each suited to different terrain and gear. Know the differences and coach them accordingly.

Anyone who has skied at a resort probably already knows the downhill kick turn. It's remarkably underutilized in the backcountry, so keep it in your quiver for the appropriate times. Obviously, changing the direction of one's skis during a descent is prime time for it. Consider, however, a teammate on tele bindings that lack a tour mode—it can be difficult to get the ski's tail to drop during an uphill kick turn, and in steep terrain that's a deal killer. Maybe a downhill kick turn is your touring partner's only option.

As mentioned above, you might stand above a partner and hold his pack's haul loop to spot him. Whatever gives him the confidence to step around. On a steep slope, the sensation of leaning out "over the void" can be mighty intimidating.

If a rider's hips are tight, the full downhill kick turn (getting one's feet to "fifth position" in ballet terms) can be challenging. In "no-fall" terrain, the motion of stepping fully around can be daunting, so coach a skier to plunge his tails backward and into the snow (so he's facing out). Then he takes baby steps and walks the skis around slowly, always facing out and hopefully feeling secure.

Now we'll dive into the uphill kick turns, highlighting two main versions: "the boot cuff" and the "windshield wiper." Note that I've invented the names for the kick turns solely to help you distinguish between the two with a little element of each to remind you. I hope this helps keep the different kick turns distinct in your mind. Again, try to avoid kick turns, but if and when you need one, consciously

With good technique and loose hips, you can stand more comfortably in "fifth position." This makes a downhill kick turn easy and controlled. This is nearly 50-degree terrain with serious fall hazard, so a botched kick turn here would be unpleasant at best. ROB COPPOLILLO

choose which particular version suits the situation.

The Boot Cuff Turn

The boot cuff allows a kick turn in a cramped or confined space. Imagine a super-deep day, with a meter of storm snow sitting on the surface, or with a rock wall or tree just upslope of your turn. You'll need to be able to make a turn without any space to maneuver uphill of you.

DELIBERATE PRACTICE:
You can practice this technique by getting into this terrain or by placing a friend's pole uphill of you and making sure your ski or split tips don't cross that plane.

1. Arrive at your chosen spot for a kick turn, flattening your skintrack so your skis are perpendicular to the fall line, if possible. Drop your heel risers if they're up.

2. Plant your poles to provide balance and security, uphill of you wherever you can. Lift the uphill ski and place its inside edge against the boot cuff of your downhill leg.

3. Begin rotating the uphill ski while sliding it backward, maintaining contact between its edge and your other leg's boot cuff. The tail goes downhill and out into space, while the shovel comes back toward your

As he arrives at his kick turn, the skier flattens his track a bit. REBECCA YARMUTH

Preparing for a "boot cuff" turn, he lifts the uphill ski, bends his knee, and moves his heel backward, behind his standing (left) leg. He places the inside ski edge against the boot cuff on his standing leg, bracing against his poles for balance. REBECCA YARMUTH

The ski edge remains in contact with the boot cuff as the skier pivots the turning ski toward the new direction of travel. Notice that he doesn't bend at the waist to do this. Rather, he turns the ski, guiding and controlling it by keeping it in contact with the boot cuff on his standing leg, and balances against his ski poles. REBECCA YARMUTH

standing leg, sliding the edge along the boot cuff of the downhill/stationary leg. Stand upright and bend the uphill knee as you slide the ski backward, rotating it around the downhill leg. Maintaining edge contact with the downhill boot's cuff guides the ski around and sets you up to then slide the uphill ski onto the snow above you, into the new leg of your track.

4. Once you've rotated the uphill leg around and it's facing uphill and toward your new direction, slide it out and away from your downhill leg until the tail of the ski has cleared the boot cuff. Now plunge the tail of the uphill

The ski pivots around the standing leg until it's facing the new direction of travel, then the skier moves the ski (while still in the air) uphill until his ski tail clears his standing leg and he can plunge the ski tail into the snow, just uphill of the standing leg. Once in the snow, he slides it backward and downhill, getting his heels as close together as possible. REBECCA YARMUTH

ski into your platform so that it goes under the downhill ski.

5. Plunge the uphill ski backward, sliding the tail under the other ski until your heels are fairly close together. If you're on firm snow, consider pre-punching a small hole with your ski pole's grip or ice ax, allowing you to plunge the ski tail.

6. Transfer the weight onto the ski you just plunged into the snow. This has been the uphill ski, but it will soon become the downhill ski after you've completed the turn. Readjust your poles as necessary to maintain balance. Remember, this is a technique often suited to steep slopes, so a fall here could be bad news!

7. Now lift the downhill ski, placing its inside edge against the boot cuff of the ski you just turned. Keep the ski lifted, and slide the edge along the back of the other leg's boot cuff as you bend the knee and move the leg backward.

8. Once the shovel of the lifted ski is almost to the stationary leg, guide it around by maintaining contact of the ski's edge with the other leg's boot cuff. Keeping it in contact will help guide it and keep it from hanging up in deep snow or snagging on vegetation or rock.

9. Rotate the lifted ski around the other leg's boot cuff until it's parallel; slide forward, setting it down.

10. High-five yourself—you've just performed a fluid, gorgeous kick turn in tight, treacherous terrain.

The boot cuff isn't quite as fluid and fast as its cousin, the "windshield wiper," but it allows a much more

The downhill ski's edge is against the back of the standing leg's boot cuff. This helps guide it around in tight quarters and complete the turn. REBECCA YARMUTH

Keeping the ski in contact with the boot, the skier guides it until parallel and then takes off on his next leg. Try this type of kick turn and see how little your skis need to travel uphill while doing it—it's a great tool for confined, awkward stances. Perfect it! REBECCA YARMUTH

Video Replay!

For an excellent, succinct video primer on kick turns, check out my buddy Margaret Wheeler in this AMGA video: youtube.com/watch?v=pmn3IgGPKfg. Note that she calls the "boot cuff" turn a "wishbone turn," and she doesn't totally distinguish between it and the "windshield wiper" described below. Don't let the terminology confuse you. Take what you already know, add it to this information, then view Margaret's expert demo and up your game.

controlled kick turn in confined terrain. Remember to prep a firm skintrack by punching a hole for the ski-tail plunge. Not doing so invites ripping the skin off the ski, which becomes its own hassle. Knowing this turn's application is key; it can turn a nervous kick turn into a positive experience for a buddy or guest.

The Windshield Wiper

This is the more familiar of the two uphill kick turn techniques. Skimo racers pop these out in less than 2 seconds and make it look easy—which it is once mastered. Problem is, without that mastery, it is time-consuming and requires significant effort.

Encourage newer skiers and guests to practice these techniques so they'll have them when it counts.

1. Approach a turn as you normally would, flattening out the skintrack and seeing how your turn will lead you into the upcoming terrain.

2. Before anything else happens, open your shoulders uphill and place your uphill pole beside the tail of your uphill ski. Stay balanced, and don't continue until you're happily perched on your lower leg.

3. Making sure your uphill pole/arm has opened to give your uphill ski the space it needs to rotate around, lift the uphill ski and turn it around to

Approaching the turn, the skier flattens his track a bit and opens his shoulders uphill. He's turning to his left, so his left arm opens up and he pole-plants back by the tail of his skis. This allows his uphill leg to windshield-wiper around when he starts his kick turn.
REBECCA YARMUTH

In one fluid motion, he has "windshield-wipered" his left ski around and it now faces his new direction of travel. This is "fifth position" in ballet. Having his heels close together allows him to easily transfer his weight to the uphill ski without a dynamic movement. Tight hips make this more difficult. REBECCA YARMUTH

face the opposite direction. It should move across the uphill slope in one motion, like a windshield wiper. If your hips are flexible, you should arrive with the feet facing opposite directions, ideally side by side. This can be difficult for anyone with tight hips, and herein lies one of the pitfalls: If you can't get your heels within 25 centimeters of each other, this move will feel off-balance and "tippy." For these folks, the boot cuff kick turn might be more appropriate, or perhaps some hybrid of the two.

4. You should now be in fifth position (again, from ballet). Transfer the weight from the downhill foot to the uphill foot. If the feet are too far apart, this becomes a "dyno" of sorts, whereby you have to make a lurch between the two feet. This invites slipping and/or a fall—heads up!

5. The weight transfer should be easy and controlled. Once complete, the downhill pole pivots around and onto the slope above you. Positioning is key here: The pole should be high enough that when the downhill ski windshield-wipers around to become the uphill ski, your newly placed uphill pole doesn't inhibit that motion. Fluidity is key here.

6. As you lift the downhill ski, you turn the hips to face the new direction of travel and snap the lifted leg straight, knocking the ski a bit with the heel. You should feel/hear the heel tap the ski, and the motion coincides with the hips turning to face the new direction. If completed energetically, the shovel of the turning ski should snap up and into the front of the leg.

The uphill pole plants high enough on the slope that it allows his downhill leg to snap/kick/turn into position and become the uphill leg. The uphill pole should also be a balance point. REBECCA YARMUTH

Now he lifts the downhill leg, bends the knee slightly, and prepares to snap/kick his heel against the ski to force the tail to drop and the shovel to rise, allowing him to turn his hips and align the ski with the other one in the new direction of travel. REBECCA YARMUTH

The hips square to the new direction of travel, he places the ski down and begins traveling in the new direction. REBECCA YARMUTH

7. Set down the new parallel to the standing foot, and away you go.

He's just snapped/kicked his heel against the ski, which knocks the tail down and the shovel up. Just a fraction of a second after he does this, he rotates his hips toward the new direction of travel, aligning his skis to parallel. REBECCA YARMUTH

Once mastered, the windshield wiper will become a two-step, fluid, and fast technique. The pole positioning and ski motions blend together, and your teammates will gasp at your speed and grace. In closing, after the hours, days, and weeks of training you will devote to these techniques, I challenge you to leave them in your toolbox and instead rely on Jedi tracksetting to avoid kick turns at all cost.

Specialized Techniques on the Up

Experienced recreationists probably have solid fundamentals for setting tracks and turns on both firm and soft snow, but hopefully the previous sections introduced a few new concepts. Guides will be expected to set comfortable tracks and demo a variety of kick turns with ease. Practice! Coaching our teammates and guests to competence

Deep Snow and Stiletto Heels

Many guides might sound as though they're against heel risers and kick turns. Anything but. We simply encourage you to apply them only when necessary. One oft-overlooked use of risers is tracksetting in deep snow. We're talking meter-plus deep snow. You'll find yourself eventually so blessed by Ullr and setting a track through bottomless pow. Before you awaits hard work and an eventual run that will be described as "all time." Popping up your heel risers to the tallest setting will keep your shovels from diving a bit and spare you some pain. Keep it in mind.

in the fundamentals will allow them to focus on bigger objectives and make leaders' and guides' jobs easier.

As we move into more specialized applications and techniques, it's easy to consider them only relevant to guides—but don't be fooled. Much of the following content can be deployed by avid skiers, riders, and ski-mountaineers to great advantage. Much like the rock and alpine techniques presented in *The Mountain Guide Manual*, recreationists can greatly improve security and efficiency by "stealing" some of these strategies and tricks from the guides. Practice them first, and then incorporate them into your craft.

Crampons, Ski-Pole Self-arrest Grips, and Ice Axes

Removing our flotation for the up often means considering an ax and/or boot crampons. The choices are many, so let's look at a few of the options.

A traditional piolet has been standard equipment for alpinists and mountaineers for more than a century. The design traces its heritage to the long alpenstock of shepherds and crystal hunters. Since the early twentieth century, the traditional piolet has featured a straight shaft, small spike on the base of the shaft, an elegantly curved pick, and an adze wide enough to chop steps or a platform.

Over the past few decades, wooden shafts have given way to steel, aluminum, and even carbon fiber. Innovative companies have integrated aluminum heads to shave even more weight off the designs. One company in particular, Italian manufacturer C.A.M.P., has made an aluminum piolet with just a small tip of hardened steel on the spike and pick.

For everyday, versatile use, a traditional piolet is your best bet in terms of both steel construction and design. You can chop ice with it, swing it into hard ice, and even use it as an anchor. On unfamiliar terrain or with the potential for hard ice, having the durability and swing weight of a steel ax is probably worth it.

For routes like the Ford-Stettner on the Grand Teton or the Flying Dutchman in Rocky Mountain National Park, you might even bump into one or two superlight technical tools. These models will be steel and feature reverse-curve picks for water ice. The Dutchman, for example, has a single short pitch of water ice (most years), so some skimo athletes carry a short dynamic rope (30 to 40 meters) and a single set of lightweight tech tools between two partners. They use one each on the steep snow, then the leader for the crux section uses both tools to surmount the ice.

Once on top she can pull the rope up to her and lower the tools back to the follower. If she doesn't have enough rope to lower the tools on a loop, she can either untie and use her end to lower them or have her second untie and pull all the rope up and to her and then lower the tools on the end of the rope. The second collects the tools, ties back in, rechecks his tie-in, and sends the pitch. Remember to clean any gear the leader placed (the rope won't be through it after the leader has pulled the end of the rope up to her).

Above the crux, the team divides the tools again and tops out.

Solutions like this require an honest appraisal of the team's competence and a realistic sense of the compromises being made. The last thing you want is to find yourself mid-pitch on spooky terrain, bouncing an aluminum ax off blue ice!

Crampons will present you with the same challenges. Especially for guides, we have a med kit, repair kit, a rescue sled, and possibly a rope in our pack, so saving some weight on tools and spikes is tempting. Dull or fragile crampons are a real hazard, arguably worse than an inadequate ice tool. Before saving those precious grams

An example of a lightweight boot crampon. C.A.M.P. builds this "Skimo Tour Nanotech" out of aluminum, save for the stainless steel front points. Compromise on weight when you can, but also consider conditions. Long days on rock will trash aluminum crampons, and bulletproof ice is not the place for a superlight piolet. Do your homework, and take the right tool for the job.

COURTESY C.A.M.P. USA

with aluminum crampons, carefully consider the terrain.

A lightweight steel crampon gives you better durability over a day- or weeklong tour, particularly if you'll be scratching up rock. C.A.M.P., Petzl, Grivel, and Black Diamond all craft viable aluminum options too. If you're going to be climbing purely on snow, aluminum is a good choice. In a rockier environment, like Colorado, aluminum tools can end up beaten down in a matter of hours. Keep in mind that on bulletproof ice or if you're trying to chop steps, aluminum tools and spikes won't do much.

Whatever you choose, make the decision consciously. Don't just do the "light is right" thing without assessing your objectives and the demands of your mission. Steel is durable but heavy. Aluminum saves weight and energy but will dull more quickly. Beware of aluminum center bars on crampons—they bend over rocks and fatigue (then break) quickly.

SELF-ARREST GRIPS

Some ski mountaineers swear by the self-arrest ski-pole grip. These tools are simply a ski pole with an integrated pick in the grip. The pick looks almost identical to an ice ax's pick, although slightly smaller. These tools offer some ability to self-arrest in the event of a fall while steep skiing, though they also present a bit of a hazard—sliding at high speeds with a sharpened blade in one's hand can seem sketchy.

These self-arrest poles can arguably be more useful on the up than the down. A piolet and self-arrest pole make a pretty capable set of tools on steep terrain. The overall set is lighter than two tech tools and offers yet another solution to diverse challenges on skimo routes.

Roped Techniques

There's nothing more iconic than a confident-looking mountain guide, rope coiled perfectly around her powerful torso, steely glint in her eyes.

Not so fast! As we begin discussing the use of the rope, a reminder: Make sure the rope is necessary. Could you solve the "problem" with terrain? A less "techy" solution? When we deploy the rope, no matter how efficient and dialed we are, we begin slowing down. Often it's totally necessary, so no sweat. But do consider when a simpler, less-technical solution might be appropriate.

The endless debate over rope choice continues. What diameter? Dynamic or low-stretch? What length? These are worthy discussions and ones you should have with teammates or fellow guides. Your objective(s) may determine what cord to take, but often there's gray area. How light can you go? How likely is a crevasse fall? I'll try to inform your discussions with some common considerations.

DYNAMIC VERSUS LOW-STRETCH/STATIC

There has been remarkable development in rope technologies since the early 1990s. By the time this book comes out, we'll probably have three more choices on the market. Before you get into length, diameter, and the like, you'll need to decide if you're going dynamic or low-stretch/static. Research these terms in-depth and decide what's the best solution for your problem.

With any real leading to be done above gear on rock, ice, or snow, you'll need to take a dynamic cord, period. Many teams opt for a longer twin rope that they'll double over when leading and then have at their disposal for rappelling or crack rescue. It's an option, for sure.

Other teams achieve the same end by taking a shorter section of single rope for leading (singles go down to 8.5 millimeters these days) and have the same length of static tag line stashed in another teammate's pack. One advantage of this approach is that the team then has two separate ropes; the weight can be divided, but they also have two individual cords, which guards against the person carrying the rope falling into a slot. Two cords offer some enhanced risk management.

LOW-STRETCH/ STATIC CORDS

If there's no leading to be done and you're less worried about crevasse fall, a static cord might be the ticket. Petzl's "RAD Line" (6mm diameter; 22 g/m) is fashioned mainly of Dyneema and offers no effective stretch at all, making it inappropriate to hold leader falls but fantastic as a haul/rescue cord. It's light, strong, more abrasion-resistant than other Dyneema cords, and expensive. Petzl tested the RAD Line with a Micro Traxion and Tibloc, and it passed spec for hauling with those tools. Their testing revealed significant sheath damage on the RAD Line at as little as 1.7 kilonewtons (kN) with other rope clamp devices, so be aware that its use requires care and practice.

Whatever you choose—if you're using the RAD Line or any super-skinny static line—practice with it and treat it gently in the field, especially if using a toothed device like the Micro Traxion or Tibloc.

Edelrid's "Rap Line II" (6mm diameter; 31g/m) is another interesting option—it will hold two UIAA falls when rigged as a twin rope but acts essentially as a low-stretch cord when single. How? Edelrid weaves a percentage of Kevlar into the sheath, which functions statically until forces exceed its holding power. The Kevlar in the sheath fails at that point; the nylon sheath and core then take over, and the Rap Line II functions as a dynamic rope. Whoa, serious engineering!

Again, its dynamic capacity is engineered as a twin rope, meaning both strands are clipped through every piece of pro. Note that Edelrid engineered this as a tag line so that climbers could re-lead a pitch on a doubled Rap Line II without sacrificing security.

Either of these options makes for a good "just in case" rope for glacier skiing. There's also some compelling testing showing that a static cord functions better in certain crevasse falls. Petzl testing showed a higher rate of successful catches with their RAD

Hitches for Skinny Cords

If you're considering using a sub-8mm rope, you need to know both the Munter hitch and its burly brother, the Monster Munter. Don't know 'em? The Monster Munter simply adds another pass behind the hitch and offers more friction than the plain Munter. Grab a mentor, hire a guide, and have her show you the ins and outs of these two indispensable hitches.

Oh, and by the way – most of the English-speaking world knows the Munter as the "Italian hitch." Why? Ah, good story there, but one I could not verify. I'll share the story with you on a ski tour someday!

Line than they did with a 7.7-millimeter twin rope. Evaluate how you'll use the rope and what you need it to do and then practice with it. These are specialized tools requiring expert technique.

DYNAMIC ROPES

If you decide a dynamic rope is the way to go, you've got endless choices. For mixed routes involving rock, snow, and glacier travel, the growing number of triple-rated thin ropes is heartening. Beal, Sterling, Edelrid, and Mammut make triple-rated ropes—they're all single-, half- and twin-certified. This keeps all your options open in mixed terrain or when guiding. If you'll be short-roping, a slightly thicker rope is called for. Beal's 8.5-millimeter "Opera" and Edelrid's 8.6-millimeter "Canary" are both great options.

If you're just managing crevasse hazard and perhaps short sections of leading (and no short-roping), a super-skinny half or twin (like Edelrid's 7.1-millimeter "Skimmer") is a lightweight option. You can perform an effective crevasse rescue, double it and lead a steep pitch of ice, and have a knot-free rappel rope too.

(We'll discuss the pros and cons of dynamic versus static ropes further in the "Technical Solutions" chapter.)

What type of rope you choose—dynamic or low-stretch/static—will depend primarily on what you foresee the rope's main use will be. Will it most likely stay stashed in the pack? Will you rope up for crevasse hazard? Will you rappel with it? Is there a chance you'll need to lead a steep section or out of a moat? Proper prep and planning will answer most of these questions, but if you're unsure, keep your options open in terms of length and material.

TRANSITIONING FROM UNROPED TRAVEL TO ROPED TRAVEL

Touring toward the Illecillewaet Glacier from the Asulkan Trailhead, you have ample time to scope the toe of the glacier. Early in the season or on a low-snow year, you'll transition from ascending unroped to roped just before the toe of the glacier. You know it's coming. Heading toward a couloir with a nervous client might present a similar transition; you'll go from relaxed skinning to short-roping in boot crampons. Transitions like these can go smoothly with a little practice and forethought.

If you and your team are already in harnesses, many experienced ski-mountaineers have the rope stacked loosely inside their pack, near the top. They then leave a single end of the rope within reach and, when the time comes, simply start pulling the rope from the pack. Stacking the rope loosely inside a silnylon stuff sack can facilitate easy pulling from the pack too. This makes handing the free end to your rope mate easy, and while she ties in, you can continue pulling. Stacking the rope like this saves you the time of removing your pack.

Spacing will depend on your objective. If you're a guide going to short-roping, have the guest tie into the end, continue pulling the rope until it's all free, and then tie in as normal, shortening the rope to as long as you need based on the upcoming terrain.

More frequent, though, is going to glacier-travel mode. Your spacing on the rope will depend on the number of teammates and what system you'll use in the event of a crevasse fall. (If you're rusty, check out the glacier chapter in *The Mountain Guide Manual* or Andy Selters's excellent *Glacier Travel and Crevasse Rescue* for specifics.) Consider having your spacing already determined and the appropriate knots pre-tied in the rope.

Taking a quick belay (perhaps when approaching a corniced ridge or negotiating an exposed scramble) will mean judging where you place your belayer and how much rope you need out. This is classic "short pitch" terrain on which you might take a quick belay then begin moving together with the rope looped around terrain features (rock, hopefully) or be counterbalanced on either side of the ridge to protect one another.

Another common situation is fixing a handline for guests or partners. These sections are usually short and steep, where a fall might be unlikely but the additional handline gives confidence. Consider tying a bulky knot every few meters to give a good handhold, should someone slip and start sliding. An alpine butterfly works, or use a braking knot (from your crevasse system) if you need to add bulk.

If you're pre-stacked and know the terrain (or did excellent homework), you can tie into the rope as you approach the pitch then pause and pull all the rope from your pack as your teammates or guests catch up. As they arrive, you fire the pitch, fix a quick, secure anchor at the top, and the rope will already be hung. The infamous "Burnie Step" pitch comes to mind above the Burnie Glacier Chalet, as do many top outs where the final meters can be noticeably steeper than the slope below.

Braking Knots

Testing by the Ecole Nationale de Ski et d'Alpinisme (ENSA) demonstrates that adding braking knots to the rope during glacier travel is effective in helping to arrest crevasse falls, provided there is enough snow on the glacier. My take? Especially when traveling as a roped team of two, you should consider knots in your rope!

The type of rope you choose for glacier travel will determine what type of braking knot you use. Above, I describe skinny ropes that save weight and bulk—but these "pros" becomes "cons" when employing braking knots, for no other reason than the resulting knots are small.

ENSA's video on the topic (youtube.com/watch?v=IgNR-VZMwHo) is worthwhile viewing for determining what knots to use when. Give it a look.

TRANSITIONS TO BOOTING

Steep terrain and icy conditions will necessitate a transition to booting—the term we use for uphill travel on foot. Hopefully you've anticipated this transition, because there are few things as nerve-racking as having to transition on a bulletproof slope while managing guests and the potential for a fall or lost gear.

Expected Transition

Knowing the terrain, having good vis to preview, and/or good beta will help you plan for a seamless transition to booting. Inexperienced teammates and guests will probably fumble for their first booting transitions, so plan on having additional ski straps, and find a spacious, flat (hopefully) area on which to transition. Guests won't remember that their skis' brakes might be in tour mode. Warn them as you head into the transition to (a) watch others' skis and splits so they don't inadvertently kick them down the slope; (b) engage their brakes before setting down a ski, especially if they're removing skins; and (c) be careful of others once they've mounted skis/boards on their packs.

Consider having the group transition above you so that you can potentially catch a sliding ski or backpack. If you lack flat(ish) ground on which to transition, consider shoveling. A co-guide or another dialed teammate can jump on this task while you prep everyone for the transition. Sure, shoveling takes time and effort, but balance that against the likelihood of someone's ski sailing off the top of your summit and ending up on the highway 4,000 feet below. Ouch!

You should have a decent idea of everyone's attachment systems on

Decision Points

We build decision points into our tours to allow the team to check in and reassess the plan and/or conditions. Try to remember to get as much done during a transition as you can: Preview upcoming terrain, check in with the group, share observations, make a weather observation. Guiding solo makes all this a juggling act, but psyched clients are often willing to help with weather or a quick pit. A well-practiced team can knock out a bunch of tasks at once, all while eating and drinking. Strategically placed decision points not only make for a more efficient day but also enhance risk management as well as enjoyment.

their packs. If someone shows up with a glorified laptop bag, you might be shipping two pair of skis on your back. Again, think ahead to the prospect of having to retrieve a dropped set of skis. Your temporary pain of carrying extra skis might pale in comparison to descending the slope to retrieve those lost boards.

Double-check everyone's rigging and make sure it's going to survive the booting. If harnesses are on, remember to double-check buckles and tie-ins. Crampons must be secure and adjusted properly. Ideally, you've done this during a pre-trip meeting, but take the time to correct an ill-fitting crampon before you're mid-slope.

Spacing will be critical if guests are tied together. Remember, they'll have skis or a board off the top of their pack, potentially sharp points on their feet, and maybe an ax in their hand. A few inches too close, and somebody could end up knocked unconscious by an errant movement. Booting in steep terrain also means adequate spacing to prevent someone having a hand impaled.

Once moving, set a reasonable track with evenly spaced steps. If you're tall, consider the shortest member of the team: Is he dying at the vertical spacing in your steps? Likewise, lengthen your stride a bit if your buddy is 6-foot-plus and you're 5-foot-nothing. Compromise is everything.

Often a bootpack ends with a brief short pitch for the top out. A rock anchor calms the nerves if you're negotiating a tricky cornice. Several versatile pieces like tricams, Metolius SuperCams, or Omega Pacific Link Cams offer a better chance of finding good gear. Once on top, take the time to find a secure anchor if you're belaying several people at once. If there's a real falling hazard, consider spacing them before you leave the belay.

An Unexpected Transition

It happens: Try as we might, mid-slope we decide the snow surface is too firm or the terrain too steep, and we have to start booting.

First attend to your least-secure partners. If that requires an immediate spot, get below them and plant your poles firmly just below their downhill ski's edges. Get them into a balanced position. Fixing their heels might afford them more edge control and give them a sense of security.

Perhaps just descending to a point immediately below wobbly teammates or guests is all you need to calm them. Demo and/or talk them calmly through the transition, showing them each step. Remove a pole and plunge it into the snow. If you need to remove an ice ax and plunge the shaft into the snow, so be it. You can then loop the shoulder strap of your pack around the ski pole or piolet. Help them perform the same.

You might also take the time to shovel out a stable platform below them and let them side-slip onto it. Consider how much faster they'll move with a flat working space and how much more secure they'll be. Is it worth the time?

Once they're in a position to remove skis, coach (or help) them step out of their uphill ski and immediately plunge its tail deeply into the snow. Make sure they have a secure spot for their ski boot, like a chopped step, or have their boot crampon waiting. If they're at all wobbly, have them hold on to the plunged ski, help them into the crampon, and fasten it to their boot. Do the same on their downhill ski. Have a ski strap ready to secure both skis to the pack. A diagonal carry will probably be easier to manage for them, if their pack is set up for it. If not, you can fashion a diagonal carry with a shortened sling girth-hitched through a bartacked loop of webbing on their pack. Consider taking their skis too if it will save time and prevent a fall.

With spikes on their feet, and a pole or ice ax in hand, they should feel more secure at this point, giving you the chance to button up your system. If having them tie in is hazardous, allow them to clip into a locker clipped to the rope. Be careful moving around them, as inexperienced guests often forget their skis jutting above them. If they bend toward you, they could give you a good knock to the head.

As soon as you're ready, tie off to them at an appropriate distance. If you're guiding, are you moving into short-roping? Recreationists should avoid short-roping or simuling if at all possible. It's an advanced technique and one requiring an honest appraisal of the fall hazard and snow surface. A sliding fall on firm, 20-degree terrain can generate impressive forces, ones impossible to manage while short-roping. Don't inadvertently increase your hazard by deploying the rope!

The Summit—You Made It!

Going uphill requires fitness, a keen eye for terrain, and a genuine

Falling Off, Falling In, or Falling On . . .

A wise mountain guide once said, "You're either worried about falling off the mountain (slip and a fall), into the mountain (crevasse fall), or the mountain falling on you (avalanche)."

Ascension techniques are well and good, but if we misidentify the hazard, they can become deadly. Recall the accident on Mount Hood in 2002, when seven climbers on three separate ropes—two teams of two and a team of three—became entangled in a fall and ended up sliding into a crevasse. All the teams were roped together as if they were managing a crevasse hazard, when in fact the real hazard was a slip and a fall. Had the teams had intermediate protection between climbers, they likely would've survived the incident without incurring three fatalities.

By accurately identifying the hazard throughout the day, you can modify your rope system. Being tied together with a crevasse hazard makes perfect sense. Being tied together with a falling hazard means free-soloing tied to your buddy, unless you're placing intermediate protection (pickets, screws, or rock gear). And you definitely do not want to be tied to others in the event of an avalanche.

Mastering the technical systems is relatively easy. Knowing when and where to use which system takes more experience. As you begin tackling bigger, more complicated objectives, remember to revisit your technical systems and adapt them as the hazard changes. Just as avalanche hazard can and will change throughout the day, so too can your other hazards. Stay aware.

appreciation for crafting a beautiful uptrack. Take pride in moving a group to a summit or col so that they arrive relaxed, psyched, and better informed for the down portion of your tour.

From a diligent trip-planning process, we arrived at the trailhead prepared and moved into the uphill. Expert decision making has infused the entire tour thus far; now it's time to consider letting gravity do its work—the down.

The whole day or week flows together, equal parts of the overall experience. Up to down to up—all the while sharing information, enjoying your team, and reveling in the landscape. Your up should prepare you for the down, and each should be its own reward.

CHAPTER 3

The Down

There is more to life than simply increasing its speed.

—Mahatma Gandhi

America is all about speed. Hot, nasty, badass speed.

—Will Ferrell

After a long, elegant uptrack, we reward ourselves with a pristine summit, unforgettable view, and usually a wonderful down—the descent! A few times a season we harvest a phenomenal run, whether that's perfectly softened steeps or a thigh-deep payday with great friends. Sharpen your senses, though, and appreciate the down no matter what—even in tricky conditions. Moving competently through the terrain requires an expert eye and refined movement skills. We draw on our experience to mitigate any hazards, often without mentioning it to guests or our teammates. The down gives us the chance to shine and interact with the mountains, often at speed.

Making turns on snow requires considerable planning, prep, and teamwork to carry out safely. Doing our homework increases our chances of getting the goods too. A guide or competent team needs to formulate a trip plan that accounts for the day's hazards, where those hazards exist in the terrain, the weather forecast and how it will impact conditions, assessing and mitigating hazards during a tour, and of course the team's skill and compatibility. With those considerations in mind, the team chooses its uptracks and descents and, just as important, devises a plan to have some fun.

I hope you devoured the chapters on trip planning and the up. Any discussion of the down comes in the context of a completed trip plan identifying potentially appropriate descents, given the day's conditions. If your tour begins on the uptrack, we complement our trip planning by gathering observations as we gain altitude, localizing the bulletin to our drainage, and looking out for anything we missed.

I encourage you to remember that the trip plan isn't a finite thing; it's an ongoing process to be revisited and revised throughout the day and at day's

Mountain guide Nino Guagliano leads a group to the sea ice, Svalbard, Norway. ROB COPPOLILLO

end during a debrief. We're constantly assessing conditions, reassessing our plan, and incorporating observations into our travel. As the AIARE curriculum teaches, traveling together and deciding together means regrouping with teammates and devoting some time to error correcting, evaluating new evidence, and adjusting accordingly. Having options prevents us from fixating on a single goal for the day and potentially ignoring information that might steer us away from that goal.

Plan your tour well, give yourself options, and reassess with your team throughout your tour.

Choosing a Line: Slope-scale Decision Making

We choose potential descents based on our expectation of the hazards, our team's abilities and objectives, and where we might find good skiing. Using a topo map, guidebooks, terrain imagery, and our run atlas help us pick out our runs. During the trip

Mikey Arnold carving his bit of paradise below the Gran Paradiso, Italy.
MATT KENNEDY

plan and guide meeting, we are effectively going from a macro scale to the micro-scale once in the field. Armed with the knowledge our trip plan and meeting provides, we eventually find ourselves at the top of the slope. The theoretical has become the reality. Now we get down to maximizing fun and minimizing hazard on a micro- or slope-scale.

Where We Ski

So where *exactly* do we ski? During our trip plan we drill down from deciding in what range we'll ski, to what mountain, to what aspect, then drainage, and, finally, where on a slope we'll travel. With only one range within reach, your choice is often made at that scale, before you even wake up. But rise and shine in a place like Golden, British Columbia, and you can choose between the Rockies, Rogers Pass, and south into the Purcells—three distinct snowpacks and ranges. Choices, choices, but you see the progression.

Storm track, seasonal snowpack history, and word of mouth will all begin to inform your decision as to what mountain for the day. In North America, northeast aspects often hold great snow until a north wind rips across them. You probably already have a great sense of which mountains and what drainages do well in different storms. Rely on that experience, but ask others as well, particularly in a new zone. Guidebooks may help too.

Checking weather stations can also give you a glimpse into the "big winners" in terms of snowfall amounts. A few minutes in the morning will give you a great sense of where you're going to find the goods and where you need to be on guard for storm slabs and other potential hazards.

THE BALANCE

Your trip plan sets you up with great information regarding where you'll ski, where you'll find the best snow, and where the avalanche problems lie. You're balancing risk and reward. This process gives you a great filter with which you can choose drainages and individual slopes. A quick preview of considerations:

- Where's the avalanche problem? Can we find terrain that avoids it? For example, wind slabs up high mean look in sheltered trees.
- Identify avalanche terrain. Do you need to be in it to find good skiing? If conditions are "all-time" and you want to ride in avy terrain, is it safe? Worth it? Are the stars aligned and you can tolerate being in, and exposed to, avalanche terrain?
- Does the terrain afford you low-exposure uptracks? In a perfect world (ha!), the terrain provides you with no-exposure uptracks and wonderful downhill terrain. Do your best to find that terrain.
- Downhill terrain with great snow, top to bottom. Sure, we want this every time we ski, but can you identify the aspects on which this might be true? Wind direction, temp, and sun exposure are all factors.
- Terrain suited to your group, in terms of size, skill, fitness, and exposure. Three riders in a tight couloir, great! A team of five, though? Think ahead to how you'll manage the terrain.
- Terrain traps. Can you avoid them altogether? Minimize or avoid many of them?

MACRO (DRAINAGE) SCALE

In the trip plan we visit weather reports; ask expert friends, guides, and forecasters about conditions; look at freeze levels; consult the guidebooks—all in an effort to set ourselves up for epic skiing but also to avoid unacceptable hazards. What range or subrange of mountains has done the best this season? Where are you seeing avalanches? Once you're discussing a specific range or mountain, what drainages have been more stable and skiing well? Where have your friends and the local guides been finding the best skiing? Getting into trouble?! Make sure you have a quality, repeatable process to answer these questions—and then use it every time.

FROM MOUNTAIN DOWN TO MICRO: SLOPE, SHAPE, STEEPNESS

Once we begin drilling down to the medium- and slope-scale decisions, we begin evaluating and choosing terrain based on slope aspect, shape of the slope, and how steep it is (slope angle).

In the trip planning process, you should've identified the aspects with better snow and the ones with expected avalanche problems. Wind and sun are the main architects of avalanches in this sense in the short term, but keep in mind the long-term conditions too. In Colorado's Front Range, for example, western aspects get scoured storm after storm, which often results in a shallow (nonexistent in many places) snowpack, more faceting, and lower-quality riding. In general, though, western aspects pick up more snow, as storms push against them first and drop their snow generously through orographic uplifting. Tracking your season's conditions helps to dial in your smaller-scale decisions.

As we're touring we need to constantly revisit our choice in slope aspect. Another way to phrase this is maintaining situational awareness or "panoramic awareness": Has anything changed since we chose this aspect to ride? Since we started our tour? Since the start of the storm? During the day? Timing often affects aspect too, especially for wet avalanche problems like cornices, loose and slab wet avalanches, and even glide cracks. Thinking ahead to temperature swings, wind intensities/directions, and solar input will help you avoid hazard and find the best/safest aspects for touring.

We visit the shape of terrain during the trip plan as well, particularly when we've seen a trend in triggering of avalanches on particular slopes or features. Imagine a rash of reported avalanches in shallower, rockier areas. Or recent triggering of convexities mid-slope. We can forecast our own problem slope shapes as well, but often reported avalanches are our best indication of where in the terrain we can find avalanches. Wide, planar slopes? Exposed start zones? Identify trends in your zone and then apply that wisdom to your terrain choices.

Avalanche courses in the United States often use different language than "slope shape." Rather, they ask, "Are trigger points present?" Perhaps an even more accurate formulation would be "areas where a slope can be triggered." Rather than give the

The Notebook

Maintaining awareness sounds easy . . . until I find myself overwhelmed with a gear issue, cold teammate, glitchy GPS, or just a "bad day." Having your notebook along can help dial down the noise and keep you revisiting your priorities on the day. The AIARE fieldbook provides a checklist for maintaining awareness. Give it a look, or develop your own. It'll help keep you in touch with conditions on the ground.

impression there is a single point on a slope where a rider might trigger the slope, we try to allow that many areas on a slope are "triggerable," or weak. All this is to say that we're evaluating slope shape or asking, "Are there shallow, buried objects; convexities; sparse trees; potentially weaker areas in the snowpack?"

However you label and discuss slope shape/trigger points, try to identify specifically where you'll be able to trigger avalanches in the terrain, and then avoid those areas. A quick scribble in your notebook—something like "avoid wind-loaded convexities just below ridgetops"—might be just the nudge your mind needs to recognize that terrain in the field and get your team around it safely.

FEATURE-SCALE

Now we're making feature-scale choices. Imagine a descent with a convex rollover on the skier's right side of the slope but a more planar, consistent angle on the left. If we're at all concerned about triggering a persistent weak layer at a weak spot on the slope—like a convex roll—then we'd call out the rollover as a problem and make a plan to avoid it. Great decision, but . . .

. . . hang on a sec. Remember, we don't just decide "where to ski" once we're standing atop a run. We should've visited a macro decision within our trip plan. What drainage will we ski; what aspects will hold the best snow; what slopes should we avoid; and how will we ski once we're on a specific slope?

The point here is that "where to ski" needs to telescope from the macro to the micro. Most people put a good deal of thought into the micro, which is great. Let's make sure, though, we put as much thought into our macro decisions as our micro, and then revisit those decisions as we tour. Don't end up on the slope with no idea of what specific slope-scale features you'll avoid!

Sources of Uncertainty

Simple, right? Well, many days, it is. But what if you're dealing with flat light? Or a weather event you've never seen before, like "thundersnow" or 3 centimeters of graupel? Or a group so spread out that communication is difficult? Or you've got a teammate who doesn't speak English (or French or Spanish)? Suddenly, managing slope-scale decisions and features becomes quite the challenge. Remember, anything that introduces uncertainty into your process or decisions should be accounted for—by defaulting to a more conservative terrain choice and/or gathering more information.

Ali Vagnini steps into the sunshine and peers down the world's most famous ski run, the Vallée Blanche, above Chamonix, France. Make sure you can read French, English, or get the gist from the sign. MATT KENNEDY

SLOPE ANGLE

Slope angle plays an important role in determining where we ski on both the micro and the macro scales. We all learned that slab avalanches occur most frequently between 30 and 45 degrees. Indeed, this is a great rule of thumb, but let's really look at those numbers and what they mean. Is that the average of the whole slope? Just the start zone? How do we arrive at that average? If we drill down into the nuts and bolts of a "35-degree slope," we might find there's more vagary in the term than we like.

When we throw the term "slope angle" out there, most of us mean on a "slope scale," meaning an individual run we intend to ski. Too often, though, and especially in the age of digital tools, we default to using an average of an entire run or larger slope. For many, and for all digital apps, slope angle is merely rise-over-run—an average of the slope from point A to point B.

Let's try to define our terms here. A feature indicates a bit of terrain on a specific slope or ski run; for example, a feature like a roll, cliff, or one side of a ski run. Among your teammates, are you evaluating slope angle on a larger slope, or are you looking at a particular feature on a slope or run? Make sure you're using the same language.

Let's be specific and accurate when using the term "slope angle," and I

Guiding and Digital Mapping Technology

by Marc Chauvin

Marc Chauvin, the third American to receive IFMGA certification through the AMGA MARC CHAUVIN

About fifteen years ago, a fellow guide and I spent 20 hours over two days creating a route plan for a weeklong ski tour. That's 40 person hours—a week's worth of work for one person! These days, one of us could create the same tour plan in one 8-hour day. How and why?

The short answer is digital mapping technology. And just as important, the average person's ability to access that technology. CalTopo, Caia, FATMAP, along with country-specific programs and apps, are commonplace and affordable now.

The problem of course is that there are errors in the digital maps. Nowhere are the errors more talked about than in digital elevation modeling (DEM) and the ability to colorize a map based on its steepness (slope shading).

To come to grips with errors in DEM and the resulting error in slope shading, it might be a good idea to see how we deal with error in other products that we have dealt with and accepted.

The first thing that comes to mind are forecasts. "Forecast" is defined as a prediction or estimation of a future event or trend. The very word is practically a synonym for error! Yet we manage that error and use forecasts regularly. Not only that, but we would consider not acquiring a weather or snow/avalanche forecast prior to a ski tour as irresponsible.

We obviously see the value of these products despite the inherent error. So how do you deal with the errors in those forecasts? We accept some uncertainty and adjust our planning and behavior accordingly.

The same attitude you bring to forecasts needs to be channeled as you deal with slope shading.

Having said that, let's drill down a bit on how significant the errors in digital mapping and, specifically, slope shading can be. Remember that 40 hours of work using paper maps with rulers and compass? We were measuring distance, counting contour lines to get elevation gain and loss, and comparing the distance between contour lines with the scale on the side of my notebook to figure out slope steepness. Consider the potential for error!

Not only was that process fraught with human error, the data was no more accurate than the data we use today and likely had more error. What I see is not the error of digital mapping and slope shading but the remarkable comparative accuracy of it. I'm comparing it to what it replaced, not perfection.

So, do I use digital mapping and slope shading? You bet. It saves me 32 hours of work, which means I get more skiing in. Do I expect perfection? That seems too much to ask.

In practice, how do you use a route plan that has error? I would be remiss not to mention that first you need to admit it has errors. But if that admission means you don't use the tool at all, that would be an even greater error.

I use slope shading in conjunction with the avalanche forecast. If I have an avalanche forecast that is "Low" or "Moderate" with an avalanche problem that is not likely to go deep, remote trigger, or propagate a long distance (so, more manageable consequences) and I can see that there are no terrain traps, I feel pretty comfortable relying on slope shading to identify the avalanche slopes. If at any time I feel the slope is steeper than the map indicates, I'll take appropriate measures either by modifying my route or using mitigation techniques like one-at-a-time, etc.

When the avalanche forecast is "Considerable" or there is the potential for deep weaknesses, remote triggering, or propagation (think: persistent problems), I will be conservative in my interpretation of the slope shading. I will not trust the slope shading if it is within 3 to 5 degrees of the angle I am trying to avoid unless I have direct information—either because I have been in that area or I have a trusted source or colleague confirming that the slope shading is accurate.

In short, I need more than just the map data. If the avalanche forecast is "High," I'm scared and act appropriately. In this case, I venture onto only confirmed low-angle slopes that are not connected to steeper slopes or have steeper slopes above. Under "High" danger and with (deep) persistent problems, slope shading plays a very small part in my decision making. The digital map, however, will help me stay in the area I want to stay in and keep me from bumbling into areas I want to avoid.

In "Extreme" hazard, I am likely to get a lift ticket.

Of course avalanche hazard is aspect- and elevation-dependent and can have errors. As I travel, I assess the accuracy of the forecast and adjust my reliance on the map accordingly.

Weather also has an impact on my use of the map. In poor visibility, being able to pinpoint your location within 10 to 20 meters is a great advancement compared to map and compass, but again you need to be very conservative when it comes to slope shading. Anytime you are threading a needle because you want to avoid a steep slope on either side of you, STOP! It may be appropriate to ski a lower-angled map-indicated section of a slope you'd be willing to ski anyway, but thinking you are avoiding the hazard should not be the goal of skiing the map-indicated lower-angled line.

Another use of slope shading—and one I use a lot—is not to avoid hazard but to find a nice comfortable uptrack. I like my uptracks to be well below the bull's-eye angles of the avalanche hazard, and I have had great luck finding good uptracks where a few degrees of error is of little consequence.

There is error in much of the data we use to make decisions ski touring. This introduces uncertainty to our planning and terrain selection. This is a fact we must embrace—and account for in our behavior—because we have no other choice.

Marc Chauvin earned IFMGA certification through the AMGA in 1999—the third American to do so. Coauthor of* The Mountain Guide Manual *and a former AMGA examiner, he lives in North Conway, New Hampshire, with his wife, Jane.

caution you to really investigate how you're determining slope angle and on what scale. A common mistake in the age of digital elevation modeling is averaging the angle of ski run or slope and then using that imperfect number to make a terrain decision.

When determining the angle on a specific slope, you should take the steepest piece of terrain that's 20 meters or more along the slope, or in the start zone, and use that as your slope angle—NOT an average of the whole slope. If there's one bit of terrain advice to take from this book, this is it. Too often, backcountry skiers get surprised by an avalanche and then say, "But the slope was only 30 degrees!"

If there is a portion of the slope large enough for an avalanche to initiate and slide, that should be your working slope angle for that run.

After getting an approximate idea of slope angle from topo maps and digital tools, we need to begin determining slope angle in the field in real time. To reiterate: We are not interested in an average over the slope as much as we are identifying portions of a slope or start zone that are big enough to avalanche. For example, a slope that averages 28 degrees but has a 50-meter (downslope distance) section of 37-degree terrain on it should be considered a 37-degree slope. While not a hard-and-fast rule, forecasters and expert guides identify any steeper portion of a slope that's big enough to slide and many days use that as the slope angle. So that slope that averages 28 degrees but has a 37-degree rollover at one part of the start zone—consider it a 37-degree slope that could be triggered with the presence of a weak layer under a slab.

DELIBERATE PRACTICE:
Challenge your team to accurately identify slope angle in start zones and on specific features. Everyone guess the angle, then (safely) measure it with a clinometer as accurately as you can.

Standing there in the terrain, ask yourself, "Is that steep section of the slope large enough to initiate an avalanche?" If it is, consider that your slope angle more than the lower-angle portions of the slope. A 20-meter (measured in horizontal distance) section of slope is a good rule of thumb to use when identifying terrain that could avalanche. For us gringos, that's only a 65-foot stretch of slope. Heads up.

Apps Are Nice, but Trust Your Eyes

Nestled in the trees on the east side of Vail Pass, on a forested slope above Corral Creek, is a fun ski run below Lynx Point. Observed on a topo map and/or with slope shading, it appears to be a fairly consistent slope, with no terrain steeper than a tiny blip of 32 degrees. The reality on the ground, though, is quite a bit different than the map might lead you to believe. Lurking just into the trees is a 40-plus-degree rollover ending in sparse timber. Were you to slavishly trust the topo map and/or a slope-shading app, you wouldn't be ready for what could be a triggerable feature above a terrain trap. The slope is plenty big enough to produce a size 2.5 avalanche—and sometimes does.

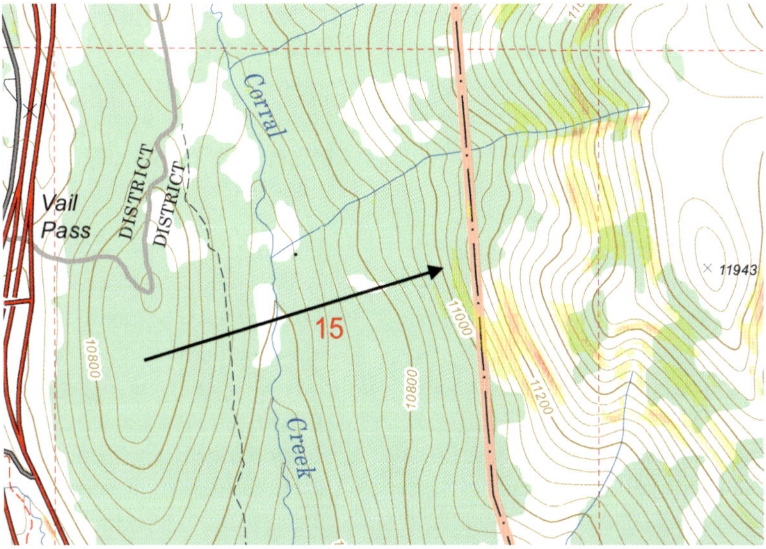

A screenshot from CalTopo showing Lynx Point (Pt. 11943 on the map) and the run below. The arrow indicates a 40-plus-degree rollover in the trees that could easily produce a size 2.5 avalanche. Note that the shaded colors (yellow and light orange) suggest a blip of low-30-degree terrain rather than a significant rollover of 40-plus. COURTESY CALTOPO.COM

* * *

We use an accurate assessment of slope angle to dial back our terrain choices. In touchy conditions, we often manage the hazard by limiting our skiing to slopes with no large features steeper than 30 degrees. For example, working at Sunrise Lodge in the Esplanade Range near Golden, British Columbia, in 2019, there were two touchy surface hoar layers buried approximately 45 centimeters and 70 centimeters down. They were most reactive below 1,800 meters, as the layers hadn't formed as well in the alpine. Generally speaking, as skiers descended, the problem grew touchier, and Avalanche Canada warned users about it. Above tree line, we could push our terrain choices above 35 degrees; below tree line, anything above 30 kept us puckered for the week.

Managing terrain like this requires discipline and attention. It's easy to get carried away on the down, especially in sheltered old-growth. Isn't this where the safe skiing is?! For our week at Sunrise, it most certainly was not, and we had our guard up. We would check our maps to identify potentially steep areas, but once in the field, we had to keep the groups tight and our eyes peeled for rollovers and gullies

During an AIARE 2 outside Nelson, British Columbia, a blissed-out student applies his decision-making—and ski—skills during a fabulous storm cycle.
MAHTING PUTELIS

that might not be indicated on the map. Skiing shorter pitches helped manage the group, but a team decision to post up above any steep pitch or rollover helped too. In short, besides total avoidance, an accurate slope-angle determination is one of your best defenses against avalanche hazard.

IDENTIFYING PROBLEMS IN THE TERRAIN (SO WE CAN AVOID THEM!)

We should head into the field with a solid idea of where we will find avalanche problems, and other hazards, in the terrain. This can be done by elevation band, aspect, and, most important, by a solid description of the terrain in which you'll find a particular problem.

A couple minutes reading the bulletin and checking local weather stations will help us determine where we might find wind slabs, for example. If the wind blew from the west all night, with snow available for transport, then you can reasonably expect to find wind slabs on lee aspects. We certainly discuss this in our morning meeting and probably note it in our notebook for the day.

Once in the terrain, we approach any lee aspect with caution. Note that we said, "any lee aspect" and not simply any northeast/east/southeast aspect. The reality on the ground doesn't conform to the compass rose or the nearby weather station. Forecasters necessarily have to give us a general idea of which aspects are lee and where we'll most likely find wind-deposited snow—but by no means does that mean these aspects will be the only places to find wind slabs.

Consider the Vail-Summit zone in Colorado, which encompasses almost 4,000 square miles. As you travel to the eastern portion of the zone, the wind becomes a bigger influence on the snowpack compared to the western end of the zone. Forecasters at the CAIC have a tricky problem—giving the general public an idea of avalanche problems throughout a maddeningly diverse area! Shading a portion of the avalanche rose in the eastern end of the zone might not be totally accurate in the western end; that's why they also give us a written description in the "Summary" portion of the bulletin, describing what wind slabs look like and on what sort of terrain they might lurk. Taken in total, the avalanche character, avalanche rose, and written description should give us a highly detailed and accurate idea of the overall avalanche problem.

One useful exercise is to look at avalanche accidents/involvements and then go back and not only match the avalanche problem and aspect to the accident but also read the textual description on the bulletin for that day. Usually we see that the forecasters accurately described the terrain in which the accident occurred in the summary, even if an involvement occurred just a few degrees outside the forecasted aspect. During debriefs you frequently discover that a backcountry rider turned off her brain the moment she left the aspect on which the forecasters listed the problem, only to find herself on a slope that matches the description of problem terrain.

Some days Mother Nature makes it painfully obvious where the wind slabs lie. On a typical Colorado Front Range day, Dirk Friel does his best to identify safer skiing below the Citadel. ROB COPPOLILLO

We need to remember to take the bulletin as the sum-total of the rose, avalanche character, nearest-neighbor observations, and text/summary, without missing any element or overprioritizing it. We also do our own morning meeting to discuss the danger trend, how the weather might have influenced the snowpack overnight, and incorporate our own local observations. In short, it's our job—whether as advanced recreationists or mountain

With the wind raging and wind slabs building, this team opts for safer and better skiing in the trees, just downhill of the Asulkan Hut, Rogers Pass, British Columbia. ROB COPPOLILLO

guides—to localize the bulletin for our subregion, drainage, slope, and each feature in the field.

STAYING HIGH

In general, being higher on a feature or slope minimizes exposure and reduces consequences rather than being lower. We can certainly find exceptions to this rule, but generally speaking, you want less terrain above you rather than more when managing a hazard.

Tour planning with this in mind will help you reduce your exposure and consequences, so consider it when you're working at a macro scale. Once in the field, apply this strategy on the micro scale too. Any time you can regroup or ski on a bump, ridge, or rib, do it. Avoid terrain traps as a matter of habit, even on low-danger days.

Staying high in the terrain shouldn't introduce other hazards to your descent or uptrack. Use the strategy to keep you and your team safer.

TREED TERRAIN

When it's nuking in the alpine, we instinctively head into the trees. On many days this is an easy sell if there are high winds or flat light. Particularly with wind-slab problems, treed terrain is often safer than alpine skiing. Trees shelter the slope from wind effect and often hold better, softer snow.

This is not a hard-and-fast rule, however. Less-experienced skiers often assume that trees anchor a slope—which they can—but for trees to reliably anchor a piece of terrain, they need to be dense enough that ski quality begins to suffer. If you can hold your poles in your hands and extend them horizontally around without hitting trees, there's less anchoring going on than you might think. If you're able to make fun, casual turns between trees, they're probably not anchoring much.

Use tree skiing to your advantage on the right days. When the alpine is blown out, much of that snow might be hiding below tree line, in lee aspects. Get some!

THE RIGHT RUN FOR THE GROUP

Group size, skill, and goals inform our trip plan on the day. Touring in a group of three might make total sense for a narrow couloir, while a group of six in the same feature might invite carnage and reduced ski quality.

As you're choosing terrain during the trip plan, fast-forward in your

Looking down the slope, the guide cut high above the proposed ski line and sluffed loose dry snow. He did this before sending guests down the run. By traversing high, he not only protects himself but also can cut any unstable snow threatening his ski line. Guests had a great ski, the guide was safe, and the whole operation took just a few seconds. Outside Golden, British Columbia. ROB COPPOLILLO

Headed into the narrows in the Dragontail Couloir, a team of three made sense for the day. With 30 centimeters of fresh overnight and wind drifting in the start zone more than 250 meters above the team, avalanche hazard was increasing. Narrow terrain meant fewer safe zones on the up and the down, and managing a larger group would've required more time exposed. By keeping the team to three, full mountain guide Eli Helmuth, AIARE avalanche course leader Andrew Ogden, and the author moved more quickly, could ski pitches one at a time . . . and got the goods that day! ROB COPPOLILLO

mind's eye to managing your group. Are there safe regroup spots? Enough snow for everybody? Easy enough to maintain communication and visual contact? Do your teammates or guests work well together, or is it a gong show of crossing lines and people splitting up? From a guiding perspective, if the terrain is convoluted (think micro-features on a forested slope with diverging drainages, for example) and you're working with a group of six skiers, the prospect of managing all of them becomes daunting. Will that be manageable for you? Fun for the guests?

When you match the terrain to your team and its capacities, you've effectively pre-managed some of the hazard and set everybody up for a better day of riding. Narrow, committing gullies require a disciplined, skilled team and teammates who won't fall while descending. For a gang of chargers who want to make GS turns without regrouping during the run,

Wide-open, safe skiing in the glades and bowls of Vail Pass, Colorado. A larger group poses fewer problems in forgiving terrain like this.
ROB COPPOLILLO

look for a wide-open run that feeds everybody into the same drainage. Let a natural terrain feature manage the group for you. Choosing terrain suited to your group delivers great skiing as well as better risk management.

How to Ski

We've chosen where to ski during our trip plan. We have a bunch of tools at our disposal to decide at the slope scale where we'll ski once in the field. Now we need to consider *how* we are going to ski. One at a time? Spaced out, or perhaps closer together? Do we need radios? Or even—uh oh—a rope?! Let's try to imagine a few scenarios and when we might or might not use the tools.

COMMUNICATION IS KEY

No, we're not relationship counselors, but good communications stand as the first rule in group management and how we ski. Whether you choose radios or agreed-upon hand signals, having clear communication among teammates helps reduce mistakes and hazards. Effective coordination and communication in the field should be part of any strategy you use to travel and manage the team. Wind and blowing snow make even a quick chat difficult, so keep an eye on overall conditions like weather, language barriers, and team dynamics when deciding on a communication strategy for the day.

ONE AT A TIME

Most backcountry skiers default to skiing one at a time. This exposes only one skier to avalanche hazard—provided the group waits in a truly safe spot. It's usually a solid strategy.

Getting the down one at a time also increases enjoyment. Particularly with less-confident guests, they feel less pressure if they can ride a slope at their own pace. Having a pitch to themselves and the freedom to look around and relax, they're less likely to make mistakes. In a couloir or gully, we send one guest at a time for safety reasons, but don't discount the technique on an open bowl; your skier might appreciate it.

There's a common myth that we space out to reduce "stress" or "weight" on the slope. In reality, a backcountry rider usually only affects the snowpack 1 to 2 meters around himself. We space out mainly to reduce the chance that multiple members of our team could be caught. If we've made a mistake in our terrain choice and we get somebody buried, we want our whole team available to effect a rescue. Skiing one at a time is a hedge on our bet. For high-consequence terrain, touchy conditions, and/or shorter day tours, defaulting to "one at a time" makes a ton of sense.

TEAM SKIING

We need to weigh the downside of riding one at a time too. If our audience is more experienced backcountry riders and mountain guides, these people can begin to identify exceptions to the rules. Add to that the increased fitness levels and ambitions of expert practitioners—i.e., bigger, longer days—and we need to ask ourselves if we're creating another hazard by skiing one at a time.

The practice certainly slows down the team. Are we going to end up on a sunbaked, sunny slope later than we want because we spent all morning going one at a time on relatively safer slopes? Or will we end up being out after dark because we moved too slowly during the day? If we can't manage the avalanche hazard while completing our tour safely and/or in time, we need to ask ourselves if we've chosen the right tour and terrain for the day.

On many slopes, "team skiing" can be appropriate. This might mean teaming up with one other partner while tree skiing or having the whole group riding the slope together. When considering the technique, we need to make a conscious decision that it's safe enough and we're not upping our risk to an unacceptable level. Tackling longer tours will mean having to move through the mountains efficiently, and that requires identifying slopes we can ski as a group. Low-angle terrain and lower avalanche danger are the obvious situations in which we can save valuable minutes by allowing the group to enjoy a run together.

As soon as we decide to jump on a slope as a big group, we need to have a solid plan—either decided upon by the group or described clearly by the guide—on how we'll ski and where we'll regroup. How far shall skiers space themselves? Are we in the trees and agree not to ski below a certain elevation?

Don't dismiss riding a slope together out of hand. Just make sure you've consciously considered the decision and have a reason to do so. You're betting the whole farm on the decision. A mistake with the whole team on the slope could easily end in tragedy.

PARTNER SKIING

We often partner ski when it's critical that we not lose sight or contact with any particular team member. On the guiding side of things, it would be nearly impossible to have "eyes on" every guest for the entirety of a tree run without skiing such short pitches that your guests would hate you for it. Skiing longer, enjoyable pitches means giving folks a bit of the freedom to do it. Tree wells or an unexpected avalanche—even a small one—can be deadly hazards in treed terrain, though. The solution: Grab a partner.

Too often we ask guests to partner up; then, at the regroup, the front skier rolls in and turns to face uphill with no idea of where his companion is. That's not partner skiing! When trying out the technique or asking others to, we need to be diligent and clear in practice and explanation. Partners need to be in visual/auditory contact for the entire pitch or run. The second rider on the slope has an easier time doing this; he can simply follow his partner's track while watching her too. The lead skier, though, must make the effort to keep in touch. She does this by listening for the occasional "whoop-whoop" (or whatever kooky sound her partner agrees to) from her partner and/or occasionally turning her head. The moment she no longer has contact with the trailing skier, she needs to post up and wait.

Those of you with mad pow disease (it's a thing; consult your physician) are already shaking your head: "Yeah, but the poor guy chasing her down never gets freshies!" You are exactly right. Take two deep breaths, and when your cortisol levels have returned to acceptable levels, consider this technique: You either swap pitches in the lead or, especially for longer runs, have the lead skier pull off every 30 seconds and let the trailing skier slide by. Yes, you need to alternate turns in the lead, but you will get some untracked.

Believe it or not, partner skiing takes a little practice. Remember, the person in the front is identifying hazards and avoiding them, spotting alleys in the trees, and potentially keeping an eye on other pairs nearby. She might be skiing a bit more slowly than the charger following her tracks. The trailing skier needs to keep this in mind and adjust pace accordingly. It's easy to roll up on the front skier.

WARMING UP AND EASING INTO TERRAIN

However we decide to travel in the terrain, getting a warm-up and easing ourselves into the day and run will make for a better experience. I, of course, have not aged a bit past 31 years old, but for the older skiers out there, getting a warm-up will allow them to ski longer and more comfortably during the day. More important, a casual first run affords the team a chance to assess conditions, get acquainted with one another (if necessary), and gather obs.

Those of you lucky enough to have visited the legendary Sorcerer Lodge know the fantastic tree runs that start just 200 meters to the north of the hut. You can literally walk out of the lodge, slide a few steps, and arrive at steep, entertaining terrain. Nearby, though, you can take a slightly mellower run near a glacial moraine. While it sure is tempting to dive into that rowdier treed terrain, it's also a higher-consequence maneuver.

My dear friend Martin Van Pelt enjoying the morning below Sorcerer Lodge, British Columbia. One of the all-time great guests, Martin could ski, tell a joke, roll with any situation, and tour all day. He's no longer with us, and I miss him every time I step into skis.
ROB COPPOLILLO

Leaving the hut one morning to 35 centimeters of new snow, we opted for the more relaxed run between the trees and the moraine. It gave us a warm-up and allowed us to poke some small, low-consequence rollovers—and wouldn't you know it, just about every rollover popped a little slab out. A quick call on the radio to the other team and we'd assessed conditions, identifying a touchy storm slab that we had wondered about in our morning meeting.

If you're starting the day with an uptrack, this often gives you the time to make observations. Heads up if you're lucky enough to start your day with a nice run, though. Ease into it, get the legs warm, and get a feel for conditions before jumping into "real" terrain.

SPACING

Above, we discussed the idea of skiing a run or pitch together as a team. We jokingly call it "gang skiing" a slope, but in reality we need to make a deliberate decision about getting everybody on the slope. If it's flat light, perhaps having a skier just five turns ahead will help the followers with visibility and perspective. An alpine bowl on a bluebird morning, with 40 centimeters of fresh and low avalanche danger, begs to be skied fast and in long turns! Spacing skiers 30 seconds apart will keep people happier than keeping them closer together.

Spacing refers not only to distance on the slope but also to distance between tracks. We've all shared a slope on a powder day. If you left the house or hut early and made it to the top first, well . . . good on ya; there's no rule or law governing the way you ride the slope. Common courtesy, however, might suggest keeping your team's tracks pretty tight to leave some untracked goodness for others following you.

You might also elect to keep the team's tracks tight to avoid a hazard. If you notice a rollover on skier's right and the light is flat, you might ski as close to the rollover as is safe, then simply tell guests to stay left of your track. That might be enough to keep a disciplined group safely away from the rollover.

Now add a second hazard. Imagine that it's flat light and, in addition to the rollover, you know there are crevasses 80 meters skier's left. Now you have two dangers to manage. You might ski the same line, but now in addition to deciding to have your teammates ski just left of your track, you want to make sure they don't stray too far left, toward the crevasses. You can simply add to your original instructions, "Ski 1 to 2 meters left of the track ahead of you." You ski the line, the next skier slides just a bit left of your track, and the next skier does the same. Everyone stays left of the rollover, but close enough to the tracks that they also avoid the crevasses. So, without going into tedious detail (like I'm doing here), you've managed two significant hazards with simple, quick instructions. Good job!

Keep your eyes peeled for opportunities to apply spacing as a risk-management strategy. For example, coming

The team stacks tracks and moves together in non-avalanche terrain. A larger group needs to keep moving on such a long day—1300m vert! After ascending the Illecillewaet Glacier, the team rides lower-angle terrain to the start of the Lookout Couloirs. On this approach pitch, the terrain allows for gang skiing, though the guide asks his guests to "ski either side of my track; wait five seconds and the next skier can go." This keeps everybody together, guarantees pow for every skier, and moves the team efficiently to the start of the "real" skiing. It's also a means of keeping the group tight and away from hazards.

ROB COPPOLILLO

off the Col de Valpelline into Zermatt, midway on the Vallée Blanche above Chamonix, or the ski out from Pearl Pass near Aspen, Colorado—all these routes have spots of very mellow skiing with potentially lethal overhead hazard. Stopping the group to ski across them one at a time would add a bunch of waiting and delay, but skiing with the whole group stacked beneath the hazards makes no sense either. Deciding as a team, or coaching guests, to leave 100 meters between skiers means only one person is exposed at a time while keeping the team moving. In the unlucky event a teammate is hit by falling ice or an avalanche, at the very least his teammates will be able to respond. Adequate, accurate spacing ensures this.

STOP ABOVE THE LEADER

Whether guiding or skiing with your regular posse, having the team stop above the first skier on the slope accomplishes a few important goals. The first skier or guide has the responsibility to identify the best line, impending hazards, a change in snow quality, and truly safe regroup zones. If you're the second skier on the slope and the leader posts up, she might have seen a crevasse, reconsidered the terrain choice, or just wanted to rest the legs. We need to trust her judgment, dial back our speed, and stop above her. At that point we can check in and eyeball the next pitch.

If this becomes a team's default setting, the leader can ski a pitch, and when she identifies a reason to stop, she knows her group will arrive above her. This allows her to control the gang without having to radio, yell, or gesture. Easier, quieter, safer.

A word on the technique: A good friend and colleague of ours had her knee blown up by a guest coming in hot and crashing into her. Ouch! When coming to a stop above the leader or guide, skiers need to downshift two turns before the leader and slide in slowly and in control. Coach your ski partners to do this!

REGROUPING AWAY FROM THE HAZARD

Hazards range from crevasses to rockfall to avalanches to seracs to polar bears. Guides and team leaders need to be alert to various hazards throughout the day and, when possible, regroup the team away from them.

We try to ski fall line whenever possible and give enjoyable pitches to guests. This is usually possible, but not always. The leader needs to keep his eyes peeled to both expected and unexpected hazards; if that means

DELIBERATE PRACTICE:

For any of these techniques, challenge yourself to manage your team with as little instruction as possible, using simple phrases and even silently through the terrain. Ask for feedback, and actively seek out tricky sections on tours.

Skiing in polar bear habitat and with firearms—two hazards we don't normally face. In addition to avoiding curious bears, now the guide needs to be extremely attentive to where his gun is pointing, where the guests transition, and how to manage the rifle during transitions. Bear avoidance and gun safety on Svalbard, Norway. ROB COPPOLILLO

stopping short, so be it. Stacking the group up in a hazardous spot invites a bad accident, so try to read the terrain and tour plan such that you can regroup with an appropriate buffer between you and the hazard—on the order of tens of meters, not right up to the edge. There's always a surprise lurking, whether it's a cornice breaking farther back than we expected, an avalanche running farther than we anticipated, or a polar bear and her cubs.

Regroup away and before you're in the danger zone. Sheltered spots, high ground, and below dense timber are all opportunities for safety.

PITCH LENGTH

Finding the right rhythm and pace of the day comes easily to a tight-knit team that rides together all season. Guiding unfamiliar guests or incorporating a new teammate, though, requires gauging everyone's fitness level in addition to balancing hazards with fun skiing.

When fitness, whiteout conditions, or hazardous terrain demands it, keeping pitches short becomes helpful. Remember, we're not often tied to the guests (thankfully!), so pitch length is one means of maintaining contact. Being able to see a ski partner or the guide usually helps nervous skiers manage anxiety too. In a whiteout, short of roping up, keeping pitches short might be your best way of not losing a team member. In crevassed terrain, erring on the side of shorter pitches prevents a psyched (or sketchy?!) rider from straying too far and ending up in a crack. In dense trees, the riding quality has already deteriorated, so why risk losing someone by skiing long pitches?

Veteran skiers and/or strong teammates generally enjoy longer pitches, so deliver when you can. We don't want to shatter a weaker teammate or less-experienced guest, but the joy of riding a slope comes not in 15-second increments. Point 'em down when you can, and enjoy long pitches when the group and legs are up for it.

Longer pitches can also keep the group moving, managing a time hazard like nightfall, solar heating on a slope, or building wind slabs. Glacier skiing below seracs provides dramatic views and terrain, but spending large amounts of time below teetering ice towers isn't a winning strategy. As a guide or team leader, you're probably on the fitter end of the spectrum, so if your legs are burning, the following skiers might be suffering. Deliver fun skiing, but don't crush people—it's easier on them and ultimately on you too. Nobody likes bonking on the final climb of the day—not the bonk victim or his teammate or guide. Less-aggressive skiing, and our low-angle skintracks from "The Up" chapter, might save yourself and clients a bunch of pain at the end of the tour.

COMMUNICATION

Mention comms to backcountry riders, skiers, and sledders and they immediately think radios. Great idea, but before we get to techy solutions, let's not miss out on some tried-and-true old-school strategies.

We generally "point positive" while touring. By this we mean if a teammate leads a pitch of downhill skiing then suddenly posts up and points with her ski pole to skier's left, we assume that means better skiing or lower hazard, or just that she wants us over there for some reason. Maybe a photo op, even. She points where she wants us, not at what she wants us to avoid. Crossed ski poles, on the other hand, generally means "stop." Something's not right, and it's safest to just stop.

Some groups develop their own hand signals, like scuba divers. As long as everyone in the group knows the signals and uses them consistently, why not?

We discussed pitch length above. Shorter pitches facilitate easier communication. In a whiteout, even with radios, it becomes difficult to describe terrain. Getting split up eats up time and leaves teammates exposed to otherwise manageable hazards like tree wells, etc. When things start to go wrong, maintaining visual and verbal communication really helps out. (Don't discount this in climbing, either. How often do we see people linking pitches, only to lose all that "time saved" by extended shouting sessions just to determine if one is on or off belay?)

Guides and some groups rely on radios for group and risk management. For guides, having local repeaters and organizations preprogrammed into their radios greatly expedites a rescue or sharing information.

During the same Sorcerer trip mentioned earlier, the snowpack trended into a dangerous and spooky deep-slab cycle. One afternoon while touring, the team climbed out of a valley to notice a long crown running across the Upper Cheap Scotch zone of the tenure. Sorcerer Lodge shares a portion of its terrain with Great Canadian Heli, a heliski outfit. By having their frequencies preprogrammed into our radios, guides were able to share an observation with Great Canadian. We described an approximate 1.5-kilometer-long crown line at the head of the valley. The pilot seemed a little skeptical at first, but after a flyby he hit us back on our channel to say, "You weren't joking!"

Sharing and receiving an observation, especially on the front end of a deep-slab cycle, can greatly increase our safety in the backcountry. Radios let you do it in real time.

A powerful (5W or even 10W) VHF radio also connects you to search and rescue (SAR), air traffic, or possibly a repeater (which will help you connect with distant resources). Some areas require a ham license to use certain frequencies, so check in before purchasing some Chuck Norris Delta Force unit (and landing in hot water with Mr. Norris and/or the US Federal Communications Commission or its Canadian counterpart). In an emergency, anyone can use any frequency, but for routine communication, most countries have strict regulations about which bands are open to the public.

Radios can also be indispensable within the group too. A "dual-band" VHF radio not only will talk to SAR resources and pilots but also will transmit on the FRS bands (Family Radio Service, the frequencies between 462 MHz and 467 MHz). Backcountry Access "BC Link" and Motorola "Talkabout" radios operate on FRS frequencies. Expect radio chatter in high-use areas like ski resorts and popular destinations because the general public also uses these channels. Your guests and teammates are way more likely to have FRS radios, so it's nice to operate on two sets of frequencies, which a dual-band model does.

Allowing you to easily and quickly communicate with a teammate or guest at the top of a slope shouldn't be underestimated as a risk-management tool. We've all skied a slope, only to look back and think to ourselves, *Maybe a couple hundred meters left would be safer.* It's a terrible feeling to have no means to nudge your group toward safer skiing. Not that it's ever happened to me; I'm a mountain guide and therefore never wrong. But you get the gist: A quick radio call can be a lifesaver in tricky conditions or terrain.

FALL-LINE SKIING

We mentioned above the idea of skiing fall-line pitches. Given the option, most of us prefer fall-line skiing over a "diagonaling" line. Knowing this, we can lead our teammates on fall-line skiing to a safe regroup then put in a traverse in one direction or another to connect to a different part of the slope. We might do this to stay on the fall line, to avoid a hazard, or to set ourselves up for a safer exit. The strategy requires a bit of forethought, but it can be effective in "managing the group without managing the group." That is, you can move your entire group to another part of the ski line with a quick regroup and traverse without wasting time on a lengthy explanation.

LEFT, RIGHT, BESIDE, OR ON TOP OF MY TRACK!

The first skier's track can be a great guide for followers. Perhaps it just puts some texture on the slope in flat light so that your team can get better turns. Your track can also guide skiers to one side or another, toward better skiing, away from hazards, etc.

You might use your track to "fence" in guests. For example, a shallower, weaker area of snow on skier's left might be the hazard you're trying to avoid. You ski as close to the shallow snow as you like and instruct people, "Stay right of my track, spaced 10 seconds apart." Two simple instructions, but you've moved your guests away from hazardous skiing and toward deeper snow.

You might also ski "the gut," or deepest section, of a slope. You could tell folks to alternate skiing "either side of my track." (Pro tip: This also gives you a great run right down the goods.)

Once in a while, we might just surrender to conditions or terrain and say, "I'd like you all to stay right on top of my tracks." Imagine sneaking between two crevasses as you change fall lines. In this instance, rather than nudging people toward better snow, you're actively protecting them from a crevasse-fall hazard by keeping them on the strongest, deepest (hopefully un-crevassed) snow—so you set a track and tell them to stay right on top of it. Breakable crust might be another situation in which you stack the strongest skiers at the front of the team, let them break up the crust, and give weaker skiers a better chance of survival by skiing in the disturbed snow.

Reminder: We're not roped together very much while on skis, so use your tracks as a connection to your partners.

SPLIT, SKI, AND (YES) SNOWSHOE

In terms of travel mode, mixed groups require planning and forethought. Regroup at the bottom of a slope with a flat meadow ahead, and your splitboard buddies will howl in protest. Remember, it's harder to slide across the flats on a snowboard. Snowshoers will enjoy firmer snow rather than bottomless pow. So, teaching an avalanche course to a group of snowshoers, you might actually search out bulletproof, refrozen snow. You need to accommodate all your partners, so give some thought to terrain selection and what your partners have on their feet.

Splitboarders in particular enjoy slightly different terrain choices. Chunked-up, heavy chunder looks like pretty fun riding conditions when we see our split partners charge it. On superlight touring skis, though, that stuff can be challenging. Breakable crust? Sure looks easier on a snowboard than our skinny sticks.

Check in with the group and think ahead. Going a kilometer out of your way might actually save energy and time, depending on your touring gear.

Survival Mode

Eventually it happens. The weather gods, poor timing, or a hex placed upon you by local guides hellbent on sandbagging you—survival skiing. Breakable crust, rain-on-snow, bottomless facets, sun cups. There are many types of manky snow, and you have to be ready for them.

CHALLENGING CONDITIONS

Trying to describe every type of tough skiing would fry your brains and mine, so let's keep it mostly general and hit only a few of the most obvious situations.

In cold, shallow climates (ahem, Colorado), you might find yourself skiing bottomless facets. Riding wider skis helps a bit, but only so much. Assume you will be way deeper into the snowpack than usual. Avoiding rocky slopes and shallow buried objects becomes paramount. You'll be effectively sliding just above the ground if it's early season. Sometimes a sun crust just above the ground can be a lifesaver. That first snow in November then baked into a sun crust can provide a "base" of sorts on which to ride faceted snow in December and January. Keep it in mind.

Rough, chundery snow can be tricky for less-experienced guests and partners, but if the snow is at all soft, you can consider side-slipping to smooth it out. This works for a short pitch or challenging section. Side-slipping an entire slope (though it has been done!) will be a low point in your ski career, so avoid using this technique for much more than a few meters. To make the snow more predictable and manageable, however, this might be the ticket.

"Breakable crust," the words you most fear in the backcountry besides "rain" and "one-piece." Awkward, challenging, frustrating, more than a few of us have threatened to quit and sell all our gear after a long (read: more than 10-meter) descent on breakable crust.

Take faith, though; a couple pointers will help. First, consider riding a snowboard or a monoski. Short of that, you might suggest a long descending traverse to a stop and downhill kick turn (for skiers), then another long traverse to another downhill kick turn. Tedious, but pretty safe, and you're steadily dropping altitude. This is the definition of survival skiing—just get

A bit of breakable crust, with leftover chunder from previous ski tracks, transforms the first turns into quite a challenge for a less-confident skier. The guide side-slips the steep entrance and tells guests to downshift a bit when they come in. Silver Sneak, Buffalo Mountain, Colorado. MATT KENNEDY

it over with safely, without injury or drama.

Second, try to reframe the experience as an opportunity to demonstrate competence and confidence. Ever seen somebody slay a pitch of breakable, making it look like kinda-good skiing? It's impressive, and a mountain guide should be able to do it.

Another solution, mentioned above, might be to coach your guests to follow in your track and make turns where you make turns. You can break up the crust and provide a bit of disturbed snow, which is slightly more predictable. A tight stem christie turn will provide a bit more control too.

Remember to consider ordering your team from "best" to "worst" in terms of ski ability. When the last/less-experienced skiers go, they'll be skiing broken-up crust rather than an intact breakable crust.

We should seek to inspire and teach our guests and teammates, though. Merely surviving a tour short-changes them (and ourselves). How about linking controlled, elegant turns in breakable crust?! Easier said than done, but worth striving for. Keep these things in mind:

- Use both skis as one. Imagine you're skiing 95-millimeter-waisted skis; this gives you 190 millimeters of potential surface area beneath your feet. Ski with your feet together, staying balanced and centered over your feet. You're re-creating the life-saving surface area of a snowboard (or a monoski, *mes amis*!). Your feet/ankles should be working in concert here; if you're doing something with one and not the other, quit it.

- Your weight-unweight rhythm is critical here. We're trying to link controlled, fluid turns, so forget the idea of the survival traverse mentioned above. Find a rhythm that works given your ski and skill; you want to initiate the turn and get some edge-penetration into the crust and even begin to break the crust without penetrating it and submarining your skis. If you dive your skis, it's going to be tough to stay upright. Ease into those first couple turns to see how fragile/stout the crust is, then load/flex your skis into the crust and use the rebound/return energy from the turn to unweight your skis and roll them into your next turn.
- Faith. Yes, faith in the creator above will probably help you here, but also faith in a bit of speed and faith in your innate athletic ability. Some momentum and speed here will help you link turns and weight/unweight the skis.
- Don't lose track of your upper body. As with much of skiing, a tight core, quiet upper body, and upper-lower body separation are all critical components here. Start swinging your arms, using your shoulders to turn, or dropping that uphill hand behind you and you're flirting with carnage. Funny for your friends; less so for you.

As bad as breakable crust can be, remember the wise words of the legendary Doug Coombs: "There's no bad snow, only bad skiers." Good luck!

FLAT LIGHT AND POOR VIS

Riding in low-vis conditions ranks as a bit less hateful than breakable crust, but not by much. A few techniques can help, but "skiing by braille" is no fun, especially for anybody with shaky movement skills.

Consider choosing terrain with rocks or trees to aid in giving perspective to your teammates. Skiing a narrow gully lets them sight off rocks along the sides. The occasional tree island will help a ton, or just diving into some glades will deliver great skiing when the alpine is desperate.

Often, though, we have no choice but to ski in low-vis conditions, especially during traverses, tagging a summit, or switching drainages. In these situations, we need to give our companions the best chance of making turns. It's safer and more enjoyable for them. In addition to riding near trees and rocks, another strategy might be to put tracks on the slope. The first rider will flail a bit on the down, but his tracks will offer the team some perspective and reference.

Before committing to the slope, check your map for any terrain features you will want to avoid, and if you need to, roll a snowball down the fall line. Tying some flagging tape to a medium-size washer can be a lifesaver too. Have a couple of them and throw one near and one far down the slope. Now at least you have two points of reference on the slope and potentially some indication of hidden cliffs or crevasses. If you don't see one of the washers, assume it went down a crack or cliff—and that there's a hazard below you.

(The downside of the tape-and-washer trick is the potential for littering the landscape with flagging tape. It can be an effective trick in a pinch, though. Replace your flagging tape if it's getting brittle or worn and you probably won't have a littering problem.)

Often when crossing a glacier, we tie a cordelette to our pole basket in truly flat-light conditions and flick it out in front. This works on the down too, but it only gives you a sense of the next 5 or 6 meters. This makes for slow going, but it's safer than sliding along and hoping for the best. As they say, "Hope is not an effective risk-management strategy."

Short pitches will help in true "milk" conditions, allowing you to sight off your partner downslope but also keep an eye on her.

In summary, never underestimate how much low-vis hampers your ability to make observations and how much it short-circuits your decision making. You lose a ton of information on route finding and the snowpack, not to mention you can't make avalanche observations without good vis.

"Slide-for-life" snow turns manageable terrain into a veritable pucker-fest. You do not want your less-confident teammates perched on a slope with real fall potential. This is probably a mistake in your planning and prep for the day, so let's remind ourselves to avoid this situation in the first place. Find yourself in it, though, and you need some strategies to manage the terrain more safely.

Let's save steep-ski techniques for that chapter and assume your guests can't manage this terrain safely or the snow is so firm you can't get edge penetration. If you find yourself confident on the slope, with a teammate spooked, you can always side-slip below him and coach him a bit. If it's truly that firm, ask yourself what happens if he blows it and slides into you. If you won't be able to check his fall, don't put yourself in harm's way.

Tell him to forget linking turns and to get on his edges and side-slip the spooky section. If it's short, you might be able to hold onto his pack's haul loop from above. Can you truly hold him, though, if he starts to slide?

The first technique, which provides balance more than anything, to suggest is baton ramasse. Like piolet ramasse from snow climbing, the practitioner takes both ski poles, holds them together as one, and then pushes both sharp ends into the slope horizontally. Coach your skier to not lean back and into the slope, as this might cause him to lose his edges. Ramasse

Shouldering the Ax

The skier has a shouldered ax tucked between his body and the backpack—it's the thin, white strip hiding behind his arm.

MATT KENNEDY

Having an ice ax at the ready can be mentally comforting and inspire confidence. Removing one's pack mid-slope can be tricky business, though, and risks losing gear—expensive at the least, dangerous at the worst! By "shouldering" one's ice ax, we can avoid the on-off routine, speed ourselves up, and protect against losing a full pack.

Before a run in which you think you might need your ax, remove it from your pack. Once you're ready to ski, take your ax head in one hand and, with the other hand, grab your pack's shoulder strap *above* the sternum strap. Pull the shoulder strap out so that it's off your shoulder. Now, with your other hand holding the head of the ice ax, put the spike/bottom of the shaft on your shoulder so that you can slide it under the shoulder strap of your pack, backward and over your shoulder. You're sliding the spike of the ax as if you're trying to spike somebody standing behind you. Once you've slid the shaft of the ax all the way until the head of the ax is about to hit your shoulder strap, maneuver the head of the ax (pick and adze) around your head and let it nest across the top of your backpack. The pick and adze should sit behind your neck, atop your pack, and the shaft of the ax should now be diagonal and down. Nestled correctly, you should barely feel the ax.

It should be secure and stashed, allowing you to ski or climb without it thrashing around. This gives you the option of grabbing your ax mid-slope, if you encounter sketchier conditions than expected or you lose your courage on the down. If having your ax immediately behind your neck seems risky to you, avoid the technique or reconsider your terrain selection.

Remember when you remove your pack that the ax is loose back there. Don't just take off your pack on the slope; you'll lose the ax!

should allow him a third point of contact with the slope and more of an ability to lean out and over his ski edges, keeping him balanced and in control. (Joey Vallone demonstrates this in a photo in the "Steep" chapter.)

After ramasse, removing an ice ax from his pack and giving it to him might help. You allow him to leave the pack on and extricate the ax; this protects him from dropping his pack, dropping the ax, and/or losing his balance. Maybe having a piolet in hand will give him the confidence to side-slip a section, though we don't want to encourage a false sense of security with the allure of self-arrest.

Digging a quick bucket seat and letting a guest side-slip while on belay might solve a short section too. A long slope of this, though, and you're going to burn up valuable time, especially if you're using a short rope.

There may come a day when mid-slope you decide it's simply too sketchy to ski. Transitioning to booting—whether up and out or down—requires focus. People will likely drop a pack or crampon or ski, so plan on spotting them. They're probably already nervous, so expecting them to perform a tricky, complex maneuver is a tall ask. Set up below them, secure your gear and protect yourself, then help them get out of skis and into boot crampons, mount their skis on their packs, and make sure they're relatively safe before letting your guard down. If you can, anticipate this transition so you can find a safer spot. Mid-slope invites a fall or lost gear. Your shovel might help; dig out a platform if you must. Focus and help your teammates.

You can coach a person to remove her skis (but not necessarily a snowboard) mid-slope by suggesting she plunge one of her ski tails backward and into the slope. Once the first ski is secured, she can plunge the second, so now her ski tips are pointing away from the slope, into space. With both her tails plunged behind her, she hopefully feels secure enough to relax, lean into the slope, and remove her pack. You'll probably still have to spot her here, as she needs to eventually/potentially remove her crampons and ice ax (digging a small hole in which to place her gear might help), get out of one ski and kick her boot into the slope or put on a crampon, then do the same for the other foot. At this point she can turn and face in and carefully put one ski on her pack, then the other. Plunging ski poles into the slope can provide an anchor too—by allowing her to loop one of her pack's shoulder straps over the poles, securing it to the slope.

Avoid this error correction entirely by carefully considering your and your partners' ski skill and the terrain. Transitioning mid-slope presents real hazard, at the very least losing a ski or a pack.

Steep Skiing

Steep skiing—what we used to call extreme skiing—endlessly fascinates us. From the time we start sliding on snow, we wonder how steep we can go without losing it, mentally or physically. Photos of courageous riders linking turns on a 55-degree slope amp us up. Most of us wonder, *Could we pull that off too?*

Guiding steep skiing can be a nail-biting affair—it's a bit like guiding free-soloing on rock. You can only offer so much coaching, support, and safety. Later in the book you'll find an entire chapter devoted to the discipline, but a few brief thoughts here first.

Whether guiding or not, before you and your teammates venture into the steeps, you should invest the time and effort into doing it safely and sanely. As a ski guide, it would be nearly unheard of to take a first-time client into consequential steep-ski terrain. Guides willing to work in steep terrain typically spend seasons bringing clients up to a point where they can get into steeper terrain with an acceptable level of risk. It can be a tremendously satisfying partnership, training together with a goal like skiing off the Grand Teton or riding the full Marinelli Couloir.

TECHNIQUES

Steep skiing is not safe, period. Certainly we can practice it more or less safely, but we need to disabuse guests of any false sense of security. We simply cannot afford to fall in steep terrain, so by definition we need to push the needle toward "perfect." Humans and "perfect" don't mix very well, so you see the problem we're managing here.

Notice I didn't give a particular slope angle to the definition of steep skiing. Fifty degrees with a bit of edge penetration will feel far more reasonable than 40 degrees on white ice. This leads into the first bit of advice: Do your homework. On the weather, on the terrain, on your teammates or guests, on your equipment, on the snowpack. Planning and prep help manage the risk before you leave the hut or your comfy urban lair.

We took a deep dive into trip planning in that chapter, and those basics will get you most of the way to making better decisions in steep terrain. It's worth tailoring your pre-trip plan to account for the steeps. Some things to consider.

Weather. Low light, frigid temps, and/or high winds can all morph a manageable ski into a horror show. Rumor has it the author skied the Cables Route, or north face, of Longs Peak with an ice ax in hand and terror on his face. The forecasted sunny skies turned into overcast-and-cool just before he and his teammates skied the line. Instead of edge penetration and hero turns, the team found bulletproof snow at 14,000 feet! Do your best not to get surprised out there.

Know the aspect you're skiing, the forecast weather, and when the sun will hit your feature. (CalTopo has a spot indicator for this; check it out.) Often with long descents, you need to estimate conditions on the summit, midline, and at valley bottom. Skiing hero snow at the top of your line might mean slush and wet-loose avalanche activity in the lower third.

Compromise on the less-hazardous sections of your tour. By this I mean, if you plan to ski truly no-fall terrain somewhere near the lower half of the route, you might accept that you'll ski the upper half before it has softened up in the sun, then hit the super-steep section as the upper centimeters of snow have loosened a bit but before they're grabby or dangerous.

Don't limit this strategy only to timing. If you feel a particular pair of skis will provide more edge hold and stability during a steep section (or a heavier pair of boots, or a different backpack might be more balanced, etc.) but might not ski as well throughout the rest of a tour, so be it. You want to have the best overall situation—in terms of gear, comfort, and riding conditions—when it matters most.

During your planning and prep, choreograph as much of your day as possible. Where will you stage your team/guests? Will they be first on a slope or follow you down? Less-experienced skiers tend to overpack and be overprepared in terms of gear. Can you save them some weight?

We present more technical solutions to steep-ski problems in the "Technical Solutions" chapter, but here are some thoughts on managing the

All good . . . until it's not. AMGA-certified ski guide Donny Roth booting the north face of Longs Peak for a ski on the Cables Route. Minutes after the photo was taken, blue skies turned to overcast and the face refroze. It was—shall we say—less than relaxing for one team member. ROB COPPOLILLO

Peering into the Dragontail Couloir, Rocky Mountain National Park, on a stable powder day. The group skinned around the back and therefore hadn't collected direct data on the couloir itself. A quick belay as the rest of the group catches up allows gathering a few observations. In this case, a view down the couloir, then some stomping in the start zone, and the team felt more informed and less uncertain about the decision. And, yes—it was a good run! ANDY GRAUCH

group once you've tried to forecast the terrain you'll be in, the weather, and any other hazards you might encounter.

Ease into the terrain and try to provide a warm-up. If you're booting a couloir, then by all means you and your crew will be plenty warm by the time you step into skis. Maybe too warm! Booting couloirs allows you to preview tricky sections, identify ice and/or rock, and even look for anchoring possibilities for rappel sections.

We should add, skiing truly steep terrain without first booting adds a serious hazard to your mission. One small rock or a short section of ice can easily end in a fall. Don't discount the information you gain by suffering up a long couloir. Especially in venues like Chamonix or La Grave, lift access can make steep skiing a much less laborious affair. Make a careful decision about skiing a committing feature top-down.

If you can't boot your chosen line, perhaps you can add a short shake-down ski before dropping in. In addition to getting you physically warmed up, gauging snow conditions helps boost confidence and mitigate risk. It might also be worth the time to take a belay and downclimb or side-slip into your feature to gauge the snowpack.

Again, guiding steep skiing requires a thorough sense of your guests'

The Self-Arrest Ski Pole?

A ski pole with a self-arrest grip offers some measure of safety to skiers and riders pushing into bigger terrain. The thing looks like a regular ski pole, but with an ice-ax head ingeniously integrated into the grip. Adventure skier Andrew McLean took the original design developed by Paul Ramer and upped the performance a bit in Black Diamond's "Whippet." The Whippet has proponents and detractors, but wherever you fall on the spectrum, you should know about the tool.

Whippet lovers enjoy the added security of potentially self-arresting with the pick. Detractors say the risk of impaling oneself outweighs the imagined benefits of self-arrest. You decide. Some things to keep in mind, though: Make sure you ski and ride with the pick covered by a protector when out of steep terrain. That probably removes much of the hazard of a self-inflicted self-arrest in your own belly. And don't discount how nice having a single ice ax and a Whippet can be in a couloir. Booting a steep, long slope with an ax and a Whippet can go remarkably quickly and feel surprisingly secure.

Whatever you choose, make sure your guests and teammates know how to use the Whippet safely and don't incur additional hazard by having one (or two) along.

abilities. Watching them ski on the morning of your big day helps you gauge their psych levels and mental outlook. We strongly urge that you consider the wisdom of steep skiing with folks you don't know.

Once you and your team arrive at the "real" terrain, put some effort into assessing snow conditions, consequences, and hazards. You should avoid diving into the skiing and hoping the folks behind you do the same. At the least, a couple of controlled, easy turns will allow the group behind you to listen to your skis, watch how you manage the snow, and see what the riding will be like.

Your team should have a very clear idea of how you're going to navigate the terrain. Is there a reasonable regroup spot in the gully? Is it safe from a sluff, falling rocks, or even a sliding skier? Will the second, third, fourth skiers stop above or below the leader? Couloir skiing is often one of the times we have guests specifically

Belaying a skier through an awkward start and into serious terrain. The skier wants his self-arrest ski pole ready for the steep skiing, so the protective cap is off the pick. Once into position, he'll unclip from the purple rope and ski a pitch. As soon as he feels relatively secure, he can pull the protective cap—a small plastic cover weighing a few grams—from his pocket and cover the pick again. We cover the exact rigging technique for the belay in our chapter on technical solutions. MATT KENNEDY

regroup below us. Even if you have pressure from other people coming up the skintrack to ski "your line," you should put in the time to get a plan. Not doing so invites carnage.

If you're riding a confined feature, coach your less-experienced teammates to finish each pitch facing into the couloir. This means they will need to make their last turn and then slide backward into the regroup spot. Why? Often the first turn on a pitch presents the most hazard. Wobbly, nervous skiers don't have any rhythm or momentum going, making the first turn an awkward affair. By finishing their pitch and then sliding gently and backward into the regroup, they're set up for a much more casual first turn on the next bit of terrain.

For a more wide-open feature, regrouping may not be a reasonable option. Hopefully, if you're riding a slope like this, your legs will be able to send the entire pitch.

Relaxed and ready, IFMGA mountain guide Mike Arnold eyes the next steep pitch off McHenry's, in Rocky Mountain National Park, Colorado. Facing into the couloir makes initiating the next pitch easier and with better visibility.
ROB COPPOLILLO

You're Down

You and your team sent. You're down, safe and sound, ready for another lap or the casual exit to the trailhead. Awesome job!

Some days you and the team will ride a high all the way to happy hour; on others you'll enjoy the fine glow of hard effort and making it work in tricky conditions. Other times you might sulk back to the car with your tail between your legs. It happens. A near miss, an outright mistake, or just a bummer among teammates can derail your day and leave you scratching your head. No stress—here's your opportunity to learn from it in the debrief and improve the next day.

At the trailhead, on your way home, over a beer, or perhaps even later, the team debriefs and addresses successes and less-ideal moments of the day. Give yourselves credit, but also become your own critic. A thorough, sincere debrief puts your day into perspective and also identifies opportunities for deliberate practice, the fastest road to mastery, as we'll see in the next chapter.

CHAPTER 4

The Debrief

When used diligently and strategically, debriefing powers a continuous improvement engine that can elevate the performance of any team, no matter how elite it may already be.

—*The Debrief Imperative*

The process of mastery certainly takes time, but it can be expedited by one significant factor: immediate feedback.

—*Autonomy, Mastery, and Purpose*

Hindsight gets you to oversimplify history. You will see events as simpler, more linear, and more predictable than they once were.

—*The Field Guide to Understanding Human Error*

If wisdom grew on trees, we'd all be sages, philosophers, and True Mountain Jedi. You know as well as I that a master passes through our lives rarely and fleetingly. When she does, watch carefully, listen intently, take notes, and let her expertise infuse your every cell.

So how do you and I, mere mortals alone in a tempest of chaos, weakness, and incompetence, cultivate our mastery? The debrief.

We've all run into the self-professed guru, the guy (it's usually a dude, let's be honest) who says, "I've been doing this for twenty-two years, and what I know is . . ." Now, let's not rush to judgment; perhaps he is a guru, but did Yoda go around telling everybody he was 900 years old and beat down dark lords at every turn? No, of course not; as the samurai used to say, "The true master reveals it in his every action," and not by talking shite on Facecramp. Keep your eyes peeled for the real thing.

Sure, mastery requires some innate talent, but more than that, it requires what the experts call "deliberate practice." A-ha! Now you know what those pesky boxes sprinkled throughout the first three chapters mean. To practice deliberately, we need to identify our weaknesses and errors, formulate a plan to address them, and then implement that plan. Simply going ski touring for twenty-two years is no

After a long tour, you come inside, throw a log on the fire, change into dry clothes, grab a snack . . . and debrief. Ymir Lodge outside Nelson, British Columbia. MATT KENNEDY

guarantee of anything except creaky knees.

The debrief is our best, most efficient means to identify weaknesses in ourselves and our team, and improve upon them through deliberate practice. There are no shortcuts, but there is a defined, time-tested method to get it done. Here are some ideas on what it looks like for backcountry skiing.

Deliberate Practice

Imagine taking up golf (I know, I know, but bear with me). I buy clubs, I purchase the knickers and Gatsby cap, join a club, and start acting, uh, "clubby." Every morning I go to the range, buy a bucket of balls . . . and I throw down. I swing, I smack, I slay. *Buy Bushwood!?!* (Welcome to middle age if you got the reference.)

I do this for ten years, and one evening, in my sky-blue knickers and matching cap, holding court in the club lounge with a snifter of cognac, I proclaim, "I've been doing this for a decade, old boys. Now the thing about the links is . . . "

And I'd still suck. I could mansplain until Ben Hogan rises from the grave, but I'd probably be no better than the day I started. I'm the same guy that's been "just going skiing" for twenty-two years, with no real method to improve. Why doesn't this work?

Simply performing a complex skill over and over does not deliver significant improvement. No, anything we want to improve, we typically seek instruction, even if it's from YouTube, and try to gauge our progress by measuring our results. More on that in a sec, but it's plain to see the problem here: If I'm a terrible golfer, I probably don't know much about the game, the subtle technique involved in a good swing, not to mention the mental aspects of golfing. In short, I'm being coached by a punter: myself!

In their now-famous 1993 paper, "The Role of Deliberate Practice in the Acquisition of Expert Performance," Ericsson, Krampe, and Tesch-Römer researched how violinists (and other practitioners) developed "expert performance." In short, it came down to deliberate practice over the course of years.

Like much academic work, their paper attracted little attention until someone packaged it in a sexier way. In this case, Malcolm Gladwell's book *Outliers* popularized the Ericsson et al. paper but unfortunately (though lucratively!) misinterpreted the data. It's worth discussing how exactly he misunderstood the paper.

Gladwell suggested that 10,000 hours of practice results in mastery of an activity. There were several things wrong with this interpretation, which the paper's authors rebutted in a 2016 *Salon* article. Most relevant for us, they wrote:

> *Gladwell didn't distinguish between the type of practice that the musicians in our study did—a very specific sort of practice referred to as "deliberate practice," which involves constantly pushing oneself beyond one's comfort zone, following training activities designed by an expert to develop specific abilities, and using feedback to identify weaknesses and work on them—and any sort of activity that might be labeled "practice."*

Sounds like a pretty effective recipe for improvement, eh? Pushing oneself out of one's comfort zone, following training activities designed by an expert to develop specific abilities, and using feedback to identify weaknesses and work on them.

Deliberate practice involves more than just rote repetition and relies on feedback to identify weaknesses. For our purposes, merely going touring and ending the day with a high-five would be rote repetition. On the other hand, investing 15 minutes in a thorough debrief at the conclusion of each tour (or workday, as a mountain guide) sets us up for deliberate practice. You and your teammates act as experts to provide feedback, identify weaknesses, then devise strategies to address those weaknesses. Once in a while you might even bring in an outside expert—a guide, mentor, instructor, or more experienced practitioner—to help with your craft and provide feedback.

As guides, do we know colleagues who practice? Do we practice? After having earned a certification in guiding, or any other activity, do we continue to practice?

Before we move on, let's throw a bone to Gladwell. While he did flub the gist of the Ericsson paper, the original authors were quick to add in their *Salon* piece, "Gladwell did get one thing right, and it is worth repeating because it's crucial: becoming accomplished in any field in which there is a well-established history of people working to become experts requires a tremendous amount of effort exerted over many years. It may not require exactly ten thousand hours, but it will take a lot."

Gladwell got that part right. The original paper's authors used the 10,000-hour rule as an average; some folks achieved mastery faster and some slower. Guess who arrived at mastery fastest: those immersed in deliberate practice or the group just kind of winging it?

Valid Feedback

You probably already identified a sticking point. I'm a beginning mountain guide, only having had my certification since 2014, so what business do I have providing myself or anyone else feedback? Further, how do I generate feedback? And further-further, is it possible to recognize feedback in the backcountry?

Let's start with our own limitations. It's not possible for me to know what I don't know. Kahneman highlights this when he discusses blind spots and the "What You See Is All There Is" bias. This ignorance or blindness is also a main factor in the Dunning-Kruger Effect; that is, the cognitive bias in which minimally experienced people systematically overestimate their competence and abilities. In short, how can I provide myself or a teammate feedback if I don't know what I don't know?

Good question—and one that is tricky to answer. The best approach, obviously, is to engage a true expert and have him evaluate your skill and process, provide feedback, and brainstorm activities to improve (develop a road map for deliberate practice). We seek out mentors or hire professionals to help us do this. For pros, this is part of "continuing professional development" and daily debriefing. In the military, they call these "after-action reviews."

Whether you're a pro or not, time and resources (financial and otherwise) sometimes prevent or limit these opportunities. In this event, we do the best we can within our team. We assemble diverse individuals with an array of complementary skills. If I have a WFR, perhaps you're great with orienteering, while another teammate is a high-end ski instructor, while yet another is involved in SAR. We nurture a culture of openness and creativity and foster a mindset that seeks to improve and grow. We learn from one another, attend avalanche workshops, read books, watch videos, and team up to do better.

If something "just didn't go right" or seems "off" about your tour, focus on it as a team. Are you painfully slow in transitions? Not quite getting the goods, while others are? Getting separated as a team in the field? Even if you can't possibly identify why or how this is happening, at least you have an idea that something isn't working. E-mail a friend, send a note to your forecast center, search for a topic online . . . hey, e-mail me; I'll help you figure it out or find someone who can. Point is, check in honestly with yourself, and if something's amiss—fix it.

We do the best we can with what we have. We identify what we could do better and endeavor to do it. Even if we're left without immediate answers, the debrief helps us put our finger on our weaknesses and revisit them.

Valid Feedback

Ah, you caught that! I snuck in the word "valid" in the previous section. We receive feedback all day long, in everything we do. It's how we change course, error correct, adjust our behavior, gauge results, and, yeah, improve. But not all feedback is created equal.

In environments with a "significant degree of uncertainty and unpredictability," we begin to second-guess the accuracy or validity of the feedback. These are "low-validity" environments, according to Kahneman and others. In ski-guide terms, this means the feedback you get might not be the feedback you should get.

For example, we go ride on a deep day, getting fresh tracks, and return to the trailhead with stoked clients or buddies; maybe we even snag a fat tip. Oh, yeah, we're good at this!

What happens, though, after a "great day," when you return home to read of four avalanches within a couple miles of your tour? Having seen your hero footage on Facecramp, a mentor calls and asks, "Were you comfortable all being on that slope?"

The following day you return to the field nearby; you get full propagation in an ECT and observe the debris of a skier-triggered avalanche—same aspect, next drainage over from your original line. (I'm describing my own near miss in 2016. Check out my article in *The Avalanche Review*, December 2017; link in the "Suggested Reading" list.)

The smart money is on recategorizing the "great day" as a near miss. Rather than call the day a success, you recognize that you could have easily ended up involved in an accident.

We'll talk more about near misses in a sec. The point here is that the backcountry doesn't return valid feedback much of the time—and that's not just tricky, it's dangerous. Instead of learning a lesson and debriefing a near miss, we might high-five, head home to the family, and recount tales of our skill, heroism, and panache. The feedback we received—hero skiing—is not the feedback we should've gotten: You jokers barely survived!

As we acquire experience, it needs to be evaluated and cataloged, which is hard to do unless you slow down, engage your evidence-driven logical mind (or "System 2" thinking; more on this in the "Decision Making" chapter), perform a conscientious debrief with your crew, and listen.

Getting feedback in the deep Kootenay snowpack south of Nelson, British Columbia. MAHTING PUTELIS

Luck or Skill?

Running a marathon or throwing a javelin offer easy metrics—time and distance—for gauging success, improvement, and skill. But what about backcountry touring or mountain guiding? Sure, we can look at how often we're getting caught in avalanches or whether our guests survive days in the mountains with us. Those are obvious "metrics," relying on obvious feedback.

But hang on a sec; that's pretty risky feedback on which to focus. Further, we're assuming any day we don't kill a guest or get involved in an avalanche is a "success." (That's a terrible sentence to write, honestly.) If we gauge our mastery in the mountains with those metrics, when we finally do get some negative feedback—an involvement or fatality—it will be at the least dangerous and at the worst utterly tragic. No thanks.

What's more, on those "successful" days, how do we know we didn't just get lucky? The balance between luck and skill resists easy measurement, so much so that Dr. Michael Mauboussin wrote a book about it, *The Success Equation: Untangling Skill and Luck in Business, Sports, and Investing*. He argues two points that matter here: First, "deliberate practice" is essential for developing skill; second, valid feedback is essential for practicing deliberately.

Valid feedback, a solid team, and a thorough debrief helps us accurately perceive our lucky days versus our skills—and correctly identify our near misses.

Celebrate the Near Miss (avalanchenearmiss.org)

High-performing teams and organizations recognize that near misses are actually learning opportunities and blessings in their own way. This, of course, requires correctly identifying near misses in the first place. Failing to recognize a near miss, or dismissing it through a "no-harm, no-foul" attitude, is a lost opportunity for recreationists—and downright negligent for professionals.

Kahneman, in *Thinking*, phrases the risk thus: "If repeated exposure of a stimulus is followed by nothing bad, such a stimulus will eventually become a safety signal."

Jonah Lehrer reinforces this sentiment in *How We Decide*, diving into the neuroscience and neurochemistry of it, discussing dopamine reward circuits in the brain. If our brain mistakes a near miss for a "safety signal," we're actually building in dangerous behaviors to our practice and mistaking it for "best practices." Some writers have called this "normalizing deviance."

The take home for us is that near misses, if themselves missed, can actually become "safety signals," or tales of success and skill in the backcountry. Can you think of a worse outcome from the days when we just got lucky?

Firefighters in particular have profited from a culture of reporting, recording, and learning from near misses. Go to firefighternearmiss.org and give a look. Surprising, eh? Initiated in 2005, the organization has amassed thousands of near misses in its database, and tens of thousands of first responders and firefighters have learned from their colleagues' experiences. Avalanche professionals have adopted a similar platform at avalanchenearmiss.org. If you're a guide, patroller, instructor, or forecaster, share your near misses with us there.

Don't be shy. Celebrate near misses and share them with your teammates. If you can't, that's a good sign that you're not skiing with a team.

Canadian ski guide Dr. Iain Stewart-Patterson said it well in his PhD dissertation: "The role of the ski-guiding environment is of particular interest, as it allows poor decisions to masquerade as good ones."

Don't let a poor decision—and we all make 'em—masquerade as a success.

DELIBERATE PRACTICE:
When reading a report or debriefing, challenge yourself to rewind and focus on how a well-meaning team ended up "blowing it" in terms of their prep and process, not just at the moment of the accident. See how far from the incident you can get to recognize contributing elements and factors.

Outcome Bias (Process over Outcome)

Here's an exercise for the avalanche instructors among us: Select a case study for your class, but take one-half of the studies and rewrite the ending. If the study has a fatality, involvement, or near miss, rewrite it to reflect just a great day skiing. Same weather, observations, danger rating, and group, but make the outcome nothing more than a fun day skiing with buds. Leave the other half of the studies unchanged.

Now divide your class and give one-half the original case study and the other half the modified case study. Let the two halves of the class analyze the studies and present their findings to one another. Keep an eye out for general differences in how students perceive a team's decisions when there's been an accident versus an uneventful day in terms of avalanches.

Looking back at an accident, we're hypercritical of every decision, every observation. Those same circumstances *without* an accident, however, result in a far rosier analysis of the day. Professional poker star and decision strategist Annie Duke calls this "resulting." If we question the validity of our feedback or if/when short-term results don't provide valid feedback, we debrief and analyze our *process* rather than our outcome.

This protects us from hindsight/outcome bias, in addition to focusing us on our repeatable process. Mauboussin teaches this approach, and risk-management thinkers like Sidney Dekker encourage this analysis of systems and processes rather than focusing on "human error." Start reading accident reports and performing debriefs in this mindset to capture more insight than simply focusing on "mistakes" or the outcomes of decisions.

Mindset, *Kaizen*, Growth versus Fixed Mindset

I hope by now you see the power of the debrief. It sets us up for relevant, useful feedback, even in the absence of mentors, pros, and coaches. Perhaps even more so than decision making, though, the debrief requires a specific mindset and commitment within the team. In terms of decision making, Annie Duke reminds us to be more committed to "getting it right than being right." Another way to think of that is fostering a team culture of "accuracy" over "being right." Great sentiment as we head into a potentially thorny debrief at the end of a tough day.

Growth versus Fixed Mindsets

Dr. Carol Dweck describes two opposing mindsets in her book *Mindset: The New Psychology of Success*: the "growth" and the "fixed."

A fixed mindset believes we are born with an inherent intellect, one fixed and relatively unchangeable. There's only so much we can learn, change, improve, and adapt to in life. Failure, in a fixed mindset, means one has reached the limit of his capacities. Failure is threatening and an indication of a hard boundary. Acknowledge a near miss, and we might be revealed as unskilled or incapable! A growth mindset, in contrast, accepts failure as an opportunity. It sees learning, growth, and challenge in a failure, without succumbing to fear or humiliation.

The fixed-mindset mountain guide knows it all, has already thought of everything you said, and takes a more defensive tone. You've never heard him change his mind or say, "Oh, I've never seen that. Can you show me again?" The guide with a growth mindset says, "I don't know" once in a while, changes her mind, admits an error, error corrects early, appreciates feedback, accepts challenges, and shrugs off negativity.

Other writers have called the growth mindset one of abundance and the fixed mindset one of fear and/or scarcity. Guess which mindset results in faster improvements and better culture? A debrief among a team committed to getting it right and one with a growth mindset yields insights and leads to improvement. The team with a fixed mindset rarely confronts mistakes, let alone learns from them.

Kaizen

Kaizen, a Japanese term meaning "improvement," grows directly from a growth mindset and culture of respect and blameless debriefing. Since applying the term to business, particularly in the Toyota Production Method, it has evolved to mean "constant improvement." These improvements come incrementally, on a day-to-day basis. This goes back to our idea of improving just a bit every day, say, 1 percent.

Toyota and others have used kaizen to empower workers to streamline and "mistake proof" every element of the business, from assembly line manufacturing to logistics to productivity. At Toyota, for example, if a worker on the assembly line sees anything wrong, he can immediately signal to shut down manufacturing to address the issue. He does this without fear of punishment or judgment, no matter the outcome.

For us, if we head into our debrief with the idea that we just need to improve a bit for tomorrow, that's kaizen. Small, manageable improvements daily lead to huge improvements from season to season, and over our lifetime as backcountry riders. It takes a culture of openness and collaboration, but it's totally doable for the right team.

Putting It All Together

Yeah, this all sounds snuggly, but how do you actually do it? Easier said than done, my friends! I've played every role imaginable in debriefs and decisions—from the expert, Zen facilitator to the defensive know-it-all who ruins the debrief. Ah, the joys of being human. I will try to draw on a few personal successes but also, more important, on the wisdom of the men and women who've done this time and time again successfully, much to the health of their teams.

Name That Bias . . . and Trust

Quick, name your last two near misses. Now name your two biases that will get you smoked.

If you hesitated, you're not doing your homework!

My twin brother runs a nonprofit in Montana, and one of his hiring questions is "Name your last two mistakes at work." If the candidate can't answer or mumbles around for a few minutes, my bro considers it a sign the candidate isn't self-aware.

I'd say the same for climbing and ski partners. We've all been around the person who never says "sorry," "I screwed up," or "I didn't know that." There's a lot going wrong with that situation, but one of the less-obvious problems is the failure to build trust. By admitting our mistakes and being willing to address them, we show our teammates (and friends and partners) that we are willing to be vulnerable, to improve, and we acknowledge that people make mistakes. Now they're more likely to respond in kind by admitting a failure, learning from it, and moving on.

My two (of many!) biases? Scarcity and trying to be right. OK, one's a heuristic and one's a mindset, but you get my drift.

So you roll into the debrief with a strong team, one committed to getting it right, kaizen, and risk-free communication. Awesome, but now what?

HOW TO

Down to brass tacks. Remember, we're focusing more on process than outcome, as that de-biases our debrief. It will take a focused effort to evaluate your process if you ended up skiing hero snow under blue skies, but if process is your focus, you're halfway there.

Consider these points, culled from military and business thinkers and "high-reliability" organizations:

- Discuss observations of fact, not opinions.
- One person speaks at a time.
- Everyone leaves with something specific in her fieldbook: an "actionable" item.
- "Leaders" go first, though elite military units profess "no rank" within a debrief.
- Did the team accomplish what it set out to do, no matter how mundane? Get a workout? Perform a PST on a north aspect? Get some good views? Find the deepest snow imaginable?

- Avoid "you" statements, and stick to facts and ideas.

Experiment with having different teammates run the debrief each day. This rotates the responsibility and prevents one person from becoming the "debriefer." Extreme care should be given to eliminating judgment. The honest team realizes any member could make a mistake.

In *The Debrief Imperative*, Adm. Ron Horton describes debriefing the crew on the USS *Enterprise*:

> *We didn't care who made the mistake. Our philosophy is that if that guy made the mistake, there are 50 other people who made the mistake, or who could. We want to prevent the mistake, not punish the person. We're not going to fire or crucify anyone. Things will happen. People will make mistakes, but we want to learn from them. It's easy to shoot the operator when in fact you probably have procedure issues, communication issues, or training issues. Why did that guy do what he did? I can guarantee it wasn't because he came in that morning and said, "I'm going to screw this up." Debriefs are nameless and rankless and they help you be a better team. On* Enterprise, *they saved taxpayers a lot of money. On that cruise we had maybe $100 in flight deck damage. That's extraordinary.*

Culture, tone, and language matter in your debrief. You and I will even mangle our debriefs some days. We can debrief those too. Point is, the debrief is your chance to turn "just skiing with friends" into a lifelong learning of deliberate practice. And in a high-stakes activity like backcountry touring and/or mountain guiding, that matters.

THE AIARE DEBRIEF

The AIARE fieldbook offers a ski-specific approach to the debrief, one worth copying, emulating, or performing. It requires all the "cultural" components mentioned above.

Note that the AIARE prompts connect your observations from the day to maintaining awareness of how avalanche conditions are changing. First, in "Summarize Conditions," you simply note conditions and observations; you're not forecasting/predicting at first, merely reviewing notes from the field and then asking yourself, "How does this impact conditions?"

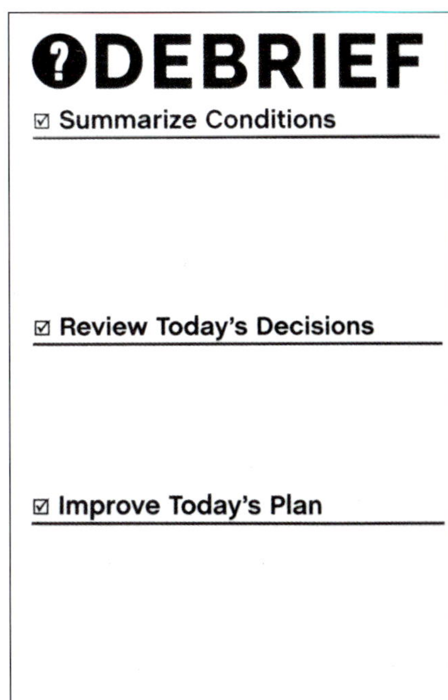

The AIARE debrief COURTESY AIARE

(If you're going out the following day, you apply that knowledge to the morning meeting, incorporating nearest-neighbor observations and the updated bulletin.)

After that, we debrief the day's decisions, impartially and without blame. If somebody royally screwed up, remember Admiral Horton's attitude: "Any one of us could've made the same mistake." Follow up with "What about our process led to that mistake? How do we avoid it in the future?"

Other questions that guides often ask are "Where were we in the most hazard?" "Knowing what we know now, if we were to do the same route/tour tomorrow, what would we change?"

This leads into the final prompt, "Improve Today's Plan." What could you do differently next time? Warmer sleeping bag? Tarp instead of a bivy sack? Larger shovel? Bring skin wax? More food? Less food? Better mapping prep? Shorter morning meeting?! Avoid convex rollovers?

OTHER SUGGESTIONS

One navy writer suggested a set debrief time after the event, with a maximum length for the debrief. This is sometimes difficult with traffic, weather, and life obligations, but if your crew knows you like to debrief 20 minutes after returning to the hut, great. Later that night via e-mail? Not ideal, but if that's all you can do—awesome.

A maximum time keeps everyone on task and lets teammates know the conversation can't drag on. Fifteen minutes is totally reasonable. Thirty minutes on an avalanche course seems doable, as it allows for referencing informational texts like *Snow, Weather, and Avalanche Guidelines* (SWAG) or its Canadian analogue, *Observation Guidelines and Recording Standards for Weather, Snowpack and Avalanches* (OGRS), or watching a short video on a snowpack test or mapping technique.

In a larger organization, anonymous reporting can be an effective tool to empower teammates to speak up. Some people fear personal conflicts or reprisals, so at a larger operation or ski patrol team, this can help broaden the discussion. Solicit anonymous topics, then discuss them as a team.

RADICAL CANDOR

When I'm resisting accountability or offering up some dim excuse, I put myself at odds with reality and honesty. Often, if I'm being unreasonable or stubborn, my friends politely demure and change the subject. Fine if we're discussing the latest Schwarzenegger film, but sketchy if we're trying to debrief. Once in a while, my teammates need to say, "We're in this together, Rob, but we disagree with you. What you did was dangerous." Or risky, or useless, etc.

We have to try to hold our teammates (and ourselves) to account. We do this politely but firmly when the time comes—and this is "radical candor." The term's a bit hokey, but take the point—you're doing your teammate a disservice to "just drop it." You

A long day of touring ends at Sunrise Lodge, in the Esplanades, British Columbia. Wood fire going, chef in the kitchen, and time for a relaxed debrief with teammates. ROB COPPOLILLO

owe it to her and to yourself and the team to persist a bit and pursue accuracy over being "right."

If a teammate can't or won't get the point in the moment, absolutely drop it—but come back to it later. If a teammate repeatedly derails the debrief with arguments and closed-mindedness, maybe that's a sign you're incompatible ski partners.

TWO FINAL QUESTIONS

In the "Decision Making" chapter we'll dive deeper into a paper by the organization Swiss Re. For now, though, let's poach two questions from the paper's conclusion. First, does your repeatable process allow for shortcutting and sketchiness (I'm paraphrasing here); second, why might a person take such a shortcut?

These are important questions to answer within your team, especially the latter one. What "payoff" is there to sketchy behavior? The obvious one, in guiding and personal skiing/climbing, is ticking a big/sexy objective or a fastest-known time or some "achievement." Is it really an achievement, or just borrowed time against an accident or involvement? Answer that, identify it, and watch for it. Address your team culture and fix your process—your life might depend on it!

Conclusion

The debrief protects us and our team from lapsing into rote repetition and blindness to our errors and biases. Debriefing commits us to identifying our weaknesses then addressing and improving them—in short, deliberate practice. It's our secret weapon for acquiring mastery in an activity and/or a profession that demands it.

We debrief on different time frames. We revisit our individual days, but we should also be looking at seasonal and yearly debriefs. Don't lose sight of your lifelong learning and progression. Mentors of mine like Colin Zacharias and Marc Chauvin openly discuss their progression over the years—things they learned, near misses they survived, mistakes made, improvements measured, and career successes. Even if backcountry riding is "just" our passion, we can practice it as if our lives depend upon it—because they do.

From here we head into chapters on team and decision making. Truth is, those chapters could fit almost anywhere in the book, as they underpin everything we do in backcountry touring, from trip planning to the up to the down and the debrief. So, after introducing those topics, let's discuss with whom we're riding and how we make better decisions along the way.

CHAPTER 5

The Team

If we are cultured to respectful teamwork, the odds of spotting and correcting errors improves dramatically.

—Bruce Kay

Whether we're talking about leadership, teamwork, or client service, there is no more powerful attribute than the ability to be genuinely honest about one's weaknesses, mistakes, and needs for help.

—Patrick Lencioni

If you put individuals together in the right way, such that some individuals can use their reasoning powers to disconfirm the claims of others, and all individuals feel some common bond or shared fate that allows them to interact civilly, you can create a group that ends up producing good reasoning as an emergent property of the social system. This is why it's so important to have intellectual and ideological diversity within any group or institution whose goal is to find truth.

—Annie Duke

The Perfect Team

Our team and our teamwork underlie everything we do in the backcountry. Sure, we occasionally ski solo, but usually we're out with friends, guests, or maybe just random partners. In a perfect world, we tour with a high-functioning team made up of good-natured, reliable riders. A strong team can reduce uncertainty and keep us safer, as well as help us consider more ambitious objectives and find better snow.

We've all been there—those days when we find ourselves riding with a less-cohesive group. Not the end of the world, but also not ideal. The more our team becomes merely a group, the more our uncertainty grows. Do these people make sound decisions? Are they familiar with the day's conditions? Do they use a process in the backcountry?

Not knowing the answers to these questions should indicate higher uncertainty, which should nudge you toward a lower-commitment,

Teammates fill in one another's blank spots, check one another's biases, collaborate, laugh, disagree, and create great days in the mountains.
ROB COPPOLILLO

less-exposed tour. As uncertainty goes up, we consciously shift our terrain mindset to a "defensive" one—stepping back, less exposure, conservative terrain choices.

We discussed the "stars aligning" in the "Trip Planning" chapter, and integral to that alignment is a great team. Like most catch phrases, though, the perfect or great team requires far more than just texting a few bros and showing up on time. It takes chemistry, maintenance, and dedication to assemble and nurture your crew. Ample resources exist to help you improve your team, but this short chapter suggests a few starting points.

Why Team?

Am I overstating the importance of the team? Certainly much of the research on bias and decision making relates to individuals, and backcountry teams don't figure into much academic research. Recall, however, that a broad review of Atkins, Dr. Ian McCammon, Jill Fredston and Doug Fesler, Bruce Kay, and others captures thousands of avalanche incidents. Overwhelmingly, their research and writing indicates that groups of avy-trained, high-functioning individuals tend to get into trouble through poor decisions, despite having relevant information at hand.

These are more team/process breakdowns than they are individual errors.

Earlier I mentioned the idea of ineptitude versus ignorance. Like most perspicacious bits in this book, I ripped the concept off from somebody else: Dr. Atul Gawande. Author of *The Checklist Manifesto* and a professor at Harvard, he frames decision making in modern professions as a problem of ineptitude rather than ignorance. We have enough information to reduce ignorance, but that doesn't guarantee a better decision through integrating it.

Gawande points out that we can be marvelously well informed but totally inept at incorporating, interpreting, and applying our knowledge. In short, our process or algorithm falls short. Add group dynamics to the equation and things get trickier still. Too often we read of a team that had all the information it needed to make "the right call" but somehow didn't. Ineptitude, rather than ignorance, wrecked the mission.

Teams can break down for a variety of reasons, but they can also vastly improve decision making and reduce errors—when they're functioning. Investing legend Charlie Munger (Warren Buffett's business partner) warns that cognitive traps and biases usually occur in concert and that these "compounding errors" can turn our brains to "mush." Solid teams help us short-circuit that risk.

A white paper prepared by Swiss Re, the multinational Swiss insurance company founded in 1863, reinforces the qualities and advantages of teams in high-risk professions. Swiss Re drew on the aviation, nuclear, and medical fields in their paper—so, not as serious as our day-to-day mega-sending, but you get it. Teams can help keep us safer. (The original Swiss Re paper is listed in the "Suggested Reading" section.)

Teammates making observations, collaborating, and checking one another for bias, blind spots, and anything overlooked.
ROB COPPOLILLO

So if we're riding in the backcountry with several other people, why not make it a team rather than just a group? Think of your team as its own quality-control app, or antivirus software, protecting the algorithm of your repeatable process. Your crew double-checks operations and catches errors before they turn into accidents. The team debugs your process and keeps

Teamwork as the Antidote to Bias

by Bruce Kay

Perhaps the most fascinating aspect of teamwork is the insight brought to bear on problems by teammates from whom you'd least expect it. These are, of course, people lowest on the totem pole of competency: the rankest greenhorn client on a guided ski tour or your old high-school chum you are trying to impress by dragging him up some rock climb.

As hierarchies go, these people are at the bottom, and their contributions to decision making tend to be relegated as such, yet no one can dispute they are equal stakeholders in whatever outcome transpires. No one will dispute that of course, but what is often disputed is their ability to see things that "their betters" cannot, to hold valid insights where they have no experience. It is just plain counterintuitive.

One minor parenting moment from my distant past reveals this intuitive error. My son and his mates were upstairs doing the video game thing—probably *Grand Theft Auto*, the favorite of that particular era. I snuck into the room to watch, assuming the role of wise yet tolerantly observant adult, curious to see the depths of the next generation's depravity. They knew I was there but remained transfixed by the bloodbath unloaded on the various animated victims of their bloodlust, chatting occasionally among themselves, but generally ignoring me.

Like most parents, all this lawless mayhem at the push of a button didn't sit well; I was intent on making a point, biding my time for an opportune moment. Finally, perhaps the end of a particularly bloody mowing down of innocent old grannies and puppies, I made my play:

"You guys were going to go play road hockey—remember?"

Instantly, my own son kneecapped my clever gambit: "Relax, Dad. Just because we play these games doesn't mean we will grow up to be ax murderers."

His friends said nothing, but it was obvious they saw through me too. I managed a "Uh, I see, well maybe later, eh?" then slunk off to mull it over.

The fact is, and despite my worldly wisdom, I didn't know any better. I just assumed they would grow up to be ax murderers. Where did I get that idea? God knows, our own adolescent games were no less bloody, just less digital.

Why had I completely forgotten that? It really helped to hear their opinion. In fact, since then, the actual behavioral science has proven their rather astute observation: Violent video games do not produce violent individuals.

A similar evolution occurred with the heliski industry: They learned over time that even the tail guide might see valuable insights where the crusty old veterans are blind and stuck in the mud. It did take time, some real-life carnage, and no small amount of humility, but eventually they had to admit that even the least likely can at times provide a unique and valid perspective, which, after all, is what teamwork is all about.

Bruce Kay is the author of* Autonomy, Mastery, and Purpose*, an insightful meditation on decision making in avalanche terrain. He grew up in western Canada and spent summers alpine guiding. During winters, Bruce worked as an avalanche forecaster for Blackcomb Skiing Enterprises—what would become Whistler Blackcomb. Since 2004 he has provided safety-consulting services to the logging, mining, sporting, and film industries.

you safer. Hopefully this chapter shares some ideas about how your team can improve and what sorts of teammates you might be looking for.

THE AIARE TEAM

I return to the AIARE model because it's the one I know best and the one in which I learned the fundamentals of avalanche decision making. Note that their approach to team lists some rules of engagement; that is, the agreed-upon rules by which our team interacts, travels, and functions. Different instructors and organizations, like the wise folks at the Alaska Guide Collective and the American Avalanche Institute (AAI), will have their own take on the process, and I encourage you to compare methods.

For our specific discipline, the AIARE team prompt marks a good starting point. Long-term AIARE practitioners like Jean Pavillard, Tom Murphy, Howie Schwartz, Margaret Wheeler, Brian Lazar, and Colin Zacharias have debated and refined these principles over the last twenty-five years, arriving at a concise checklist that backstops our activities.

Consider each prompt and how it can help your team. For example, travel together and decide together. The Pucker Face accident, eloquently described and debriefed by Alex Do (link in "Suggested Reading"), illustrates how losing touch with teammates, verbally and physically, can have tragic consequences. Radios help, but if you're not regrouping at critical

The AIARE team prompt
COURTESY AIARE

TEAMWORK

- ☑ Travel together. Decide together.
- ☑ Listen to every voice.
- ☑ Challenge assumptions.
- ☑ Respect any veto.

decision points, ask yourself if you're really communicating.

Expert halo, over- and under-confidence, and social proof stand less of a chance of derailing our decisions if we not only listen to every voice, but we solicit them too. We've all toured with that quiet teammate in the back of the group. It's always worthwhile to ask, "Hey, you haven't said much in a while. What are you thinking?" Maybe my buddy is starving. Maybe he's in a foul mood, shy, or just fried. Maybe, though, he's got a lingering feeling that I'm blowing it, but he doesn't want to speak up. I should ask him to.

Challenging assumptions keeps us in the mindset of the skeptic. We second-guess our assumption that it's "good to go," or that wind slabs are only found northeast-to-east-to-southeast today, as an example. Did we miss anything? What don't we know? What can't we know? Did we account for those uncertainties in our trip planning and terrain choices?

Lastly, the AIARE team respects any veto. Each team member leaving the trailhead gets to say, "This doesn't seem right; we should bail." I think as practitioners we need to have valid, evidence-driven reasons for our decisions, but we need to also honor our intuition at times.

Revisit that Pucker Face accident and notice the moment when two riders split from the group. Alex Do writes, "Mike volunteered to go first and test the slope with a ski cut. Before he committed to the slope, he asked if everyone was okay skiing the face. Two of the group members mentioned that they might choose to go a different way but indicated that they would stay around and watch at the very least."

Great job, "checking in" with teammates . . . but let's also recognize what two gents are communicating by considering a "different way." They don't come out and say, "This doesn't seem safe enough for us; we're not doing it." I assume they're trying to be considerate and not shut down the party, but in hindsight they're having reservations about the terrain choice.

Hindsight is easy; I concede that. No judgment on these guys. Remembering Dekker and "human error," looking at the moment of an accident

Leveling Up Your Team: Better Playmaking, Better Playbooks, Better Leadership

By Alex Do

I remember the first tour I took with my regular, longtime partners after I had thought hard about the lessons I needed to learn and integrate into my touring approach following the Pucker Face avalanche accident in 2013. (I was not skiing with my regular partners at the time of that accident.)

At the trailhead, after we were done with the usual chit-chat and joking insults, gear ready and skins on, I asked for everyone's attention. We had already made our terrain plan based around the forecast avalanche problems before driving to the trailhead, but I still wanted to talk through a few things as a group before we skinned out. From the inside cover of my

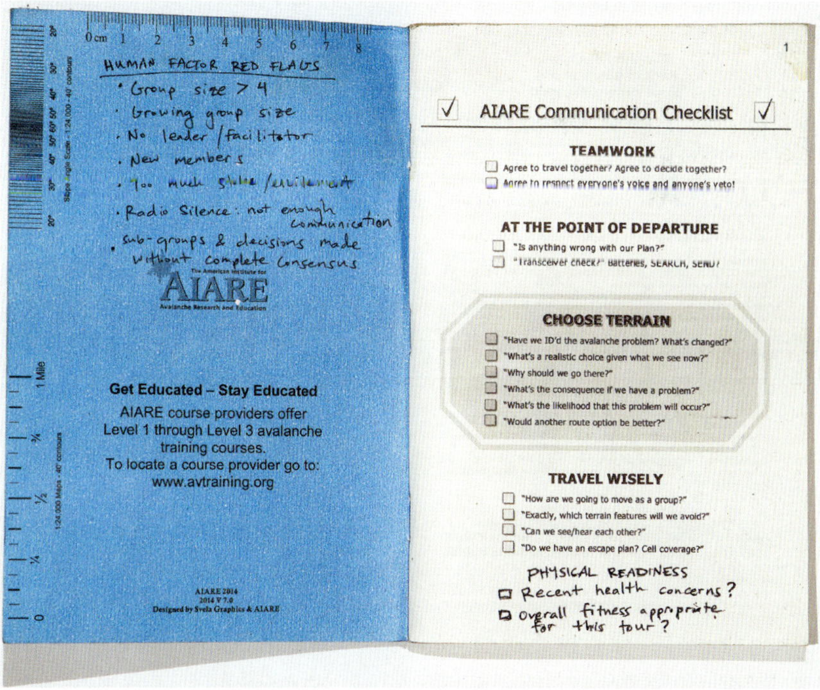

Alex's fieldbook ALEX DO

blue fieldbook, I reviewed all the questions on the AIARE Communication Checklist, plus a few of my own "Human Factors Red Flags" that I'd scribbled in the adjacent blank space.

We again talked about the forecast avalanche problems, agreed that our terrain and travel plan was reasonable, planned what observations we wanted to collect and where, and agreed to travel together before setting out. From a holistic perspective, we really didn't "do things" differently than we had before my accident: The overall communication, travel, and terrain management before and during the tour were pretty much the same. The one change was that I stood in front of everyone with a list in my hand to make sure we didn't miss anything, that everyone participated in discussing all the key aspects of the known avalanche problems, our trip plan, and our group dynamics, *before* we left the trailhead.

At the end of the day, I asked one of the partners in the group how he thought things went. "Honestly, it felt kind of weird and forced," he said. Some of the discussion felt perfunctory, and no one was accustomed to discussing things in that style, with these specific friends, on a typical weekend ski tour. But he didn't have any objections to the change either.

Months earlier he had been on the other side of the phone with me after I had just gotten down the mountain from Pucker Face, listening to me sobbing, unable to form complete sentences because "Mike just died" and "I let everyone down." In that phone call, he reassured me we'd be out there again, that this accident wouldn't necessarily change what we did, but it would change *how* we did it.

Since that day, my regular partners have come on board with, and are accustomed to, my use of the communication checklist. I've also adapted the specific manner in which the words come out of my mouth, making it more conversational while ensuring that the specific checklist items have been discussed face to face with all group members present. It didn't occur to me until years later to ask each person in our group how they thought we've collectively evolved our backcountry touring approach—"how we did it"—since my accident. Overall, our group agreed that we've taken a more avalanche-problem-based approach to terrain selection and management—making sure that we correctly identify the main avalanche problems and agreeing that our terrain exposure is deliberately appropriate for them.

There has also been a lot more general caution around partner choice and skiing with a smaller circle of more trusted teammates, specifically those who would respect partner concerns. And the one thing that surprised me the most: I learned that when I wasn't present ski touring with our regular group, no one else was using a printed checklist or printed decision-making aid to double-check that everything was in line.

I had mixed feelings about this feedback. On one hand, we all had clearly gotten better at the "playmaking" aspects of our skills and teamwork, such as listening and paying attention to our partners, factoring specific forecast and observation details into our plan, and being intentional about our travel and exposure decisions. On the other hand, we still weren't necessarily running off the same "playbook," meaning that our approach and processes could deviate depending on which team members were "on the court" on any given day.

The situation made me realize that becoming a stronger leader isn't necessarily about "taking the ball in my hands" and deciding how we should execute, but that campaigning to build robust consensus around our overall approach strategy and our processes, just like we build consensus on specific terrain decisions, would lead to an even stronger and more resilient team.

Alex Do COURTESY ALEX DO

Alex Do is a recreational backcountry skier, husband, and dad, and in his spare time a product marketing and development professional who has worked in manufacturing and technology industries. While not a snow-industry professional, he has a passion for outdoor education and safety. Alex cut his backcountry teeth in the central Sierra Nevada and now explores the Oregon/California Cascades near his residence in Eugene, Oregon.

deprives ourselves of looking at how reasonable people ended up in that situation in the first place—the process. Assuming we would never make the same decisions in the same circumstances misses the point. We have the benefit of hindsight; we know the outcome. What we need to do is put ourselves there, at that moment, before anyone knew what the outcome would be.

In a perfect world, perhaps other teammates could've glanced at a checklist at that moment and asked, "What specifically about this slope makes you nervous?" By soliciting their opinions, the team could've more accurately identified the hazard and decided if it was manageable. The takeaway, for me, is that if my team can't reach consensus on skiing a slope, that's telling me something is out of whack—too much uncertainty, too much risk, too difficult a slope, incompatible goals, etc.

As an aside, and thinking ahead to decision making, imagine if the team had asked, "How are we going to die today?" Or could they have conducted a premortem right there on the ridge? We'll talk more about these concepts in the next chapter. Again, zero judgment; we're trying to benefit from a thorough debrief on the accident, not assign blame. We're looking at process: How did the team arrive at that decision at that moment? Alex Do does an excellent job of talking us through the accident, and we should accept his offer to learn from the event.

Creating Team Culture

I keep mentioning "functioning" teams and warning about "breakdowns." Let's really consider what kind of team we want. I'd argue that we need more than buddies "who have my back." Sure, that's part of it, but you also need a diverse gang, people willing to disagree respectfully, communicate effectively, commit to learning, and agree on a collaborative process. Guiding, climbing with friends, even just a road trip to go skiing—if we can't agree on the "how" of the activity, there's little hope of putting together a resilient, capable team, no matter what we're doing.

TALK EARLY, TALK LOTS

Sexton and Helmreich, writing in the *Journal of Human Performance in Extreme Environments*, state, "NASA researchers analyzed the causes of jet transport accidents and incidents between 1968 and 1976 . . . and concluded that pilot error was more likely to reflect failures in team communication and coordination than deficiencies in technical proficiency."

Just like Dekker warns us that "human error" is usually more indicative of an error of process, NASA's research reveals that breakdowns in communication are often mistaken as mere pilot error rather than a problem in team, communication, and/or process.

The Sexton-Helmreich paper goes on to explain, "Crew performance was more closely associated with the quality of crew communication than with the technical proficiency of individual pilots. . . . No differences were found between the severity of the errors made by effective and ineffective crews; rather, it was the ability of the effective crews to communicate that kept their errors from snowballing into undesirable outcomes."

All teams make mistakes, whether in the backcountry or outer space, but it's the high-functioning team that catches the mistake, error corrects, and stays safer. Remember, though, error correction requires the humility to admit an error in the first place.

Their paper goes on to harvest insight from bunches more research, including decades-long NASA findings, but they stress that successful crews tended to communicate more and earlier than lower-performing crews. That is, teammates discussed the mission, what was expected, how they'd go about it, and identified problems before and during their work.

In researching the topic of teamwork, these themes of effective communication resurfaced time and time again. I highlight here the Sexton-Helmreich paper because it so expertly explains that a strong team trumps individual talents, and concludes, "Such findings are not unique to aviation, as similar results have emerged in other safety-critical systems."

DELIBERATE PRACTICE:
Next time you're touring with friends, jot a little reminder to discuss five things before midday . . . and then make sure you do it! Spend a sec providing feedback to one another on your communication frequency and effectiveness.

TURN-TAKING AND PSYCHOLOGICAL SAFETY

In decision making and debriefing, collaborative and respectful communication helps facilitate our process. Obviously these characteristics should infuse our teamwork too. Easier said than done, especially when we're sometimes operating in a stressful environment.

In 2012 tech giant Google, in its "Project Aristotle," investigated why some of its teams outperform others. Studying 180 teams across its empire, at first researchers were stumped as to why some of them excelled while others faltered. High-performing teams seemingly behaved differently; what derailed some teams became a strength in others, and so on.

After months of confounding observations, the Google researchers at last identified two shared characteristics among all of their successful teams. First, teammates generally spoke equally among themselves. The teams had "equality in distribution of conversational turn-taking." In short, everybody spoke about the same amount over the course of a project. Team members didn't necessarily speak equally on every task, but over a given project, "As long as everyone got

Communicating in a Ski Partnership

by Sheldon Kerr

I think of my ski touring partnerships as high-stakes, intimate relationships. I am choosing to spend my precious time with these people. We are going to make extremely consequential decisions together. And they may even hold my life in their hands. Ski partnerships require the same qualities of trust, respect, and open communication as the other partnerships in my life. The success of my ski day is fundamentally determined by my ability to talk with these people, be heard by them, and my ability to hear and understand what they have to say. This is easier said than done, but here are a few tips that help me.

Prioritize touring fitness and self-care on the trail. It is more difficult for me to communicate if I'm tired or way off the back. It is challenging to contribute if I'm showing up to the break 5 minutes late. If I've trained in the preseason and kept myself fed and hydrated all day, I'm way more capable of talking at the 2 p.m. transition to downhill.

Establish communication expectations well before clicking in. It is w-a-a-a-y easier to reference a previously agreed-upon communication expectation than to try to summon the nerve to share my opinion after the socially dominant extrovert has already presented his perspective as fact . . . and started ripping his skins. I might say, "Hey, remember how we agreed to listen to each other's stability assessments without interrupting? Let's go ahead and do that now before we make a decision."

Pick places on the map to regroup and talk. If we've agreed on places to stop and talk, it takes the social burden off folks who might hesitate to stop the whole group to raise a concern. The night before a tour, we'll circle check-in locations on the map. Logical spots include any significant navigational points (left turn at a creek, east turn into a cirque), whenever entering or exiting tree line, before working through any avalanche terrain, or at any up-to-down transitions.

Keep the group size low. I'm more likely to talk in a group of three than I am in a group of six, so I try to travel in smaller groups. If I'm in a big group at a hut, or more people have shown up to the trailhead than I was expecting, I see if we can split up. I've also just said, "No hard feelings, but this is just too big a crew for me," and gone home when a friend who brought a friend brought two friends.

See contribution and opinion-forming as a duty rather than an option. If I see my speaking up as something I owe my partners, I'm more likely to do it. Maybe I'm trying to be chill, deferential to a more experienced person, or keep another cook out of the kitchen, but it isn't fair to repeatedly put the burden of decision making on my partners.

Make room for others' voices. Perhaps I'm the most vocal one in the group, am an intimidating presence, or have been "expert haloed" unwittingly. Instead of asking, "Is everyone comfortable with this decision? [2-second beat] Great, let's ski it!" I'll say, "Hey, let's each share our comfort level with the decision we just made." And end each group conversation by asking, "Is there anything else?"

Don't go skiing with assholes. If a group always drops me on the skintrack, makes decisions before I catch up, intimidates me, or makes me feel like anything less than an equal partner, I don't go skiing with them again. No amount of pre-rigged communication best practices will make up for crappy ski partners. And the stakes are just too high and our time on this earth just too precious to put up with that kind of bullshit.

When I'm ski guiding, rather than out with friends or colleagues, the communication fundamentals really don't change much. In some ways, communicating is easier at work; the formalized guide-client relationship means that my partners are literally paying me to share my observations, form opinions, and make decisions. But there are ways our guide-client partnership can make communicating more difficult. Maybe a client disagrees with my snowpack assessment but stays quiet because she doesn't want to come off as disrespectful or uncooperative. Or perhaps a guest assumes I already noticed the avalanche activity across the valley, so he doesn't point it out. Or maybe my student is too embarrassed by his lack of experience, or ashamed to admit he's hungry, or fears the group's judgment if he admits that a pitch scares him. Gosh, it is tricky to be a human in a group! Here are a few tips that help me at work:

Sheldon Kerr COURTESY SHELDON KERR

Ask guests to think of themselves as partners. They may not know that I am expecting them to think, observe, and share. I ask them to take ownership. "I welcome your thoughts! I am depending on you to help me observe, assess, navigate, and keep each other safe." They'll have more fun, and I'll have less work to do!

Physically set yourself up to communicate. I get out of the wind, speak up loudly, and bring people close—really, really close. Before I give a morning briefing, I have guests put their ski tips together in a circle so we can all hear and see one another. When it is time to ski, I remind them to "Stop close to me and stop above me," and I wave them toward me if they stop more than 15 feet away. This is also a hack to help avoid the heinously gendered accusation of being "shrill" or, God forbid, "bossy." We're all due for bigger conversations about women-who-yell and whose jobs necessitate authoritative directions, but we don't want to unpack all that mid-slope.

Give simple, clear directions, and check for understanding. At the top of a pitch, I say as little as possible. "Stay right of my track. Ski to me one at a time. Watch out for rocks." Guests will retain these three simple phrases rather than a long explanation of the entire pitch, including a description of the snow, warnings of specific rocks and trees to avoid, and a timed interval between skiers. Where, when, how. That's it. And I'll ask someone to repeat it back to me to make sure he or she got it.

Keep your guests socially safe. We spend a lot of time thinking about how to keep guests safe from physical harm. I also think about their social comfort. I establish communication norms at the beginning of the day, figure out pronoun preference, set an appropriate pace for their abilities and our objective, solicit observations from the quiet ones, and nip rude or disrespectful behavior in the bud. If I create an environment where my clients feel safe talking, they will speak up with concerns, and we will all have a safer day.

Sheldon Kerr is a guide and athlete who works off skintracks, chairlifts, bootpacks, ski planes, and helicopters. She holds certifications in the rock and ski-mountaineering disciplines through the AMGA. She is currently finishing her alpine examination on her way to her IFMGA certification.

---

a chance to talk, the team did well," reported the *New York Times*.

Second, the better teams all shared a culture of "psychological safety," defined by Harvard professor Dr. Amy Edmonson as "a sense of confidence that the team will not embarrass, reject or punish someone for speaking up."

Edmonson began her career researching hospital units. She assumed that "better" teams would make fewer mistakes, but what she found shattered her view. Higher-performing teams were making more mistakes. She dug deeper. In fact, the better teams were openly acknowledging their mistakes and addressing them in a collaborative, productive way. Mistakes weren't hidden or deemphasized; they were highlighted and dissected, with an eye toward learning and prevention.

So the openness was there, and it led to better outcomes, and based on her work, it had to do with a sense of safety among teammates. She cautions, though, not to interpret this as a fuzzy, touchy-feely sentiment. Interviewed on *Harvard Business Review*'s "Ideacast" podcast, she explains: "What it's about is candor; what it's about is being direct, taking risks, being willing to say, 'I screwed that up.' Being willing to ask for help when you're in over your head."

This naturally circles back to our debrief, near misses, and respectful team communication. To get there, we need to continuously create and foster a sense of this psychological safety among teammates. It is not something we do in the fall and then let it grow stale throughout winter. It requires

Homicidal Impulses (and Hydration)

I've learned to interpret my homicidal impulses not as alarming signs of criminality but rather as reliable indications that I need to drink. Immediately. Preferably Skratch Labs, or maybe water, but perhaps a beer in these situations would work too.

What am I talking about?

Years ago I followed a buddy up a long climb in the Selkirks, listening to the sound his bindings and boots made with each glide forward. *Tock-tock, tock-tock*, and on it went for a few thousand feet. The nearer we came to the col, rather than rising stoke levels at upcoming turns, I realized I'd grown wildly annoyed at the sound of his gear. I had grown edgy and frustrated *by the sound of his feet clacking against his skis.* In short, by his skiing. His existence. My fevered imagination flashed images of backcountry homicide across my sweat-stung eyes. Madness!

By now you've realized I am a deeply flawed and shallow person. And now this admission. So be it. But this homicidal rage, provoked by nothing more than the sound of my friend's feet—this was a new low, even for me. And then . . . an epiphany. I realized my bloodthirsty visions amounted to nothing more than dehydration. I had run out of water and lapsed into desiccated hallucinations of carnage. A few slugs of Skratch and I was back to the flawed, shallow, peace-loving man I'd been. So simple!

Now when I find myself imagining strangling a touring partner because his leg vents aren't unzipped to equal levels or his jacket and

ongoing attention, in guide meetings and trip plans with buddies.

Edmonson stresses the importance: "And so I always want to explain, there is an observed and quite robust correlation between psychological safety and learning and performance."

A high-performing team commits to excellence, improvement, and learning from its inevitable mistakes—and all this comes more easily in a supportive, safe team environment. And ask yourself, What are the consequences of riding with a low-performing team?

GROUP SIZE

We can debate the merits of two, three, four, or five members, but a growing body of research seems to indicate that six or more in many teams starts to be a problem. Harvard, the University of

Imagine if I'd strangled this dude! Paul Rogers, well, just being Paul Rogers, above Selkirk Lodge, British Columbia. MATT KENNEDY

pant colors clash a little bit, I stop, take a drink, and the little voices stop. The demons leave my head—at least for the time being.

I'm living proof that even a profoundly damaged human can learn to work with his weaknesses. Learning to manage our own quirks and dramas, and tolerate those in our teammates, helps us to be better teammates ourselves. Try hard!

Iowa, and any number of business publications tweak the number by one or two, but the consensus is that pushing beyond six group members generally reduces decision quality for small-team activities.

Knowing this, as backcountry skiers, we usually assemble a team between three and five riders. More than five and communication begins to break own—in addition to "trust" and "cohesion," according to doctoral research at the University of Iowa. Touring with just two teammates stacks a lot of responsibility on each member, particularly in the event of an accident or injury. Three to five teammates harnesses the decision-making prowess of a small group and offers more resources in a rescue—hence the prompt of "Optimal group size, 3–5" on page 2 of AIARE's fieldbook.

I've certainly toured with larger groups, but I try to remind myself that as the group grows, so does uncertainty—and that means dialing it back in terms of terrain.

COMPATIBILITY

Most of you have at least done your level 1, spent a few seasons in the backcountry, and been part of more- and less-successful teams. Think back to what made your team "click." Often we identify incompatibilities within our team or between teammates only after a couple downer tours or even a near miss. Knowing what you're looking for in a teammate and team helps you determine compatibility on the front end.

We've all endured a tour with a partner who has a dramatically different level of risk tolerance. Perhaps she's a charger looking to ski "no-fall" terrain or a friend who saw mortal danger on every untracked slope. These are extreme examples, but you get the drift: If you're riding with someone unwilling to accept similar risks as you, it's not going to work very well.

More communication on the front end can help avoid these mismatches in teams. Often just discussing a prospective partner's "all-time" tours will reveal what he finds fulfilling and fun. If he describes epic after epic, you know he's into going for it (perhaps without proper preparation!). Coming right out and asking about risk tolerance, no-fall terrain, and "what's fun" is probably your best bet.

Disparate fitness levels have derailed many a tour too. If your buddy has a busy medical practice serving disadvantaged kids, he might not have much time to tour, let alone train. Good on him for having a worthwhile career, and he might also not be the best partner for a 14-hour day in tough weather. Save yourself and him the stress of hoping it works out—choose a suitable tour (from your run atlas!) for both of you, or acknowledge that perhaps you're not compatible touring partners.

Group Diversity

"But while a group can function to be better than the sum of the individuals, it doesn't automatically turn out that way. Being in a group can improve our decision quality by exploring alternatives and recognizing where our thinking might be biased, but a group can also exacerbate our tendency to confirm what we already believe"

—*Annie Duke*, **Thinking in Bets: Making Smarter Decisions When You Don't Have All the Facts**

Before going on a tour, I'll often ask newer partners, "What's your process?" Hopefully they have some defined approach to gathering information, making decisions, and selecting tours. If not, no big deal but—you guessed it—uncertainty just went through the roof. That tour wouldn't be a good time to see if we can pull off a first descent in big terrain. How about meadow-skipping just to see how it goes?

Gear, fitness, mindset, and process can all combine to increase or decrease compatibility. The wise skier gets a sense of the team's compatibility before leaving the trailhead.

Leadership

Any team naturally has a leader or leaders. We shouldn't pretend this isn't the case. If the leader is up to the task, she can be a great asset to the team. Keep in mind, however, that ineffective or corrosive leadership can damage a team's dynamics, pre-rigging the team to make sketchy decisions.

MISTAKING MOVEMENT

Often, leadership duties fall to the person with the strongest movement skills. Notice how we afford exceptionally strong or fit skiers (and climbers) extra standing within a group. Because they're senders, their opinions and observations gain "weight."

We need to remind ourselves that movement skill doesn't necessarily translate into decision-making, leadership, or guiding skill. These weighted discussions can also nudge us toward succumbing to the expert halo, so we should guard against it by soliciting everyone's opinions and acknowledging that sometimes a less-experienced partner in terms of skiing might actually be a better leader in terms of our teamwork.

TEAMWORK

But leaders emerge in groups and teams, for better or for worse, and these leaders assume tremendous responsibility. Leaders, whether they enjoy the role or not, need to protect the culture of psychological safety and respect within the team. A quick scan of the "Teamwork" box in your AIARE fieldbook or a reminder to keep your best team ideals in mind can reset the leader's behavior and attitude if things feel out of whack.

LAST ON STRATEGY, FIRST ON ACCOUNTABILITY

A useful rule of thumb for me is "Leaders speak last on strategy but first on accountability." Thinking ahead to some of our decision-making strategies, the leader may intentionally speak last so as not to taint the discussion or influence anyone's opinions through "priming" or the expert halo. This allows for a freer discussion of ideas and ultimately to more creativity for the team. During the debrief, though, she might choose to speak first to cultivate trust among teammates and to show that it's safe to self-critique and/or admit one's mistakes. Committing to accountability or showing vulnerability builds trust and shows teammates

Oops!

How many times have I started a *mea culpa* with the words, "I was trying to make a joke"? Here it is again. Face-palm! After a week of training with students at a hut-based AIARE 2 in Canada, we were prepping for a rescue scenario. I had been hammering the idea of checklists and process and collaboration throughout the week, and before we headed into the field, a student asked, "Do you want us to use our rescue checklist?"

Of course I did, and I felt some consternation that we were still questioning whether to use checklists! I tried to answer with a joke about the checklist being nothing more than an excuse to sell $22 fieldbooks, but within a minute I realized the joke had fallen flat; the student felt criticized, and my frustration had been apparent.

Fail.

As an instructor on the course, I was obviously in a leadership position—and I'd just thrown a flash-bang grenade in our "psychological safety," the "vibe," our fun. However you want to put it, I'd been worse than an ineffective leader; I'd actively soured this student's experience and subtly discouraged other students from asking questions.

Two teammates of mine that night, a tail guide and a co-instructor, politely debriefed the misfire with me and gave me some thoughts to take into the future. To this day, I still wish I'd handled the question better.

that a leader accepts mistakes as part of operating in a tricky environment and is willing to learn from them.

MANAGE THE SITUATION, NOT THE TASK

Being a leader takes on particular significance during stressful moments. The most obvious example is a rescue or avalanche involvement. In this case, effective leaders manage the situation and don't get lost in individual tasks. We try to teach this when using a rescue checklist, encouraging a rescue leader to take a bird's-eye view. He can delegate tasks, allocate resources, and keep an eye out for the obvious while teammates focus on transceiver searching, assembling a probe, checking for a cell signal, assessing a patient, and any of the dozens of other details that need attention.

The leader keeps track of the team and its progress by staying a step behind, reviewing the rescue checklist (you have one, right?), and identifying a potential error before it becomes another accident. By managing the overall situation, the team has a more effective response. Individuals can focus wholeheartedly on one element of the rescue, performing it at a high level, while the leader ensures that all the discrete tasks of the rescue are covered.

Aviation research provides some useful context for leaders in high-stakes environments. A 1994 National Transportation Safety Board (NTSB) study showed that crash rates were lower when the first officer was flying the plane rather than the captain. A Swiss follow-up study echoed this finding, rating crew performance higher when the captain took more of a bird's-eye view of cockpit operations and left the flying to the first officer.

Teamwork, leadership, and life-or-death decisions require serious forethought. Any skill improves with practice, but we need to ask ourselves, "Do we practice our backcountry skiing?" Do we practice our team decision making? Leadership skills? Do we practice our guiding? Really, we're so good we don't need to practice?

Put some time into thinking about your own role within your team and if you're comfortable being a leader. By virtue of taking avy courses, reading this book, and practicing your companion-rescue skills, you're going to be seen as a leader. Pursuing certification as a mountain guide involves leadership, whether you want it or not. Effective leadership, instructing, and facilitating are all skills, ones you can improve through practice and rehearsal.

Teammates not into it? That tells you something right there.

> ***DELIBERATE PRACTICE:***
> On days when you are a leader, explicitly or otherwise, downshift and challenge yourself to implement one or two leadership techniques. Facilitate a discussion without dominating it. Nudge a conversation without influencing everyone's responses. Get a teammate to improve without him or her even realizing it. Ask for feedback after the interaction and grade yourself.

Guiding and Avalanche Instruction

The dynamics of team change as we pull on our fancy guide badges and/or avalanche-instructor hats. Being hired to lead or teach someone in the backcountry introduces a hierarchy to the structure of your team or group. As guides, we are skiing with "random partners" all winter long. We're supposed to make that happen safely and in a fun atmosphere too. Avalanche instructors have an even trickier role—taking students near or into avalanche terrain while both teaching and facilitating them as they learn and apply skills. And many of these instructors are not trained guides. Heads up.

Don't underestimate how a guide-client or instructor-student relationship changes the dynamic of your group. I use the term "group" consciously here—it can be difficult to build a team vibe if all you've done is swapped a few e-mails, taken payment, and then met the guests at the trailhead or cable car. What if it's an unhappy couple, squabbling in the skintrack? Two psyched brothers, but also their definitely un-psyched cousin from Toledo? You've got your work cut out for you!

GUIDING

A friend once recounted to me the story of his "pin ceremony"; the ritual of receiving the pin internationally certified guides earn after passing all their exams. During the ceremony, older, more experienced guides typically remove their pins and award them to the younger candidates. (I was extremely honored and psyched to have internationally renowned Swiss guide Jean Pavillard give me his!) During my buddy's ceremony, an older guide approached, removed his pin, affixed it to my buddy's sweater, and then said, "Now you're always right . . . until you're dead."

The older guide laughed of course, but it's a stark reminder that guides often receive an undue amount of confidence and deference from guests. This presents two main challenges: the first in our own decision making; the second in our group leadership.

A rigid hierarchy in the team can lead to decision-making errors. Having a military-style structure in a group builds in expert halo and impaired communication. As long as we acknowledge this to ourselves, we can at least account for it to some degree in our decision making as guides, instructors, and facilitators. We must project confidence to allow our guests to climb and ski with confidence. We need to keep in mind, though—especially when we are guiding alone and managing tasks like weather, snowpack, logistics, and group—that we are fallible. Allow for the potential to make a mistake; build in a buffer, check yourself, and on most days choose your terrain knowing you might have blown it.

Our second challenge, leadership, requires a different balancing act. Maintaining a fun vibe with a guiding group requires some good customer service, clear communication, and confidence. Ours is a delicate, internal conversation, one in which we remain the skeptic inwardly while outwardly reassuring our group, our guests, maybe our team, that what we're doing is sane—and safe enough. Having a blast in a beautiful landscape while maintaining firm, resolute control on the group requires a mature, clear read on people and your own skills. Don't underestimate how difficult this is, or the consequences of losing the confidence of your group, not to mention control of it, in big terrain.

Younger guides, guides with "mellower" personalities, and women all face an additional layer of difficulty in the face of all this: the potential for older men to challenge or question your competence and authority in the field. I've had numerous colleagues describe inappropriate comments and questions from (almost without fail) older men. Comments range from questions like "Are you sure you know what you're doing?" to a woman who had a client ask that she refer to him as "Daddy" during their days climbing together.

Uh, yeah; digest that for a moment.

Situations like these may require a firm and difficult conversation, but one that will establish a proper, and indeed safer, working relationship. If the offending guest balks, well—some things are more important than a day's wage.

Conclusion

A gang of bros charging in the backcountry might be an all-star team, or just . . . a gang of bros. Which am I skiing with? And if my buddies and I do make up a team, what kind of team is it? Low-performing teams generally have what outcomes? And high-performing teams? As little kids, we play on soccer and swim teams. Teams win and lose. As snow-obsessed adults, what game are we playing? And what are the consequences of losing this "game"?

When we start asking ourselves about the backcountry and our team, it forces us to ask some important questions. All of us love to be on the winning side, but are we willing to do the work? Remember, half the teams you see out there are below average. A bunch are right around average. Recreating and working in a high-consequence environment requires excellent performance. Average will get you smoked.

I hope by now you have some good food for thought on strengthening your team for the upcoming season. High-performing teams keep us safer, find better skiing, and have more fun too. Do your best to be on a winning team.

CHAPTER 6

Decision Making

The first rule in decision making is that one does not make a decision unless there is disagreement.

—Peter Drucker

Three, or four, or five of these things happen together and it turns human brains to mush.

—Charlie Munger

When it comes to effective decision making, not knowing that you cannot predict is a bigger sin than not being able to predict.

—*Harvard Business Review*, May 2015

A million times a day we decide. What to eat, how to dress, where to ski, with whom to ski, mohair or nylon, tastes great or less filling. Our decision making underpins every aspect of our lives, so we ask ourselves: Are we any good at it?

Before we answer, let's cut ourselves some slack. Do we have a college degree in decision making? Did we take a semester of it in high school? Do we have an app on our phone that quizzes us and improves our decision-making prowess? No, no, and no again.

We spend almost no time improving and practicing this fundamental skill that every one of us needs and employs daily. No wonder we buy rickety cars and make goofy investments and date the wrong person. No wonder smart, skilled, experienced, and expert riders get caught in avalanches. While we get it right most of the time, our decision making fails us too often. And as Tremper reminds us in the opening pages of *Staying Alive*, "most of the time" isn't good enough in avalanche terrain. You and I need to make better decisions, day to day, and year to year.

Decision science grows from psychology, economics, and neuroscience. This chapter draws on the research of thinkers and organizations contributing to this emerging field, in addition to avalanche experts with decades of experience. You'll recognize many of

Definitely the right decision! Bluebird, new snow, and the place to ourselves. The Vallée Blanche with a great crew in 2018. MATT KENNEDY

the names and hopefully discover a few new ones.

From poker players to fighter pilots to Swiss engineers to business-school professors to avalanche professionals, I poached liberally to share a few ideas here, in the hopes that we can improve our decision making and stay safer in the backcountry. First we'll discuss the problem we face and then move into specific techniques and strategies you can incorporate into your own process.

Really, a Whole Chapter on Decision Making?

Truth is, this chapter could work as a foreword, a conclusion, or an appendix. I decided to discuss decision making at this point in the book in hopes of getting into the flow and content of some more concrete techniques and strategies. Now that we're deep into the meat of ski guiding and touring, let's pause and discuss the one skill that informs every step of the process, from assembling your team to prepping for the season to daily trip planning to maintaining situational awareness in the field to the debrief: decision making.

But come on, do we need a whole chapter on this stuff?

Dale Atkins, a former forecaster at the CAIC, analyzed accident data in the United States from the 1990s and presented his findings at the 2000 ISSW. Concluding his paper "Human

Getting It Right versus Being Right

Standing on the shoulder of Lookout Col, Joey and I had the valley to ourselves. It was the end of the season, temps rising, and most of the locals were already migrating to the desert to mountain bike or hopping flights to surf in Costa Rica. We were alone up there.

Rogers Pass, between Golden and Revelstoke, offers some of the best ski touring on the planet—and instead of charging, we were shouting at each other. I can't even recall the subject of the argument, but it was an argument. Dumb, pointless, and ultimately a step in the wrong direction if our priorities were staying safer and "getting it right." The argument ruined our day and temporarily strained our friendship, mostly because we were trying to be right.

Important distinction, eh, getting it right instead of just trying to be right? Getting it right means finding good snow, avoiding avalanches, coming home better friends than at the start of the day. Being right protects our brittle egos, forgoes accountability, preserves our puffed-up perceptions of ourselves.

I'm as guilty as the next guy of lapsing into this trap. Propose an idea or route or snowpack test and then a teammate disagrees. Instead of evaluating evidence and options, the discussion swerves into an argument and I'm focused on being right rather than on getting it right. Evidence gives way to stubbornness and verbal trickery. Listening to understand a teammate takes a back seat to merely waiting for my turn to talk. Pointless.

I trust you've done it too. Dare I say, maybe even at work or with a spouse? As soon as you feel your blood pressure rising or you're feeling "attacked," it's time to remind yourself and your team—"Hey, we're all buddies here; let's get this right." If you can't get on the same page, maybe there's more uncertainty on the day than you thought. Worse, maybe the team isn't quite the team you thought it was. Worth considering.

Fortunately Joey and I resolved our disagreement that day, and we're better friends because of it. We returned to Rogers Pass the following season, 2014, to pass our ski exams together—no arguing, no shouting, no avalanches. I doubt he remembers the fight, but I know for a fact he's a great guide and teammate to this day, committed to getting it right.

The Evolution of AIARE Decision-Making Tools

by Tom Murphy

Speaking from my experience, there was a time when avalanche education programs felt as if we were fire-hosing course participants with information. Courses were often run in a seminar fashion in which various instructors would present well-informed discussions on the various topics relating to avalanche formation, avoidance, and rescue. Often these topics were discussed in too much detail. It was also clear that most avalanche accidents were attributed to "human factors" and that more emphasis needed to be placed on those.

Although students had spent multiple days in an avalanche course, they still didn't have a clear-cut method or process to take the information they had received in the course to make an informed decision in avalanche terrain. Something had to change.

A variety of "decision-making tools" and checklists were emerging, such as the Nivo Test, Stop or Go, Munter's 3 x 3 Reduction Method, and, later, the Avaluator. While each one of these (and other) methods had its pros and cons, none of them felt appropriate for the programs we were developing at AIARE.

Additionally, the commercial airline industry had identified that many of the accidents occurring in their industry were tied to "pilot error" or what could also be referred to as "human factors." We began to tap into the well-funded research they were doing. A key finding of that risk-management research identified communication and teamwork as an important component for reducing human-factor frailties, along with a repeatable decision-making process.

Using the research being done inside and outside of the avalanche industry, AIARE set out to provide the best possible method for assisting students in making informed decisions as they gained experience in the field.

The first rendition of the AIARE Decision Making Framework (DMF) was designed to encourage communication and teamwork in an effort to "derail" human factors as well as provide a model for assessing hazard and

Tom Murphy COURTESY TOM MURPHY

managing risk in avalanche terrain. While courses had done a good job of discussing bias and decision-making errors, students were often left with nothing much more than "watch out for those human factors." The AIARE DMF addressed that gap.

ISO 31000 was published in 2009 as a standard on the implementation of risk management; it was updated in 2018. This provided AIARE with further guidance in the development of the AIARE 3.0 curriculum and the updated AIARE Risk Management Framework that is being used in AIARE courses today.

Tom Murphy cofounded AIARE in 1998, just as the United States entered the international guiding community and the International Federation of Mountain Guide Associations (IFMGA/UIAGM). A longtime Alaska and Crested Butte skier, "Murph" taught AIARE programs, both professional and recreational, for nearly two decades before retiring to ski and ride both mountain and road bikes. Last heard from in Bormio, Italy, he's always sharing research with the current AIARE staff and instructors.

Factors in Avalanche Accidents," he wrote, "Human factors are the cause of most avalanche accidents involving avalanche-aware people. Staying alive is not as simple as being able to recognize avalanche hazards. The problem is seldom a lack of information regarding terrain, weather, and snowpack. The problem is how that information is processed."

His findings echoed and confirmed what Jill Fredston and Doug Fesler had shown in a 1994 paper at ISSW. They stated nearly the same, writing, "Human factors are a major influence in almost all avalanche accidents."

Depending on whose data set we use, these "human factors" (or, we might say, cognitive biases or mental lapses or errors in judgment) account for somewhere around 90 percent of all avalanche accidents. In short, humans making poor decisions—not acts of God, not unusual storm events, not a failure to recognize hazards, not ignorance of a snowpack test—account for most accidents and fatalities.

Dual-Process Theories

Oh boy; here we go with the jargon and tedious white papers. Far from it! This stuff is interesting and cool, and I encourage you to scan the suggested reading list for books, podcasts, and articles on the topic. If you find this stuff boring, it's because I've blown it in the presentation. Do yourself a favor and dive into some of the source materials. They're fascinating, confounding, and ultimately of great help in understanding ourselves, our teammates, and our decisions.

Weighing options and deciding MATT KENNEDY

Several years ago, it became de rigueur to say, "Our brain is the most important tool in the backcountry." Nowadays, though, the thinking has evolved to accept the fact that our brains don't always work when making decisions in a wicked environment. This chapter is my best effort at updating our "operating software" in the backcountry and when making decisions. None of this is mine; I've stolen everything in this chapter from someone smarter and more experienced than I.

The field of decision science has exploded within the past decade but goes back to the 1970s at least. Perhaps no authors have done more to introduce decision science to the general public as Drs. Daniel Kahneman and Amos Tversky. Though at one point rival academics, the duo eventually collaborated on some of the most interesting research you'll ever read.

Their achievements earned Kahneman a Nobel Prize in 2002. Sadly, Tversky had died, and a Nobel is not awarded posthumously. Still, Kahneman mentioned Tversky in the opening of his acceptance speech for the award. They were great friends and academic partners, and if we take their advice, we'll all be better backcountry partners because of it.

The Systems

Kahneman's most popular book, *Thinking*, has become essential reading for any avalanche practitioner. He presents the idea of a "dual-process" system of thinking, System 1 and System 2. The theory is not his alone. Other academics had proposed the concept, but Kahneman, in his approachable, articulate way, presented the ideas and the supporting research to great effect in *Thinking.*

In our little world of mountain guiding and avalanche work, innovators like Tom Murphy, Bruce Kay, and many others incorporated Kahneman's ideas. Knowing what Fredston, Fesler, McCammon, Atkins, Roger Atkins, Zacharias, and others had shown—that our flawed decisions usually get us killed, not our knowledge of facet development or transceiver skills or ski skills—avy pros recognized that our approach to decision making and our processes in avalanche terrain are what matter most. How do we decide? What habits and practices can protect us from our potential for terrible decision making?

Kahneman describes System 1 thinking as quick, reflexive, intuitive, and highly adaptive, but only in certain situations. System 2, on the other hand, is effortful, slow, often laborious and tedious, and by no means our default setting. System 1 is your reaction when a sketchy-looking dude comes out of an alley at night. System 2 is trying to make a sound investment decision. Think of System 1 as autocorrect—it spits out a solution before you even realize you need one. To access System 2, you must open a folder on your computer, double-click an app, let it load, sign in, and input some information before you get a decision. It takes up RAM and processor speed on your machine. If you're streaming a video, uploading photos, and trying to do a backup, System 2 tends to bog down, even quit.

Guess which one we default to. Guess which one we default to even when we think we're making a careful decision. Now imagine you're 6 hours into a ski tour, you've been out of water since the morning, your legs are tweaked, and it's minus 25°C. Guess which system you'll most likely use. You got it, the easy one, System 1—and, most dangerously, you might not even know you're relying on it.

I'll mention these dual processes and quote a bunch of people who know about it. They'll discuss decision making in the context of the lazy, quick, often helpful, but sometimes not System 1 and our process-driven, tiring, occasionally essential System 2.

WHEN?

Above, I mentioned that each system has its place. System 1 protects us from things like surprise threats, random noises in the jungle, or a hazard for which you have almost no time to react. A snake slithers across your toe and what do you do? If you're like me, you jump like a madman and catch your breath later, even if it's a garter snake. You hear rockfall and instinctively huddle into the rock and get small, even if it's on the next route over. Why?

Before you can say "snake!" or "rock!" your brain recognizes a phenomenon that could be deadly. Most of the time it's not, but do you engage System 2—for example, get a photo of the snake, search online for a chart of venomous snakes in your area, compare the images, read about the snake to see if it's aggressive, and finally draft a risk-mitigation strategy before enacting it?

Damn straight you don't; you jump out of the way, your buddies heckle you, and then everybody carries on. Think, though, over the last few thousand years: Who survived and who didn't? The guy who decided to pick up the black mamba and investigate it or the dude like you and me, who leapt out of the way in a panic?

System 1 is the domain of snap decisions and gut-level intuition. It's always running in the background; you can't turn it off, and most of the time it keeps you safer—provided you're in an environment with which it has some experience. The sketchy dude coming out of the alley alerts your System 1 instantaneously because it has experience with dark alleys, people who seem "off," and stories of crime and mayhem.

System 1 shortcuts a deliberative, energy- and time-consuming process and produces a decision or feeling in milliseconds. These shortcuts are also known as heuristics. These mental shortcuts are adaptive at times, but in an unfamiliar, complex environment, they become dangerous.

WICKED PROBLEMS AND SYSTEM 2

McCammon has written extensively on these ideas, elsewhere and in his

Is today the right day? How do you decide? Leaving the top station at the Punta Helbronner, Ali Vagnini makes the call. MATT KENNEDY

seminal paper, "Evidence of Heuristic Traps in Avalanche Accidents," presented at the 2002 ISSW. Heuristics not only work, they're essential in daily life. How you dress for work, how you travel to work, crossing the street—all these behaviors come down to quick-and-easy decisions.

Writing in 1974, Kahneman and Tversky explained, "People rely on a limited number of heuristic principles which reduce the complex tasks of assessing probabilities and predicting values to simpler judgmental operations. In general, these heuristics are quite useful, but sometimes they lead to severe and systematic errors."

It's this last bit that concerns us—the "severe and systematic errors." Heuristics work for simple problems rather than long, effortful decisions involving a repeatable process and/or algorithm in a wicked environment.

If this begins to sound jargony and obtuse, let's keep in mind the bird's-eye view of ski touring as a wicked problem: We have a team of diverse individuals—each (hopefully!) with his or her own perspective on the day's weather, snowpack, and terrain—making decisions in a medium (snow) that's often within a few degrees of turning from a solid to a liquid, changing altitude and aspect throughout the day while the weather and snowpack change around them. Add to this new and unfamiliar terrain, climate change, hydration and hunger status, fatigue among teammates, and navigation. Wicked, indeed!

Dr. Michael Mauboussin, business strategist, author, and professor at Columbia University, expands on this idea in *The Success Equation*: "Intuition works when the environment is stable and an individual has the opportunity to spend a great deal of time learning about it. . . . Trouble arises when individuals rely too heavily on their experience in making automatic decisions. When we age, we tend to avoid exerting too much cognitive effort and deliberating extensively over a decision that needs to be made. We gradually come to rely more on rules of thumb. This means that we make poorer choices in environments that are complex and unstable."

I hope by now you can see that a quick, gut-level, System 1 approach to

Another Take on Intuition

by Ken Wylie

One of my disappointments is that intuition is being usurped by the notion that it requires experience. The problem with this idea is that it sets up a hierarchy in the workplace and on recreational endeavors. Hierarchy leads to chaos in my experience and view because it silences other opinions, narrowing much-needed perspective. I have seen an entrenched pecking order create desperate tragedy.

One thing is clear: In a high-risk environment, we are all gambling with the same thing, our lives. To be fair and equitable, each person deserves a voice in the decision-making process should he or she decide to claim it.

Intuition is linked to feeling, not thinking. It is access to source in a moment that brings clarity. In my view, in all seriousness, George Lucas has it right. Listen to the force. Mystery is an important tool because it nurtures wonder and humility. Without those, we are at risk of being too arrogant to make safe choices.

Werner Heisenberg, the father of quantum physics, once said: "The first sip of a glass of natural science will make you an atheist, but at the bottom of the glass, God awaits you." Great leaders listen.

Ken Wylie is an IFMGA/ACMG mountain guide based in Mill Bay, British Columbia. He's the author of* Buried*, a public speaker, and owner of Mountains for Growth.

Intuition

Some of you may have already exclaimed, "Yeah, but what about my gut feeling?!" You hold your intuition near and dear, thinking it offers more wisdom than I'm realizing. I get that, and you might be right. A passionate group of practitioners and some very thoughtful academics agree with you. I have reservations about intuition, so I count myself a skeptic about my gut.

For me, the most revealing thoughts on the topic come from Gary Klein, inventor of the premortem. In his book *The Power of Intuition: How to Use Your Gut Feelings to Make Better Decisions at Work*, he argues that intuition can be an accurate and powerful decision maker, but with the caveat that you must have broad, robust experience in the environment in which you're deciding for intuition to serve you well.

As I'm writing this, I head into my forty-second winter of skiing and fifteenth year of guiding, which might sound impressive at first glance. I need to ask myself, though, how much of that time have I spent actually managing, for example, surface hoar layers? A couple months? Mere weeks? Is this enough time to develop mastery and therefore rely on quick, intuitive, snap decisions?

When asked about snap judgments and intuition, Kahneman cautions us here too: "One basic rule is slow down. Especially if you have an

many of the decisions involved in ski touring is not the way to go.

Most Level 1 avalanche courses are at least mentioning heuristics, human factors, cognitive biases, and different approaches to solutions/mitigation strategies. Kahneman and a process-driven System 2 approach has certainly infused the AIARE risk-management framework. Whatever you and your team's approach, within a complex and unstable environment and when faced with a wicked problem, System 2 offers your best hope of avoiding severe and systematic errors.

Pre-bias, De-bias, and a Ski-Guide Process

The wicked problem of recreating in avalanche terrain resists simple solutions, apart from total avoidance. If we're going to enter avalanche terrain on certain days, we need to accept that humans routinely succumb to bias and shortcuts, making decisions that

immediate conviction, slow down. There are procedures, you know, there are ways of teaching better decisions. If you really want to improve the quality of decision making, use algorithms wherever you can. If you can replace judgments by rules and algorithms, they'll do better. If you can't use an algorithm, then you slow yourself down."

Most thinkers agree that intuition requires accurately recognizing patterns and signals. Getting a bad feeling from a person, no sweat; I've been dealing with people since 1970. Feathery crystals that grow only in certain conditions of humidity, wind, sky cover, and temperatures? I'm sticking with System 2 for the next few decades.

Kahneman has more concise and insightful thoughts on the matter. Discussing cognitive biases and intuition, he writes, "I've been studying this stuff for more than 50 years and I don't think my intuitions have really significantly improved."

If you do rely on intuition, he advises, take note of your gut feeling, then review the evidence and revisit that initial feeling. "Do not simply trust intuitive judgment—your own or that of others—but do not dismiss it either."

If intuition is your thing, awesome. My strong advice would be to listen to it when you have a "bad" feeling and double-check yourself if your intuition screams "good to go."

in hindsight seem bananas. Our hope resides in System 2 and a solid team—but what does that mean, specifically, in the context of guiding and touring?

Above, I used the phrase "a Ski-Guide Process" rather than the ski-guide process. By no means are the ideas here the only way to get things done. The approach and interpretation here draw heavily on the twenty-five years of debate, wisdom, and innovation generated within AIARE and the AMGA, as well as my time spent with personal mentors. Neither they nor AIARE, the AMGA, the ACMG, or any other organization have a monopoly on solid decision making and safer backcountry skiing. This is a collection of suggestions from different thinkers, practitioners, and mountain guides, filtered through one writer's keyboard. Keep this in mind. Steal what you like; disregard the rest.

The unavoidable takeaway from much of this is that teams and organizations devoted to a process make better decisions. Kahneman argues, "Organizations are better than individuals when it comes to avoiding errors because they naturally think more slowly and have the power to impose orderly procedures. Organizations can institute and enforce the application of useful checklists, as well as more elaborate exercises, such as reference-class forecasting and the premortem."

As a masterful recreationist, your organization might be your team. As a mountain guide, I sure hope your organization/team has a process, employs guide meetings, and relies on some of these strategies and more. We can all agree that the problems we face and our inherent glitches as humans present a tricky situation. When preparing and executing a ski tour, we can employ some time-tested, evidence-driven strategies to pre-bias and de-bias our guiding and riding.

Pre-bias

Decades of research from academics and our own observations confirm that we all have biases. Every reader probably shares this one with me: mad pow disease. You, like I, love riding bottomless pow under blue skies with a posse of good friends.

Imagine that exact situation on the last day of a ski trip during which your team missed two days due to travel drama. The avy danger is "Moderate"/ level 2, with a deep persistent-slab problem. Left to make a decision at the top of a 1,400-meter run, standing shoulder to shoulder with your favorite ski partner, what do you think your mad pow disease does to the discussion and decision making? Is your perception of a low-probability/high-consequence event skewed because of the snow conditions? Is your missing two days of your trip affecting you?

In *Thinking* Kahneman reminds us, "A happy mood loosens the control of System 2 over performance: when in a good mood, people become more intuitive and more creative but also less vigilant and more prone to logical errors."

Mad pow, your A-list team, and blue skies? Sounds like the ingredients for a pretty happy mood to me!

Can pre-biasing ourselves help to manage all this?

MINDSET

If you've employed a pre-bias, you will probably have a clearer discussion about the run. You might even be able to "manage your stoke." Did you select a terrain mindset on the day? (Maybe you even closed terrain during your trip plan.) These exercises, done *before* you are presented with the object of your desire (an untracked hero run), tend to pre-bias your decision making toward a reality- and evidence-based decision rather than allowing bias or System 1 to nudge you toward risk.

Bruce Kay summarizes a pre-bias well: "Mindset is a willful effort to establish an appropriate biasing in our thinking determined by mountain conditions."

We pre-bias ourselves to mountain conditions (hazard, snowpack, closed runs). Some even call this "re-biasing." However you think of it, we're actually harnessing a cognitive bias in service of the team. We put a name or mindset to conditions, and that anchors us to reality. We're activating anchor bias, via the mindset, to keep us sane in the field. We're less likely to let our perception of the hazard or problem drift if we've written it in big block letters in our notebook.

THE NOTEBOOK

Don't discount the power of trip planning, mindset, and pre-biasing—also write it down. Having a fieldbook in your pocket provides a written record of your hard efforts and your pre-biasing strategies.

A good buddy of mine is a professional forecaster and helps run an avalanche center in the United States. While on a ski trip in Canada's Coast Range, he, his wife, and several other very experienced avalanche professionals were enjoying all-time conditions, with a bit of avy hazard too. Having ruled out certain terrain features and slopes in their morning guide meeting, the gang headed into the hills around McGillivray Pass, British Columbia. Soon the group found itself beneath a complex approach to a col, where beautiful skiing awaited.

Dr. Lee McNeely enjoys the big terrain around McGillivray Pass, British Columbia, above the legendary Whitecap Alpine lodge. ROB COPPOLILLO

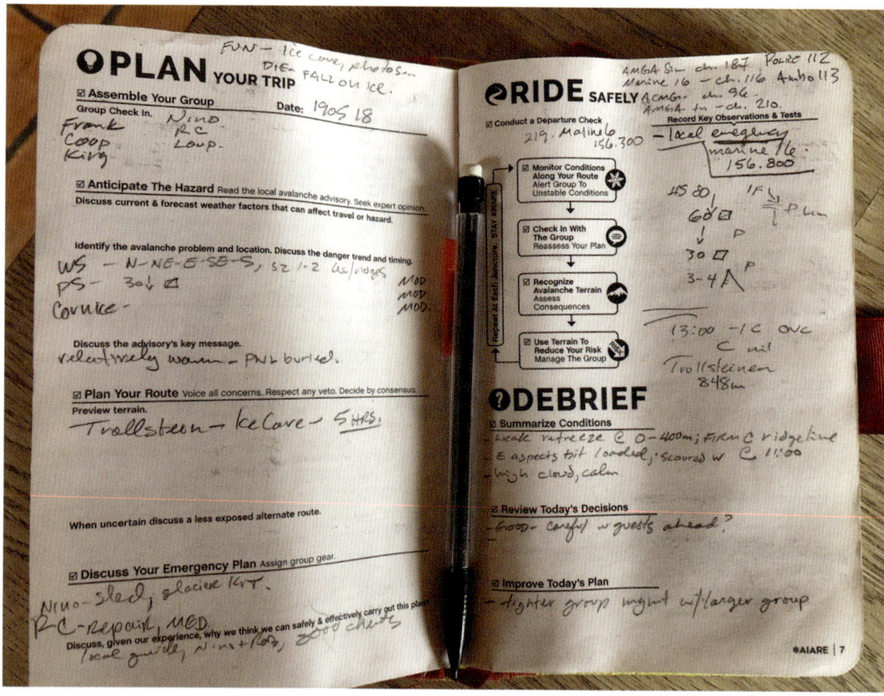

A filled-in fieldbook at least reminds you of your morning meeting and at best anchors you to present conditions and mindset. ROB COPPOLILLO

The most experienced of the riders began eyeballing a tricky, though possible, line to the col, discussing how they'd get there, how they'd manage the terrain. Others joined in—it might just go!

From the back of the group my buddy's wife finally spoke up, "Hey, didn't we say we're not going to thread the needle today?"

The experts paused and looked around. Someone produced a notebook and sure enough—they'd agreed in their morning meeting not to take on complex, more exposed terrain that day. A pre-bias isn't a pre-bias if you blow it off. Use your notebook!

HOW WILL YOU DIE TODAY?

In the book *Horse Soldiers*, an American Green Beret describes leading men in the opening days of the conflict in Afghanistan after 9/11. Each morning the unit prepares its mission and prebriefs on the goals and execution on the day. The last thing the team leader asks before heading into the field is "How will you die today?"

This is a cousin of the premortem (discussed below) but constructed with more powerful language. In the top of my notebook, I often write the word "DIE." Beside this one word, I list the biggest threat the team identified in the morning guide meeting. It's a bit like a mindset in that it anchors my or the team's decision making, frames our risk management in that box, and acts as a simple reminder that the hazard on the day is, for example, wind slabs or polar bears or extreme cold.

As guides, we probably should forgo the question with our guests so as not to bum anybody out or alarm someone unnecessarily! We can certainly ask ourselves, though. See if it works for you.

De-bias

The pre-bias anchors us in the reality of our situation, be that team, weather, avalanche, or travel conditions. De-biasing, on the other hand, helps us make clearer, smarter, safer decisions in the moment. We're trying to identify and defeat bias. It's a set of practices and strategies to plug into our decisions, as we make them, in real time. This might be nothing more than what skis to ride on the day, but more likely we remind ourselves to de-bias our decisions as consequences increase.

DELIBERATE PRACTICE:
Your first ten tours after reading this, simply challenge yourself to implement one pre-biasing strategy and make note of it in your book. Try several. See which ones click . . . and consider using them. Compare feedback with teammates and see what strategies work for you and why.

I'll propose some techniques and strategies to directly de-bias your process and decisions.

ENCOURAGING AND MANAGING DISAGREEMENTS

High-stakes decisions, cold, fatigue, hunger, and passionate people occasionally make for rocky discussions. We have to accept and even nurture disagreements in the team. Don't perceive disagreements or even a vigorous debate as a weakness or sign of incompatibility. Quite the opposite; the absence of disagreement is itself a red flag!

Peter Drucker, an esteemed author and business thinker, is sometimes called the father of modern management. In *The Effective Executive* he writes, "The first rule in decision making is that one does not make a decision unless there is disagreement."

Some of us avoid conflict or a hot discussion at all costs. Consider, though, that expecting or even requiring some debate helps defuse "groupthink" and the "expert halo." Groupthink of course refers to allowing a team or organization to lapse into simply reinforcing its own decisions and methods; the expert halo involves a group deferring to one member perceived as more expert than the rest.

We have several tools for helping to facilitate productive disagreement. The first and perhaps most difficult is creating a culture of respect and openness within your team. Recall our discussion about getting it right versus being right. I've strayed from this ideal too many times to remember, so the best I can do is trust my teammates to remind me that I'm doing it, own it, apologize, and move on. This helps build trust and show my teammates I'm willing to change my mind, be wrong, and commit to a better course of action.

In an open, collaborative environment, decision making improves because the breadth of discussion widens. You get more information. Capitalizing on this culture, some organizations appoint a devil's advocate in brainstorming sessions. Some researchers, like UC-Berkeley's Charlan J. Nemeth, question the effectiveness of the devil's advocate, arguing that "authentic dissent" produces far better and more creative solutions. Problem is, the team needs a culture of respectful dissent to rely on it—easier said than done.

Either way, you get the gist: An appointed devil's advocate or authentically skeptical teammate can vastly improve decision making by raising potential pitfalls in the plan or the issue at hand. No matter which approach you choose, the team has to be open to truly listening to the skeptic and evaluating her input.

If the devil's advocate approach suits you and your team, consider rotating the role among members. This keeps the role fresh and from becoming one or just a few persons' responsibility. By appointing the person, the rest of the team knows it's her duty to troubleshoot the plan. She's derelict if she's not second-guessing decisions. This strategy prevents anyone from taking her suggestions personally. It's her job; she's supposed to be a pain in the butt!

If a debate becomes acrimonious, take a break; accept that the group cannot reach consensus and let that inform your decision making. If a group of like-minded teammates can't reach consensus on a critical decision, that tells you something. Recognize that your uncertainty just went through the roof and today is not the day to push it. Dial back exposure to avalanche terrain.

After you've done that, get back to mending fences. Cool off, take some time to relax, revisit the situation when the time comes and tempers cool. If it's in the field, it's probably a smart idea to defer to less-exposed terrain. On a day tour, you might revisit the disagreement days later. Point is, if the team has devoted itself to trust and mutual respect, it will be easy to circle back, own up to each person's role in the disagreement—and then discuss how to avoid it in the future. If Joey and I could do it, you guys certainly can.

STRONG OPINIONS, WEAKLY HELD

Dr. Paul Saffo, chair of the Future Studies and Forecasting track at Singularity University and a professor at Stanford, described one of the best mindsets I've encountered for debating serious issues among a team: strong opinions, weakly held. Have your opinions and gather evidence to support them, but be willing to discard them in the face of better, more logical facts presented by a teammate. It's a quick reminder that fosters skepticism and defeats bias in the moment.

FACILITATE EFFECTIVE COMMUNICATION

No, I don't mean change the batteries in your VHF radio. A couple simple techniques improve our communication, giving our team more and better options in the process.

Expert facilitators know that how we have conversations can dramatically alter the process. For example, a team leader can set himself up for better or worse conversations simply by speaking first or last. Years ago, as a newly minted AIARE instructor, I was pretty psyched to be in front of the class. I had committed to becoming a full mountain guide, but that fancy badge was years away. All of a sudden I'm in front of a group, and I'm feeling pretty darn knowledgeable and cool. (Dear God, I was anything but!)

After a few courses, though, I caught myself diving into rabbit holes I scarcely understood myself. I was quick to offer thoughts on topics, lead the class in discussions, offer my opinion. This "sage-on-the-stage" type teaching can be gratifying to the wannabe sage, but in the end it limits group learning, not to mention it's frickin' boring for students. (Sorry, everybody; I owe you one!)

Granted, team decision making and instructing are different beasts, but they overlap. A wise team member or leader solicits opinions before divulging his thoughts. Groups, whether they realize it or not, drift toward the

What could I possibly have known back then?! Discussing companion rescue in the field with students on an AIARE 1, "back in the day." BRETT WILHELM

"expert's" or "leader's" conclusion or opinion. Reserve that opinion and let your teammates or students speak first, and you'll get a wider range of discussion. That helps them, that helps you, and that helps you make better decisions.

Experts and academics call this habit of some leaders "priming," and it's a cousin of "framing bias," or Annie Duke's "resulting." You might want to nudge students or at least highlight certain information by saying "This is what I'm seeing" but then allowing them to connect the dots. Sharing your conclusion first can frame the discussion in a certain way, limiting topics and reducing creativity. Avoid it!

Facilitate an untainted dialogue within an open culture of respect and collaboration, a devil's advocate, and pre-biasing—now you're getting somewhere.

OVER- AND UNDER-CONFIDENCE

Believe it or not, both over- and under-confidence can be handicaps in your decision making. The overconfident team or teammate tends to overestimate his forecasting abilities, while the team risks losing the under-confident teammate's opinion because he doesn't speak up. So how do we address that?

Overconfidence, the expert halo, or "level 1 disease" all lead toward the same place—missing evidence and, potentially, confirmation bias. The overconfident guide or teammate tends to discount disconfirming evidence, if he's aware of it at all. The devil's advocate can help with this.

Another potential antidote to overconfidence is not just open dialogue but a requirement for contributing to the dialogue. This may sound a little bossy or weird, but it may not be enough to simply encourage everyone to contribute; we might consider requiring teammates to have an opinion on the day, the problems, the terrain, etc. Sure, a newer teammate might not have deep knowledge about the process or components of a tour, and we can roll with that. But in general, a full-fledged, experienced member of the team should be engaged and aware, and actively contributing to the process.

Mountain guides can authentically solicit guests' opinions at times too. Sure, in the heat of the moment, while managing a group of four skiers on a bulletproof ridge, there may be no conversation beyond a couple shouted instructions. During a more relaxed setting, the guide can model openness and build trust by offering to discuss decisions or terrain choices, demo a quick pit, or "think out loud." While we model confidence for our guests, often to allay their nerves or fear, we also want to have understandable reasons for the things we do and the decisions we make. We shouldn't be above changing our mind or recognizing that we missed something.

Having answers feels good (overconfidence); sometimes receiving them feels even better (under-confidence). I try to remind myself of Bruce Kay's wisdom on the topic: "In nearly all cases, one single element lays the foundation for all our screw ups: we think we know what we are doing in an environment where 'knowing' borders on the impossible." Whether we're holding court or listening to a teammate do it, beware the skier with more answers than questions. If that's you, dial it back. If you're listening to her, remind her to dial it back!

The under-confident teammate threatens the group by failing to speak up or verbalize a "bad feeling." Both the Cherry Bowl (March 2013) and Pucker Face (December 2013) accidents highlighted teammates who had misgivings about the terrain selection but chose not to (or could not) speak up. Requiring a chat before a consequential decision addresses both over- and under-confidence.

While it's easy to write those words, make sure you're actually doing it. Revisit your trip planning and make sure you have decision/regroup points built into your day. Get the team together, solicit opinions, listen to them, and then decide together. AIARE instructors often say, "Everyone has a voice, everyone has a veto." We might consider rephrasing this: "Everyone must have a voice, everyone has a veto."

> ***DELIBERATE PRACTICE:***
> Next four tours you take, make sure the entire team regroups and every person contributes to a critical decision, whatever it may be. This slows you down, solicits participation, encourages discussion. Check to see that you actually did it during the debrief. And what did your teammates think of it? Waste of time? Productive? Improvements?

LANGUAGE MATTERS

Above, we described priming and framing, two potential pitfalls in facilitating a discussion. Let's challenge ourselves further and look a bit deeper into our language. How we ask questions and how we respond to teammates can subtly but powerfully influence the types of discussions we create.

I recall a morning on a hut-based AIARE 2 course. The students had trip-planned in the morning, consulting maps and a run atlas as well as the avalanche bulletin and our nearest-neighbor observations. They were dialed and doing well. We approached a long ridgeline that offered a few hundred feet of good turns to hit a small drainage, from which we'd ascend the slope opposite us. But where to drop in?

We side-slipped, evaluating terrain. We side-slipped some more, evaluating more terrain . . . and losing altitude and therefore turns. I sensed a little frustration rising in the group.

"Should we ski it," one of the students asked, a bit impatient.

From down the ridge, another student responded with a question of her own: "Can we ski it?"

Bro Language

When discussing language, we should at least address "bro" culture. At best it's a goofy feature to our beloved sport; at worst it's misogynistic, dull-minded blather that threatens our culture and decisions.

I recall working at a guide service that used its own "ski quality" rating each day. A guide might post on the internal information exchange, "Ski quality was ⅖." It was a cool way to convey conditions to those familiar with the terrain and local conditions, but it also occurred to me that a subjective rating like this meant little to somebody like me, who worked only a handful of days a year for that particular service. Further, it made it almost useless to share information with another guide, guide service, or avalanche forecaster, as she wouldn't have a very good sense of what "⅖ skiing" meant.

Colloquial phrases and terms like "mank," "zipper crust," and "blower" mean different things to different people, so a mentor of mine nudged me to quit using them and instead describe things using more standardized, agreed-upon terms. For professionals that means terms found in *Snow, Weather, and Avalanche Guidelines* (SWAG), published by the American Avalanche Association, and/or *Observation Guidelines and Recording Standards for Weather, Snowpack and Avalanches* (OGRS), published by the Canadian Avalanche Association.

You're already chuckling because I've thrown around some bro language on these pages. *Touché, mon pote!*

Different questions, right? "Should we ski it?" is probably going to solicit a yes-or-no answer. "Can we ski it?" though, resulted in a longer discussion. We ended up talking about the reward of this short slope and distinguishing between "skiing the slope" and "skiing the slope safely."

Asking yes-or-no questions ends in a cul-de-sac. Using words like "why" and "how," though, provokes deeper thought and a broader discussion.

As guides, we often don't solicit opinions or input. Certainly with a time crunch due to weather or darkness or hazard, it would be less appropriate to entertain guest input, until perhaps later. As a team leader or instructor, we might fall somewhere between a teammate and a mountain guide. Consider what hat you're wearing.

On the same AIARE 2 mentioned earlier, those students gave me some insightful feedback regarding my work during the week. I hadn't realized it, but they suggested that I think about the differences between instructor, guide, and facilitator. I hadn't done a very good job of switching hats between roles during the week. These days, just a couple seasons later, I'm not sure I'm that much better, but at least I know to consider my language, the types of questions I pose, and when or if I speak at all.

Tricky business!

THE PREMORTEM

The premortem has made the rounds in the business world ever since Gary Klein developed the tool in the early 1990s. Capitalizing on the concept of "prospective hindsight," Klein and other academics claimed a 30 percent increase in the ability to identify reasons for future outcomes. That is, conduct a premortem with your team and you have a 30 percent greater chance of identifying the reason your business plan or chosen action is going to fail.

For our purposes, conduct a premortem with your team and you're 30 percent more likely to identify the reason you're about to get yourself involved/hurt/killed in an avalanche. Obviously Klein didn't intend for the premortem to be applied in touring, nor has it been tested in any rigorous way in our domain, but let's assume it's of some value, given its popularity in business schools and corporations.

Writing in the *Harvard Business Review* in 2007, Klein explains, "A typical premortem begins after the team has been briefed on the plan. The leader starts the exercise by informing everyone that the project has failed spectacularly. Over the next few minutes, those in the room independently write down every reason they can think of for the failure—especially the kinds of things they ordinarily wouldn't mention as potential problems for fear of being impolitic."

For our crew, we might do this as we approach a regroup or decision point in a tour. Without priming the group, we might say to teammates, "Let's imagine we're all dead and buried at the bottom of the slope. How did it happen?" At that point, team members begin identifying how that outcome might come to pass, but on their own. After everyone has ripped skins, taken a drink, and prepared to ski, each member can share his reasons. Once we have a list of reasons, we ask ourselves, "Can we resolve these? Did we identify something we hadn't yet thought of? Why are we comfortable with this decision?"

It's a powerful tool, but one that requires buy-in and the time to perform it. The skimo crowd doesn't like long breaks, and sometimes teammates "just want to ski." Sometimes that's OK; other times, we should slow down in the moment and engage our mental tools.

HAPPY, HUNGRY, HEALTHY

I'm confident that all of you own the film *Predator*, the 1987 cinematic masterpiece directed by John McTiernan and starring Arnold Schwarzenegger

Multilingual Situations

Mountain guides, pilots, and adventurous skiers/riders end up taking their game farther afield. That means running into a bunch of cool people with accents, different languages, colorful one-piece outfits, and way different processes than we might use at home.

The Swiss Re Centre for Global Dialogue conducted a profound study of the aviation, nuclear, and medical fields, drawing commonalities from all three. In 2004 they published a white paper titled "The Better the Team, the Safer the World: Golden Rules of Group Interaction in High Risk Environments: Evidence Based Suggestions for Improving Performance."

After five years of exhaustive research and study, they delivered a fantastic document, one well worth reading and digesting. It highlights the need for functioning, collaborative teams in high-stakes industries. Discussing the role of language in pilot interactions, they published research showing decision making and reaction times were negatively impacted by trying to process information in a second language. Whenever possible, they recommend, practitioners should consume, discuss, and process information in their native language. Interacting and deciding among teammates of different linguistic backgrounds slows and decreases the quality of decisions.

At the time of writing, my family and I have just moved to France, and I can verify that trying to incorporate information with my unbearably heinous French is a difficult task. Turns out it is for all of us working in foreign languages. Keep this fact in mind when interacting in another language.

and Jesse "The Body" Ventura. During my monthly screening of the film (my wife loves this), I particularly enjoy the scene during which the team has encountered the alien/predator. Ventura, having sustained a small injury during an artfully rendered gunfight with the monster, bleeds from his arm. A teammate remarks, "You're hit!"

Ventura, former US Navy SEAL, governor of Minnesota, and professional wrestling superstar, merely remarks, "I ain't got time to bleed."

They don't make movies like they used to, folks.

My point here, now that you've returned from your Google machines and have watched the clip (how awesome was that!), is that a hungry, bummed-out, injured teammate won't be making very good decisions—unless he's basically a superhero like Ventura.

We need to account for that during our time in the field. Low blood sugar, dehydration, or extreme weather, just to name a few things, can all derail decision making. Consider more distant influences too, like poor sleep, relationship strife, or a sick child. These can be immensely distracting problems in our lives. Check in often, and pay attention. These things matter, and the science shows they affect our decisions more than we let on.

BLIND SPOTS AND THE OUTSIDE VIEW

We're going to have blind spots, personally and as a team. Many of you have probably heard of "The Monkey Business Illusion." If you haven't, go back to YouTube (it's still open on your machine, I assume) and visit youtube.com/watch?v=IGQmdoK_ZfY. No cheating. Follow the exercise.

Half of people "fail." Note, too, that when you're anchored to a task or term, your brain actively seeks to solve or confirm it and your awareness narrows. Funny on the internet, potentially deadly in the field.

In aviation, this narrowing of awareness is related to excessive "workload"; that is, the number and complexity of tasks a pilot must manage at the moment. The FAA trains pilots to decrease workload in the event of an emergency. Have someone else read a checklist, let the first officer fly the plane while you try to maintain panoramic awareness, etc.

If I ask myself "How will I die today?" and answer that in my notebook, have I set myself up to miss something else? Maybe. It's a risk. It comes back to the team—our teammates are our best hope to fill in our individual and collective blind spots. And a team made up of individuals with diverse talents can provide a solid defense against blind spots. The devil's advocate will help, as well as an open culture of discussion.

Another mindset to adopt during planning and touring is one of the "outside view." The inside view prioritizes our skills, our observations, and what we know. It's easy to become attached to our own prowess and knowledge, but how often do we pause and ask the simple question, "What has happened to other people in this situation?"

Focusing only on our or our team's experience can be termed "ego-induced blindness," or you might call it a version of closed-mindedness. Taking an outside view allows you to jump out of our own limited experience and ask, "What generally happens to people in this situation?"

Imagine a crew of riders who regularly trigger avalanches. A couple members of their team have been caught before, maybe even injured. They've had numerous near misses. Some of those near misses even get categorized as "We knew where the line was; we're so good, we knew how to stay on the safe side of the line."

Now, step back and ask yourself, "What eventually happens to a team that's involved in a couple avalanches every year? That's always right up against 'the line'?"

Usually nothing good, my friends. By taking the outside view or jumping up to a bird's-eye or "30,000-foot perspective," you snap out of your own little world and open yourself to broader experience and more evidence.

"Recognize the signs that you are in a cognitive minefield, slow down, and ask for reinforcement from System 2. . . . The best we can do is a compromise," advises Kahneman, adding, "Learn to recognize situations in which mistakes are likely and try harder to avoid significant mistakes."

Slow down, try harder, rely on smart, open-minded teammates. And remember, we don't know what we don't know. An outside view might at least remind us of that.

THINKING IN BETS

Having made millions playing poker, Annie Duke knows a thing or two about making decisions in high-stakes situations. Today she writes on the topic of decision making and team building.

She shares her strategies in *Thinking*, and you can probably already imagine quite a few situations in the backcountry when you need a high-quality decision but can't have all the facts about snowpack, weather, your team, and terrain.

Thinking in bets steers us away from black-and-white thinking, and if you ponder it for a moment, black-and-white thinking can lead to overconfidence. Rather than put all my faith in a yes-or-no answer, I try to slow down and do what Duke advises: Ask myself, "Am I willing to bet on this?" After I ask myself that, if I'm willing to bet on it, how sure am I of that bet? Now we've introduced uncertainty and probability to our decision. We might even ask, "How much am I willing to bet?"

Sure, with twin 10-year-olds in my family, we're constantly betting $25 million or 6 tons of ice cream. But honestly, in the field take your betting seriously. How sure are you that slope won't slide? That the danger will go green tomorrow? The ultimate wager, of course, is betting your life on a decision, which is precisely what we do day-in and day-out in consequential terrain.

DELIBERATE PRACTICE:
Write the words "Would you bet on it?" on a sticky note and post it on your computer or car's dashboard. Every time you make a shared, consequential decision over the next week, ask yourself or your partner/teammate/buddy, "Would you bet on it?" and then, "How much?" A variation is, instead of asking, "Are you sure?" ask, "How sure?" See if these prompts help you to identify uncertainty, confidence, and the consequences of a decision.

Putting a probability to the discussion reveals uncertainty, encourages discussion, and also hints at consequence. If I'm betting my life and I lose . . . well, you get the gist.

I find it a tremendously useful mindset, asking myself and others, "Would you bet on it? How much? Your life?" It certainly focuses the discussion.

Wrap-up

Hopefully some of the strategies, techniques, and mindsets above will assist you and your team in making better decisions. Some will work for you; some won't. No stress, just the exercise of seeing which approaches resonate with your team will improve your decision making and force you to evaluate your process.

Suggested reading at the end of the book provides connections to some of the source material for the research and thought, but I find it daunting to read so many books, let alone buy them. I find podcasts a great resource, so if any of the academics and authors intrigue you, put a name into your podcast app and give a listen during your next kamikaze training session. Mauboussin, Duke, Kahneman, Munger, Farnam Street—get some!

Repeatable Process and Riding Safely

The "Trip Planning" chapter described a repeatable process, drawing and building upon elements of the AIARE Risk Management Framework (RMF). The RMF is by no means the end-all of processes, checklists, and/or mental models. Any serious professional organization such as Canadian Mountain Holidays or your local hill's ski patrol has a repeatable process and employs it; do some digging and find one that works for you, or develop your own.

I won't rewind and revisit trip planning but simply reiterate that the trip plan, itself a repeatable process (or algorithm of sorts), is an invitation to slow down, put in some effort, discuss options, defeat bias, short-circuit human factors and heuristics, and make better decisions in the face of a wicked problem. A thorough, robust trip plan is nothing more or less than System 2 thinking—but only if you use one. It requires energy, time, devotion, integrity, and humility.

CHECKLISTS

You'll be decision making throughout the trip plan and once you're in the field. The AIARE approach suggests a "Ride Safely" checklist once you leave the trailhead. You probably already have a version of this checklist in your head and/or among your team. It's an invitation to keep making decisions, updating your information, and staying current.

The Ride Safely checklist or any process/checklist of your own can be integral to your backcountry practice. Simple checklists prove themselves time and time again. It's not a new concept—but any checklist only works if you use it.

Checklists Are Cool

by Joe Stock

You know about the human factor. It's why, despite all our smarts, we make stupid decisions, like getting caught in avalanches. The real question becomes: How do we avoid the human factor and *not* get caught in an avalanche?

Just knowing about human factors, including biases and heuristics, does little. It can actually lead to worse outcomes as you rationalize your bad decisions. Changing your behavior to avoid human factors is also next to impossible. Even Daniel Kahneman, the world authority on biases and heuristics, says that he is no better at avoiding them. But, Kahneman says, it is possible to put systems in place to avoid biases and heuristics. The system with the most bang for your buck at avoiding the human factors is checklists.

Checklists reduce the human factor in complex environments. Backcountry skiing was once simple. We'd forecast by looking out the window. We'd grab our skinny skis and tour into the quiet wilderness after low-angle turns. Now we forecast through a morass of too much information: social media, weather stations, weather forecasts, weather models, avalanche advisories, guidebooks, maps, and testosterone-ridden horn tooters. Then, in the backcountry, we gun for steep avalanche terrain along with the masses.

Checklists are ubiquitous in high-stakes fields such as aviation, combat, and ski guiding—where things are complex, and a mistake could be catastrophic. Our mind struggles to sift through all this complexity to make good decisions. Checklists help us find the signal in the noise.

The primary reason checklists work is they are simple reminders, assisting our memory and keeping us on task. Second, checklists help reduce the effects of biases and heuristics. They force us to slow down and engage our more rational, logical thought process that weasels out blind spots where the human factor lurks. For example, a ski partner is swayed by the dump of new snow and is chomping for aggressive terrain despite a "Considerable" avalanche danger rating. A checklist would prompt a bulletin discussion, which could thump logic into your aggro partner.

The most effective checklist for backcountry skiers is a morning checklist. This is how all professional ski guides operate, and so can recreational skiers. A morning checklist ensures that your team—yourself, if solo—discusses only the necessary items to make good decisions and nothing else.

To be effective, a checklist must be simple so that we actually use it. It needs to ask the correct questions to enable good decisions. Tailor a morning checklist that suits your process.

Morning Checklist

- ❑ Current weather
- ❑ Weather forecast bulletin
- ❑ Partners
- ❑ Route options
- ❑ Gear

The gear list is another effective checklist for backcountry skiers. We're all prone to forgetting gear, no matter our experience. We switch sports multiple times a day, moving from place to place. Make your gear list easy to use. Make it short and concise. Post it where it's unavoidable in your morning routine.

Checklists also work well when learning a new process, like learning to dig a full snow profile, for example. You'll organize and prioritize the process while building your checklist. After a few uses, you might not need it anymore.

Checklists work. Keep them short and simple. Make them easy to use. Tape a morning checklist to your coffee cup. Tape a gear checklist on the wall above your heap. Tape a discussion checklist to your steering wheel. With time, you may memorize your checklist. You won't eliminate the human factor, but you'll make a big dent in it.

Joe is an Anchorage, Alaska-based IFMGA mountain guide. He has been climbing and skiing around the world for thirty-five years. His current passions are skiing in the mountains around Anchorage, rock climbing vacations with his wife, and using himself as a case study for the misuse of biases in avalanche terrain.

Joe Stock COURTESY JOE STOCK

Alaska Guide Collective LLC
www.alaskaguidecollective.com

Backcountry Checklist

1 Have a Morning Meeting

- Current weather........increasing danger?
- Weather forecast......increasing danger?
- Advisory....................danger and problems
- Route options...........snowpack and team compatible?
- Team.........................human factors?
- Emergency contact...notified?
- Gear checklist
  - Beacon, shovel, probe
  - Boards, skins, poles
  - Boots, layers, puff coat
  - Hat, gloves, goggles
  - Sunglasses, sunscreen, sun hat
  - Water, food, headlamp
  - Communication, navigation, shelter
  - Repair, fire and first aid kits

2 D'BEAST Beacon Check

- "Turn beacons on. Check **display** and **battery** strength."
- "**Electronics** 20cm away in airplane mode?"
- "**Airbag** / Avalung?"
- "Everyone to **search**." Leader checks group.
- "**Transmit** and stow." Leader checks group.
- Watch leader go to transmit.

3 Know the Danger and Avalanche Problem

Low	Moderate	Considerable	High	Extreme

- Storm Slab
- Wind Slab
- Wet Slab
- Persistent Slab
- Deep Slab
- Dry Loose
- Wet Loose
- Cornice Fall
- Glide Avalanche

Warning: Proper use of this information requires expert training. The publisher cannot and does not guarantee the effectiveness of this information. The user of this guide acknowledges that he/she uses the content at his/her own risk.

Alaska Guide Collective's checklist for a day of backcountry touring

COURTESY ALASKA GUIDE COLLECTIVE

4 Field Observations

Red Flags

- Recent Avalanches
- Whumpfing
- Shooting Cracks
- Recent Heavy Precipitation
- Recent Wind Loading
- Rapid Thaw

Traveling Tests

- Feel Underfoot
- Ski Pole Probe
- Probe Test
- Hand Pit
- Test Slopes
- Skin Track Test

Pit Tests

- Snow Layers
- Extended Column Test

5 Choose Terrain

Green Light Terrain (usually safe terrain)	Less than 25 degrees, away from the runout of steeper terrain, low consequences.
Yellow Light Terrain (moderate terrain)	25-30 degrees, and/or in the runout of steeper terrain, and/or moderate consequences.
Red Light Terrain (dangerous terrain)	Greater than 30 degrees, and/or dangerous consequences.

6 Communicate at Safe Zones

- Is there a next safe zone?
- Is there a route is suitable for the danger?
- Spacing?
- What have we missed?
- Spotter, eyes on?

→ **In Doubt?...Turn Around!**

7 Debrief and Practice

- What mistakes did we make?
- How can we do better next time?
- What skills do we need to practice?

Warning: Proper use of this information requires expert training. The publisher cannot and does not guarantee the effectiveness of this information. The user of this guide acknowledges that he/she uses the content at his/her own risk.

COURTESY ALASKA GUIDE COLLECTIVE

"Even though people are capable of making decisions in a thorough and methodical way, it appears that most of the time they don't." McCammon wrote this in 2001–02 during his research on heuristics. You can almost hear the face-palm of consternation. Have we improved? There are some signs we have, notably the relatively flat rate of fatalities in the backcountry, despite the booming number of users. Maybe we've gotten the message?

Hopefully we have, but it remains to be seen. I've not seen any data regarding the prevalence of checklists and repeatable processes with backcountry users.

Once you leave the trailhead, the potential for snap decisions, quick heuristics, and degraded decision making spikes. Recall our "hungry, happy, healthy" check-in above. Add to this mad pow disease and any of Dale Atkins's human factors (overconfidence, attitude, etc.), and I don't think it's a stretch to call it a "cognitive minefield."

Rereading Atkins's opening paragraphs from "Human Factors" helps here:

> *On January 22, 1999, a 45-year-old Aspen, Colorado man was buried and killed in a very small avalanche triggered outside of the Aspen Highlands Ski Area. The night before the accident the victim and a friend spoke about skiing the backcountry outside of the ski area but agreed the avalanche conditions were too dangerous. The backcountry avalanche danger was rated "high" and a warning issued by the Colorado Avalanche Information Center was in effect. They decided to leave their transceivers and shovels at home. The next day the lure of fresh powder led the victim to venture outside the ski area. He completed two runs and experienced extensive instability with shooting cracks and collapsing snow. For his third run his friend (from the night before) joined him. Neither man carried avalanche rescue gear. After leaving the ski area boundary, both men experienced shooting cracks and collapsing snow. They triggered a small soft slab avalanche that buried the victim. With no rescue gear, it took almost an hour to find the man. Twelve days earlier the victim had been caught skiing in a closed avalanche area. Four days before his death the local newspaper published a "public apology" written by the victim. Regarding skiing in a closed avalanche area, he wrote: "This was inappropriate and irresponsible behavior . . . it was dangerous to myself and others."*
>
> —Reprinted with permission from Dale Atkins

Despite knowing better, we often fool ourselves, grow complacent, or simply surrender to the allure of deep snow and fun turns. It's simply too facile to call the above victim "an idiot." Chances are he and we are more alike than we want to admit. Despite having overwhelming feedback and evidence to make a sound decision, he didn't.

EXEMPTIONS

So what happened? We'll never know with the victim, but it's plain to see the gentleman and his friend had correctly identified the hazard, discussed it, had the wherewithal to observe and note unstable snow, and were receiving feedback throughout their day. They had a process going. And yet they chose to ride into an extremely risky situation: high avalanche danger in an uncontrolled area and without rescue equipment.

It's almost reflexive to immediately ask, "What were they thinking?!"

Such judgments, though, have more to do with comforting ourselves with the mistaken notion that we'd never make such errors in the field. I catch myself focusing on the moments before the "mistake," or "pilot error." Time and time again, though, people like you and me do make such errors, despite having read the bulletin and taken avalanche courses. Why?

"Students quietly exempt themselves from experiments that surprise them," warns Kahneman, again in *Thinking*.

It's the easiest "out" in the world to laugh it off and tell ourselves, "I'd never be so dumb." The science, however, says we might be. It's terribly seductive to exempt myself from bias, heuristics, and human factors, despite the research proving we are all susceptible to them. When reading accident descriptions like these, we need to remember to back up and review the process.

With hindsight and knowing the outcome, it seems surprising that the gentleman above knew of the danger, knew the terrain, had been publicly sanctioned for straying into closed terrain before, and still chose to forgo safety gear and dive into avalanche terrain under high danger and a CAIC warning. Let's not fool ourselves; we probably have more in common with the victim than not. What's protecting us in the months, days, hours leading up to a potential decision like this?

Team, process, checklists, and better decision making.

EFFORT AND IMPATIENCE

With Strava, FKTs (fastest known times), human factors and heuristics, and our plain passion for being in the mountains, we have an array of forces pulling us away from slower, effortful, System 2 decision making. The trick is knowing when to engage System 2.

Ask yourself a simple question: What has cost you more in life, patience or impatience?

Remember Kahneman's simple advice: "One basic rule is to slow down."

A glaring near miss of my own comes to mind. Two great guests and I had left Chamonix in the morning for bluer skies in Italy. After several phenomenal runs in the morning, followed by lunch at my half-brother's restaurant on the mountain in La Thuile, we headed out for another lap. The wind had picked up, the ceiling had dropped, and conditions were trending to more hazard.

I've toured at La Thuile a handful of times so don't know the terrain intimately. I knew a couloir parallel to one of our morning runs would probably have fresh and blown-in snow, so we headed there. The advantage on these slopes is the presence of Gazex units across the ridgeline. Deeper instabilities don't get the chance to linger.

Near the entrance, though, I wasn't sure of the exact drop-in. I felt the pressure of cold temps and icy wind—and paying customers. I found a quick way in. It was now blowing moderate to hard, and leaving guests on the ridge seemed less than ideal. The skiing, though! No tracks—paydirt! The start zone had wind-deposited snow in it. Cold, uncomfortable guests, quality skiing below our skis, an obvious wind-slab problem.

I told my teammates I'd wave for them to come down, slid out, stomped through a pocket of snow where I expected the worst wind slab to be, jump-turned, then cut back through it again. Nothing. I descended 50-ish meters of snow to a safe zone adjacent to the path. I turned to wave and watched the first guest slide out. He made a turn and descended—great skiing, but now the start zone I'd "expertly managed" looked way bigger than before, with enough untouched snow that I thought to myself, Uh . . .

His wife started her run. Sure enough, a table-size slab pulled out behind her and had enough mass to knock her down. A size 1, but enough to knock a skier over. Not lethal, but definitely an oversight. She tumbled once, got up, and finished the run. She and I were lucky that day; we didn't get the big surprise. She didn't seem too fazed about the affair, but I was.

An extra 60 seconds and I could've evaluated the start zone, dug a quick hand-pit, or even just crisscrossed the start zone a couple more times. A slab that size, triggered from above, would've been a nonevent, but I'd let impatience dictate my actions. Luckily for us, backcountry touring rarely has an urgent time limit—unlike firefighters, fighter pilots, and ER docs, we have minutes to make decisions. I should've reminded myself of that and taken the time. Patience.

SITUATIONAL AWARENESS

Backstopping our decision making should be a commitment to the reality of the situation at hand. If we input invalid data (team, snow, weather, and avalanche observations, for example) to our algorithm, it will return invalid strategies and solutions.

Maintaining situational awareness helps us adapt throughout the day, error correct, and revise our plans—but only if we take the time to do it. Building in decision points, checking in with the team, and using a notebook will all help. If the weather forecast calls for increasing winds, maintaining situational awareness should include making weather and snowpack observations. A quick note, jotted in your fieldbook, will help you to remember this, even when the riding is all-time, 5/5, or just plain "epic, bro."

Opposite: Jen and Steve, after our morning run in La Thuile. We'd return later, after a great lunch, but with stormy skies and winds picking up. ROB COPPOLILLO

Decision Making and the Debrief

You and your team just pulled on the cognitive armor of pre-biasing, de-biasing, and making bulletproof decisions. Take it from me, you're still going to end the day with nagging doubts and maybe even the unpleasant realization that you blew it. I sure have, and I will again. Oh, the miserable uncertainty! So, now what?

We take our trip plan, our notes from the day, our culture of respectful collaboration, and we perform an efficient, productive debrief. Try to remind yourself of all the free debrief wisdom we discussed in that chapter. It's our commitment to improving daily. Remember kaizen, improving just 1 percent a day. Your touring, movement skill, and decision making will improve in leaps and bounds. The debrief delivers those gains, so make it happen.

And we're going to need it. Next I peer over the edge into the steeps, drawing on the expertise of some world-class guides. Terrain like this requires the best from us.

CHAPTER 7

Steep Skiing

Consequences are unpitying.

—George Eliot

Success is a consequence and must not be a goal.

—Gustave Flaubert

In nature there are neither rewards nor punishments; there are consequences.

—Robert Green Ingersoll

All of us eventually wonder, "How steep can I go?" The latest snow films come out in fall and, without fail, seduce us with images of brave and daring humans linking turns down 55-degree slopes. In fact, steep terrain captures the imagination of everyone from NASCAR fans in front of the TV to experienced riders hollering in theaters. For most, it's a spectator sport, but for a few adventurous kooks . . .

Riding in "no-fall" terrain requires extra care, prep, and vigilance. Skiers like Glen Plake or Joe Vallone, guys who might look a little cowboy at first glance, actually spend days, weeks, or years planning and watching a serious line before committing to it.

For the adventurous recreationist, the requirements are barely less than that of a mountain guide taking guests into serious terrain. Errors in this arena often end in injury or worse. And guiding in this terrain can feel like guiding free-soloing on rock. Consider that before taking guests onto the steeps.

This chapter hopes to share ideas to help you prepare, as an ambitious skier or as a guide, for steep terrain. I'll lean heavily on more experienced guides and better skiers than I: Joe Vallone, one of Doug Coombs's protégés and an IFMGA mountain guide since 2005; splitboarder pioneers Benja Glatz and Rob Hopkins; and AMGA-certified ski guide and free-skiing legend Mike Hattrup, star of the film *Blizzard of Ahhhs*.

First we'll look at gear, then movement, and then some guiding techniques that recreationists might consider modifying and incorporating into their own practice.

An early season descent of the "Pan de Redeau" on La Meije, above La Grave, France. A descent like this—a 50-degree entrance above no-fall terrain, crevasses and a bergschrund to negotiate, and ample early season snow—requires humility, detailed preparation, and expert awareness of the subtleties involved. La Grave local Joe Vallone styles the final meters above the 'schrund. ROB COPPOLILLO

A word on steep skiing and many of the techniques discussed below. None of this is a good idea. Few of these technical systems have been rigorously tested and studied. Everything here requires years of deliberate practice, dedication, refinement, and controlled application before using them in the field. Merely reading a book and sending a few couloirs does not graduate a person into the ranks of a true steep skier. Go slowly; proceed with caution. Dying for a ski line is not worth it. Think about consequences.

The Gear

My wife thinks I'm insane. The boots, the ice axes, the goggles, the harnesses, *the frickin' skis*. "Do you really need all this stuff?" she asks. Need versus want—the great question! Whatever the case, specialized gear has revolutionized every aspect of skiing and splitboarding. We'd be crazy not to use the best gear possible for steep skiing. Let's look at some of it and discuss the why, how, and where of it, before moving on to how we use it.

Hard Goods

I'll recount some general thoughts here, but keep in mind that much of this is personal preference. There's some loose agreement about sidecut, width, flex, weight, and length for steep skiing, but since your life depends on staying upright and balanced, you need to verify for yourself what works. Forget what the people in the movies are slaying on—find your trusted kit and use it.

LENGTH, WIDTH, AND SIDECUT

In general, the days of 70-millimeter-waisted skis are long gone, except if you're wearing Lycra and chasing skinny people uphill. As ski widths have grown, lengths have come down, and steep skiing is no exception.

For truly steep skiing—let's call it 45 degrees-plus—most people choose a ski 5 to 10 centimeters shorter than their regular touring setup and with a waist between 80 and 90 millimeters. A shorter ski provides more maneuverability in confined features and less swing weight, meaning you can whip them around more quickly. Enough waist underfoot gives you a good platform and versatility in variable snow, without being too unwieldy on superfirm conditions. You might consider going a bit narrower as things firm up; too wide a ski will feel awkward and unbalanced without edge penetration.

On the steepest lines, 50 degrees or more, too narrow a ski will result in the outside of your ski boot contacting the slope on your uphill side and actually pushing you off your edge. You don't want to "boot out," according to Mike Hattrup. This pertains to very few of us skiing in the mountains. Be realistic with yourself about how much this matters.

Sidecut comes down to personal preference. Joe Vallone, who lives and works in one of the steep-ski meccas in Europe, La Grave, rides with a bit more sidecut than most. His preferred steep ski as of this writing is a Dynastar Mythic 97 Pro (133/97/113 tip/waist/tail dimensions in millimeters, in a 177cm ski, 1,400g/ski), with a turn radius of 15 meters. He thinks this is a bit more sidecut and a lower turn radius than the average charger uses, but he loves the edge hold and quickness of the ski edge to edge.

For a couple other reference points, I find a Blizzard ZeroG 95 (128/95/111mm, in a 178cm ski, 1,200g/ski) a great steep ski. The 95-millimeter ZeroG has a 20-meter turn radius. It's superior to its little brother, an 85-millimeter-waisted model, for some of the reasons listed above. Hattrup, an AMGA-certified ski guide and the US alpine product manager for Fischer Sports, will ride a Fischer Transalp 82-millimeter-waisted

Booting Out

If pushing beyond 50 degrees sounds like your cup of tea, I salute you. At these angles, consider your ski choice carefully. On 50-plus-degree slopes, if you're riding too narrow a ski, your ski boots' uphill edges will contact the slope before your ski—effectively pushing your ski away from the slope and denying you edge grip. At least one manufacturer as of this writing makes a "steep-specific" ski and delivers it with a 100-millimeter waist precisely to avoiding "booting out." Worth considering? If you're truly going that steep, maybe so.

Steep Splitboarding Gear

By Rob Hopkins

Rob Hopkins COURTESY ROB HOPKINS

As a splitboarder I certainly enjoy surfing bottomless glades or tagging a new summit, but there is no substitute for the feeling you get from standing on top of something steep, watching the world fall away below you, nervously anticipating your descent down an improbable patch of snow.

With this type of riding, snow quality is often variable, and features such as cliffs and rock walls limit your descent options. This is when you need total confidence in your abilities and gear.

Boots are the most important component of your kit. Your boots are the only piece of gear that supports your entire weight all day, and if they don't fit properly, you don't have fun.

Comfort is therefore the top priority, but aim for something a little on the stiff side. A more rigid boot transfers more force from your weaker foot and ankle muscles to your stronger calf and quad muscles, which gives you more power and control when riding at speed. As an added bonus, a stiffer boot will also make bootpacking a little less exhausting on your calves.

The binding is the channel through which your boot and your board communicate, and as such, the key is to use a stiffer model to maximize responsiveness. A softer binding will mute board feel while providing no benefit to your riding, assuming you aren't hitting rails or tweaking methods!

Finally, the board. When choosing a splitboard for steep riding, a hybrid shape with camber underfoot and a rocker nose is ideal. Camber offers superior stability and control since it gives you a longer effective edge to slice into harder snow compared with a reverse-camber board of the same length. The rocker nose will give you some float in deeper snow without sacrificing the grip provided by the camber underfoot.

Board flex is based more on personal preference, but again you should tend toward the stiffer end of what is comfortable for you to maximize control and minimize edge slippage.

With regard to size, use the manufacturer sizing charts to narrow it down to a length range that suits your body, then choose a size that works best for your riding style and favorite terrain.

Holding all else equal, a shorter board will be lighter and easier to maneuver in tight couloirs, while a longer board will be more stable for charging fast and dropping cliffs.

Most importantly, get to know your gear! Dial it in on something mellow, then get out there and charge!

Rob Hopkins is a CAA Level 1 certified splitboarder and was previously ranked first in Canada on the Freeride World Qualifier circuit. He has been snowboarding for twenty years and exploring the backcountry for nearly half that time. Born and bred in the Canadian Rockies, his favorite pastime is hunting for steep and skinny couloirs.

ski in a 169-centimeter length (117/81/107mm; 1,050g/ski; 15.5m turn radius).

This is not an endorsement of particular skis or brands, but rather an indication that there's a "ball park" into which most steep skis fall these days. You need to find your own sweet spot. Black Crows, for example, makes a 100-millimeter steep-specific ski. Experiment, and find your trusted planks.

When it comes to rocker versus camber, most skiers prefer a bit of early rise in the shovel and even a bit less in the tail. Too much tip/tail rocker sacrifices edge contact on the snow. A bit of early rise helps manage variable snow and also releases the ski into a turn more easily. Keep in mind that forefathers like Sylvain Saudan, Anselme Baud, and Pierre Tardivel skied long, skinny, traditionally cambered skis. Wow! Watching those killers descend the craziest faces in the Alps on that gear reminds me that it's skill and mentality more than rocker and sidecut. All the skis mentioned above are lightly early rise in the shovel and barely early rise in the tail.

In summary: A bit shorter, reasonable sidecut and turn radius, reasonable weight, and phenomenal edge hold are what you're looking for. Throw in an early-rise tip and you're probably close to a good steep ski.

BOOTS

The bottom line for almost any footwear is what performs best . . . for you. Keep in mind you'll often be booting to get to steep lines, so your fit needs to allow for step-kicking, potentially in firm snow. If your toe can tap the front of your liner in the shop, you will lose your toenails in the field. This will ruin your bikini look come summer. Be advised.

Warmth and comfort matter, and the boot must perform really well. Every bit of marketing copy ever written promises you all this and more. Don't believe any of it. Ask what your friends are riding, see what gets good reviews, and try it. Your boots have to be dialed.

"I never thought I'd be skiing something this minimalist," says Hattrup of his 1,000-gram Fischer touring boot.

Indeed, at 1,000 grams, Hattrup's Fischer boot is about as light as you can get. Keep in mind that his ski skill might be a tad higher than, say, almost all of ours, but don't feel like a 130-flex boot is the call. Try what you can, and make sure it's a boot in which you can ski well and climb proficiently.

Dynafit, SCARPA, and others also make exceptionally good, circa-1-kilogram boots. And like Hattrup, many riders remove the lighter "stock" liners to add a slightly heavier, but warmer and better-skiing, aftermarket liner, such as an Intuition. While it might add a few grams, the additional warmth and performance more than make up for it. Back to the boot fitter you go!

Fischer's Travers Carbon boot
COURTESY FISCHER SPORTS

Beyond those criteria, make sure your boot matches your ski in terms of flex. By this I mean, a 130-flex boot atop a 1,200-gram ski is probably not going to work very well. If the ski is so light or short you can't drive it hard enough to flex the boot, guess what—you end up in the back seat because you can't flex your ankle forward. The back seat in steep terrain leads to carnage—and carnage is undesirable.

Too flexy and light a boot, on the other hand, means you'll fold forward and feel unstable. Time, experimentation, and testing will reveal the right combo for you.

"You're not going 30 miles per hour," says Hattrup of riding

45-plus-degree terrain. "You need something that you can push on the tongue and not fold it, that'll be consistent and fight through some irregularities in the snow, but you don't need a 130-flex boot. Even in perfect corn, I'm going 10 miles per hour, max. The better skier you are, the less (weight) you can get away with. The fresher you are at the top, too, the better off you are."

And get your boots custom fit, will you, please? Find a knowledgeable, trained boot fitter who's accustomed to working with backcountry skiers more than alpine racers, and pay him or her handsomely. You will thank yourself—and ski better too!

BINDINGS

To tech or not to tech, that is the question. This topic provokes strong emotions. Almost all of us tour on "tech" or "pin" bindings; that is, a version of the original Dynafit "Low Tech" bindings designed and made by Austrian Fritz Barthel. As we inch into steep terrain, though, some folks find these amazingly lightweight bindings inadequate.

Some of the raddest lines on the planet have been skied on tech bindings. Despite weighing almost nothing, most people have a fine time skiing everything but bumps on tech bindings. An integral feature to these featherweights is the ability to lock out the toe. This practice also elicits passionate responses, but for steep skiing, most everyone I know locks the toes. A prereleased or unexpected eject from a ski will mean certain doom, so steep skiers accept the risk of a knee injury with the added security of a locked toe. Devil's bargain, and probably worth it.

Once you're out of no-fall terrain, I'd recommend unlocking the toe. There are still some people who advocate skiing locked-out all the time, but this heightens the risk of a knee injury too much for my liking. Evan Stevens, IFMGA mountain guide and AMGA ski examiner, exploded a knee skiing "locked" and says he avoids it now, except in spring conditions. Evan charges and is well over 6 feet tall; if he can make it work, we can too.

There are, however, a vocal minority of folks who experience "prerelease" on tech bindings; obviously, for them, steep skiing on the things won't work, psychologically as much as physically. For these senders, various manufacturers offer models relying on everything from modified tech designs to lighter frame bindings, similar to alpine bindings, but with a tour function. For mechanized steep skiing, some riders just use alpine bindings.

Pick your poison, have a knowledgeable ski tech install your bindings, and inspect them regularly.

POLES

You guessed it, personal preference. That said, keep a few things in mind.

First, adjustable/collapsible poles run the risk of doing what they're designed to do: adjust or collapse at the worst possible moment. Riding deep pow in Canada, who cares? Initiating a pedal-hop turn on steep,

Les Batons d'Alain ROB COPPOLILLO

bulletproof snow, though, and the last thing you want is your pole going from 125 to 105 centimeters without warning. Don't risk it!

Fixed-length poles provide a better "push off" from which to initiate a hop turn. Carbon fiber might not be the best call, given its fragility (and cost) compared to aluminum. The rage now is fixed-length aluminum, with an extended foam grip, allowing a skier to adjust her hand position while skiing. The most popular of these, known as "Les Batons d'Alain" (LBA), were designed by steep skier, mountain guide, and Cham local Alain Desez. They've become standard gear for steep skiers—and anyone wanting a cool souvenir from Chamonix!

On steep terrain, as we'll see when discussing technique with Vallone, your hand position is critical; the steepness of the slope greatly shortens your uphill pole, while lengthening your downhill pole. Consider the LBA if you find a "regular" ski pole awkward to manage.

Now ask yourself if you prefer pole straps. They protect against a dropped pole, as well as help you affix your poles to your pack and skis when booting. The downsides, though, are numerous: You can't adjust your grip with your wrist locked in a strap. We also teach students not to use pole straps for most backcountry skiing, as you want to get rid of skis and poles in the event of an avalanche. (This last point matters less in steep skiing—if you're worried about avalanching, you shouldn't be steep skiing in the first place.)

All this is to say, put some thought into your poles and how you use them. Forgoing straps is an option, but definitely not a rule.

PACK

Don't stress too much about your backpack, as long as it's of a reasonable weight and doesn't shift around on your back. You'll want to revisit organization, as it's more important on the steeps than in "plain" touring.

In steep skiing, you want weight as close to your body as possible. This means packing your gear carefully. Anything heavy needs to go along your back and lower in the pack, nearer your lumbar than your shoulder blades. Crampons, water, a repair kit, or anything with significant mass needs to be tightly packed, without potential to slide or swing. Pack conscientiously, then compress the pack so it can't shift, jostle, or swing while skiing. Having anything moving/sliding around means you will expend energy to maintain balance against a moving mass. Not good! Imagine walking a slack line or climbing a delicate slab pitch with a liter of water (1 kilogram) swinging from your waist. Losing your balance is not an option in the terrain we're managing here.

Experiment with carrying skis and gear before getting into the serious business. I mention some ideas on ski-carrying in the "Up" chapter. Comfort, efficiency, and security all factor in.

And the Rest?

I often joke that I'm an expert at spending other people's money. Now that I've sent you out to spend $3,500 on new skis, boots, and poles, why not blow another grand on some sharp stuff and maybe a sexy harness too?

If you have the cash, then go for it. I've got quite a nice stash of superlight CAMP harnesses, crampons, and axes. I have to say, though, I've never skied something because of "rad gear." I only mention this to take the emphasis off acquiring new stuff and try to put it back onto skill and preparation. Let's outfit ourselves, but training and homework will serve us better than shiny stuff!

BOOTING, THEN RIDING, WITH GEAR

Anything truly steep, you should boot it first, if possible. This gives you a preview and intimate contact with the snow surface. Shallow rocks? Hidden ice? Runnels? Punchy snow? You need to know what will be under your edges.

Either way, coming top-down or having booted the slope, you'll want to descend with some measure of security at hand. You might be wearing a harness and carrying an ice screw for glacier skiing. The newer, aluminum screws save significant weight. You'll want a sling or two, stored compactly (not dangling!) on your harness, perhaps a lightweight belay/rappel device, and another locking carabiner. More gear than that (for a crevasse rescue, for example), I store inside my pack in an accessible stuff sack. If you think you'll need rock gear, decide if you can stash it.

You may or may not have a rope with you, depending on the terrain you're managing. We'll obsess a bit over specific ropes and materials in the "Technical Solutions" chapter, but if you're carrying a cord, have it easily accessible. The rope, too, will weigh quite a bit, even a super-skinny one, when compared to the rest of your gear. Some skiers elect to mountaineer-coil their cord and wear it around their neck and under their arms. This leaves the rope accessible and keeps the weight distributed over, and close to, one's body. You might prefer to simply Kiwi-coil the rope and tie it off while skiing. If you don't foresee needing it on the descent, another option is to stack it loose inside the pack, with just a tail exiting the top or a side-zip. In the event you want it, simply grab the free end and pull it from the pack—ideally without removing the backpack.

An ice ax can be a literal lifesaver on the up or down, and skiing with one takes a little practice. A couple backpacks exist that allow you to access an ax without removing the backpack, but most people simply "shoulder" their ax. Take your piolet, hold the head, and point the spike toward your collarbone. Your arm is away from you, with the shaft of the ax pointing toward you, and the spike touching your chest, just above the sternum strap of your pack. Now, slide the spike underneath your shoulder strap, above the sternum strap, and continue over your shoulder. Once the head of the ax arrives at your body, the shaft should be pointing behind you, over your shoulder. Pivot the head around and behind your neck so the shaft of the ax is now pointing down, toward the snow. The head of the ax should nest behind your neck and on top of the pack's shoulder straps.

Remember it if/when you take off the pack! If you simply remove your pack, the ax will fall through the shoulder strap and to the snow—and probably down the face or couloir. To guard against this, some climbers and skiers rig the ax slightly differently. They slide the shaft downward, through the haul loop, so the head is again behind the neck, but the ax slides between your back and the backpack. This secures the ax a bit more. This isn't quite as easy to do as the classic method, but it works for some pack-ax combinations.

A short (45- to 50-centimeter) piolet stashes unobtrusively under your pack's shoulder strap, allowing you to deploy it mid-slope if needed.

ROB COPPOLILLO

The type and weight of your ax will come down to your personal preference, but keep in mind that the lighter the ax, the less you can swing it into ice. Think about when and how you'll want an ice ax when riding—and don't skimp if you think you need a steel tool rather than aluminum or titanium.

Technique

This is not an instructional book on ski or splitboard movement. Great coaching exists out there, and it's way better communicated in the field with an astute instructor providing immediate feedback. That said, not sharing a few tips from a couple experts would be short-changing you.

First I'll look at movement skill as it pertains to you and me, and then in working with less experienced friends, club members, and/or our guests.

Aspen Extreme!

Joe Vallone comes from a background in freestyle in the '80s. After cutting his teeth in the "Aspen Extreme" days, he pursued mountain guiding and earned the highest certification possible, his IFMGA "pin." He now lives in La Grave and guides steep terrain as much as anybody I know.

I had Joe Vallone's attention during the off-season, so I capitalized on it. Huge thanks to him for sharing his approach. This is, again, one method for approaching steep skiing and working in steep terrain. It's undoubtedly biased toward American, French, and Canadian techniques. Steal what you like, practice in non-consequential terrain, and ease into the real thing.

MODERN STEEP SKIING

If you haven't watched films of the steep-skiing pioneers, give yourself an early holiday present and search online for "Anselme Baud," "Sylvain Saudan," or "Patrick Vallençant." Saudan, the "*skieur de l'impossible*," is considered one, if not *the*, ancestor of steep skiing. Riding 205-centimeter skis with leather boots in the late '60s, at first local guides in Chamonix wouldn't believe the slopes he'd ridden. Over time, though, he pioneered the art and madness of skiing extremely steep terrain. Watch video of him skiing routes that even today merit a "Wow" from the locals.

Nowadays, even entry-level gear offers superior performance to what Monsieur Saudan and his contemporaries used. Modern equipment and techniques have changed the game, but it's no less consequential. We need to develop near-perfect technique, whether we're sliding into the Gervasutti Couloir on Mont Blanc du Tacul or eyeing the north face of Buckner in the Cascades. So watch the masters of yesteryear work, but let's try to update some of their techniques.

THE POSITION

As you ease into steeper and steeper terrain, you'll want to commit to some basic techniques and tactics. First, do not find yourself leaning into the slope. You need to be balanced in the center of your skis, out over your feet and bindings. On the steepest slopes, this will feel as if you are leaning into the abyss. If you find yourself unable to commit to this position, you simply aren't ready for that steep a slope. No shame—we've all been there, most of all me!

With that balanced position, now we need to keep our shoulders mostly squared to the fall line so that your shoulders are generally facing downhill, with your skis across the slope, perpendicular to the fall line. You'll see and probably already know this requires fantastic upper- and lower-body separation. If you aren't familiar with this term, then pursue some coaching, watch some videos, practice on piste, and get it done.

Having your shoulders facing (mostly) downhill, with your skis

Doug Coombs would be proud: Joe Vallone during a series of balanced, controlled turns on the "Pan de Redeau" above La Grave. He has turned around his pole, traveling down the slope rather than across. That pole has now folded forward. In the photo, it's his uphill hand. His downhill pole is already reaching for the next turn. Upper body mechanics like this keep his shoulders squared to the fall line and his head looking downhill. His lower body moves separately. As his skis come around, he angles his lower legs to engage his edges and control his downhill momentum. After several controlled turns to demo the technique and feel the snow, he has the confidence to open it up and link larger, aggressive turns to just above the bergschrund.
ROB COPPOLILLO

across the slope, sets you up to reach downslope for your next pole plant and provides dynamic tension between your trunk and legs. You'll use this tension to initiate and execute a fast, fluid, powerful turn.

THE TURN

While watching the heroics of our steep-ski ancestors, you'll see them performing wild turns on 200-centimeter-long skis, perched on slopes many would be psyched to climb with ice tools. Indeed, reading Saudan's descriptions of his early techniques gives us a glimpse of how different these brave riders approached steep terrain. He describes adapting his alpine technique by leaning back to load the tails of his skis then whipping them around like a windshield wiper. In leather boots. Whoa!

Eventually steep skiers like Patrick Valleçant and Anselme Baud evolved the technique, modernizing it to something more familiar to us. For a modern turn, we want to maintain our balanced, centered position, staying in the "sweet spot" of our skis. Remember too that our skis might be slightly shorter than our freeriding boards. Our sweet spot will be even smaller, so a balanced, controlled stance is critical.

We separate our upper and lower bodies too. We don't let our pole planting disrupt the turning of our

Check Your Position

Here's an exercise to help establish "the position." Stand with your skis across the slope, perpendicular to the fall line. Have a ski partner stand below and downhill of you. Let her grab your pole baskets and try to pull you off-balance and downhill. You'll naturally set your edges and have your shoulders square to her, resisting her downward pull.

This little trick puts you into a powerful position, with edges set firmly (as if you're controlling your descent on a 50-degree slope) and your shoulders square to the fall line. Keep in mind during this little drill that you might also tend to lean back, toward the slope (in a tug-of-war with your buddy; she's strong, eh?!). Avoid that temptation, and try to maintain a balanced, strong stance *without* leaning backward. You'll know you're leaning back if your partner lets go without warning and you fall uphill and into the slope.

legs. Watch a slalom skier and how she mows down gates with her arms while her legs go edge to edge and turn. Indeed, if you couldn't see her lower half, it would be difficult to imagine how dynamic her turns are, given how controlled her upper body is. We're striving for that same separation as we get into turning.

Our modern turn leaves the shovels of our skis as much in contact with the snow surface as possible as they come around. Our upper body is quiet and we don't travel across the slope, just down the fall line, setting our edges to control our speed after each turn. This puts us in position for the next turn.

We prep for the next turn by planting our downhill pole firmly, approximately in line with the heel of our downhill ski. Our uphill pole also plants firmly, but slightly forward of our uphill foot. We use the poles to push into the snow, helping us to unweight the skis and initiate the turn.

The skis now come around, the shovels maintaining light contact with the slope, our tails pivoting around us. We lift the uphill arm to reach forward and become the downhill arm. (More on this in a moment, but the arm that starts downhill stays planted, and as we pivot around it, the arm "folds" forward.)

The skis end the turn with solid, committed edge pressure to stop or control our downhill momentum. The upper body remains quiet through the turn, to keep our momentum directly downslope, in the fall line. Any flailing of our upper body threatens to

Head facing downhill, shoulders square, downhill pole planted below and even with the heels, in a controlled position—he's ready to initiate a turn. ROB COPPOLILLO

Here Vallone is starting to release his edges; he's planted his downhill pole and he's ready to turn around that pole, letting it fold forward with his turn. Note that he is looking straight down the fall line and his uphill (left) arm stays forward. The angle here has eased from near 50 to merely high 40s—for him, relaxed terrain; for the rest of us, "real" skiing. ROB COPPOLILLO

Mid-turn, Vallone maintains contact between his shovels and the snow surface, and his shoulders stay square to the fall line. Compare his position against the skyline—he has scarcely moved across the slope. Rather, he descends slightly but generates no momentum across the fall line. This keeps him in control and tight, setting him up for another precise turn. ROB COPPOLILLO

The skis pivot around his pole; his left arm drives forward to initiate the next pole plant while the right arm and pole fold forward. His eyes still focus down the fall line, and he's slightly forward on his skis. This is safe, controlled skiing above an open bergschrund a couple hundred meters more to the runout. ROB COPPOLILLO

Completing the turn, Vallone is already reaching downhill with his left arm to pole-plant and initiate the next turn. His right (now uphill) arm folds forward and points down the fall line, forcing his shoulders to remain square and down the slope. Again, note that he has traveled downhill, but scarcely across the fall line. ROB COPPOLILLO

complicate our balance. Channel your inner Mikaela Shiffrin and keep your torso, shoulders, and arms quiet!

If we can link these turns fluidly, we're sending. On the steepest terrain, you might make a single turn and come to a complete stop, controlling your downhill momentum.

THE COOMBS "FOLDING POLE"

Now we'll address the subtlety of the pole plant. In alpine skiing, the pole plant often derails the new skier's turn. You see this from the chairlift, a newer skier over-rotating his shoulders and exaggerating the pole plant from side to side. This is why expert ski instructors sometimes give skiers "drills" to do without the poles, which in turn helps them perfect their lower body movements before integrating them with their upper body/pole plants.

Steep skiing has its own particular technique, the "folding pole plant."

"Invented by the one and only Doug Coombs," explains Vallone. "You turn around your downhill pole, not across the fall line. This is not a jump turn. The downhill/planted pole folds forward to allow us to come around. The new downhill arm is already reaching or it's ready to reach for the next turn."

Mid-turn, with the skis in the fall line. This is when skiers sometimes lose their nerve and lean back, or uphill. No! Recognize how Vallone keeps his eyes and shoulders facing downhill; he's attacking the slope. He's fully committed. He'll fold his left arm forward and finish the turn around it. ROB COPPOLILLO

Finishing a turn, Vallone's uphill (left) arm is folding the pole forward, while his right arm is already forward and reaching for the next pole plant. His lower body has turned his skis perpendicular to the fall line, controlling his speed. On a slope like this, with good ski-pen for positive turns, Vallone would normally begin linking longer, "GS" turns, but I asked nicely and he demo'd some Coombs folding pole for us. ROB COPPOLILLO

"The steeper it gets, the more people lean back to 'sit' on the snow," cautions Vallone. "Minimize the jump and keep your shovels in contact with the snow. You don't want to go too far down the fall line."

Another aspect of the folding pole (discovered, to me, as Vallone coached me to improve it!) is that it forces you to keep your hand pointing downhill. As you turn around the pole and fold it, you must keep your now-uphill shoulder square to the fall line and your hand pointing downhill, which keeps you in a controlled, balanced, and aggressive position.

You can find video of Coombs skiing online. Search and watch his technique, paying particular attention to the upper-lower body separation as well as the folding pole.

THE PEDAL-HOP TURN

Remember our definition of steep here is 45-plus degrees. Most instructional videos and steep-ski lessons tackle terrain well under 40 degrees. Well worth practicing, but keep in mind that "real" terrain requires different techniques.

Modern ski-mountaineers have evolved past the jump turns of the 1970s, refining the technique to a dynamic unweighting of the skis, pivoting around the folding pole, and controlling their descent. A very, very select few, like Jérémie Heitz, Vivian Bruchez, Sam Anthamatten, and others, can link traditional alpine turns on 50-plus-degree terrain, but I'd caution against attempting that until . . . well, you'll know when to get after it.

For us mere mortals, we can rely on the pedal-hop turn. Grainy footage going back to Valleçant's days illustrate this technique. Reserved for extremely steep terrain, it's a means to control our downhill momentum and get our skis around as quickly as possible.

1. We start the turn in our balanced, controlled stance, weight on the downhill ski, shoulders mostly down the fall line, downhill pole planted firmly by our downhill ski's heelpiece, uphill pole closer to our uphill ski's toepiece.
2. Before we initiate our turn, we transfer weight from our downhill ski to our uphill ski. Do this by loading the uphill ski edge and ever so slightly straightening the leg. As we do this, it releases our downhill ski. We lift this ski and begin to turn it, maintaining light contact with the tip as it pivots.
3. As the unweighted downhill leg begins the turn, we're simultaneously loading our poles. Our poles take a bit of our weight, and our uphill leg straightens a bit to take the rest of our weight. We energetically and swiftly lift our uphill ski and let it follow the downhill leg to pivot around our downhill pole.
4. The uphill leg pivots around to become our downhill leg. Our planted pole begins to fold downhill, down the fall line, allowing us to pivot around it and lose altitude. We land on our downhill leg with commitment and control. As we do this, our new downhill pole reaches for the next turn.

Baton Ramasse

Adapted from traditional use of the piolet, we can use the spikes of our poles similarly to the spike on our ax. Simply face both poles into the slope and jam your spikes into the snow. You now have a third point on the slope and can push in and down, increasing your security. For a short section of firm or awkward snow, where a fall would be bad, you can flip both poles and reduce your fall chances with *baton ramasse*. Use the technique any time you'd like.

Adapted from piolet ramasse, applying the same technique with one's poles allows a skier to stay upright and balanced. It should not be an invitation to lean back, or uphill, into the slope. Rather, it allows a skier to stay upright and over the skis, which to the less experienced will feel as if they're leaning into the void. Here, Vallone negotiates a short, 50-plus section above the "Y-Grec" couloir. A fall here would be fatal. With soft conditions, he's merely demo'ing the technique. Were it firm, he might have his piolet out for additional security. You can see it stashed here under his pack's shoulder strap. ROB COPPOLILLO

5. We should, in general, be able to see both our hands, at least in our peripheral vision. This keeps us driving forward into the next turn, and helps maintain an athletic stance with upper-lower body separation as well as a quiet upper body.
6. We land in control, in the fall line, while minimizing momentum across the slope. Our downhill pole is planted and ready. Next turn!

Easing Into Steeps . . . with Yourself and Others

Perfecting the steeps means . . . getting into the steeps. Pushing your limits into 45-plus-degree terrain carries significant risk, though. If we take a measured approach, we can mitigate some of that risk and help others to do the same.

Vallone routinely guides "big" terrain in La Grave. Over the years he has developed his own progression for getting clients into steeper features more safely. Again, take these methods and evaluate them for your own practice. If they work, great. If you'd prefer to customize them to your own guiding or riding, also great. And if working in steep terrain or skiing it personally isn't your cup of tea, no stress—there's tons of fun to be had riding pow and touring in the mountains.

DELIBERATE PRACTICE:

For any steep techniques, find a non-consequential slope and challenge yourself on steeper and steeper terrain. As you acquire confidence, account for an error—what would happen if you fall? The answer should be one you can live with.

RATIOS AND TEAM SIZE

"You need to think about managing groups and/or guests in technical terrain," warns Vallone.

"For starters, there are two things that don't go together in that statement. Personally, I don't like the word 'groups,' and I especially don't like it when you add the words 'steep,' 'technical,' and 'terrain' to it. Everyone has their own comfort zone and set of rules, but I'm pretty disciplined about my ratios and who and where I choose to take guests. When I'm doing really heavy stuff, I'm 1:1 or 2:1 max, and in some cases I've been 1:2."

As a posse of buddies or as a mountain guide on the clock, riding in steep terrain demands a very serious look at your team size. A steep couloir might mean two people, max. What happens if the second skier falls? Can you avoid her? Help her? Is there a truly unexposed/protected regroup zone? Probably not. Even on a serious face, with open but 40-plus terrain, is

Some Days It's 50, Some Days It's . . .

I keep throwing around the terms "steep," "real," and "consequential." I've even put a number to it, but keep in mind—numbers and adjectives might mislead you. Much of steep skiing is mental. How steep does it feel to you? Other times, conditions dictate how "real" a slope is: Is it bulletproof and refrozen but only 32 degrees? That might feel way steeper than 45 degrees with good edge-pen. Steep is a state of mind. What feels steep one day might be casual the next, and one woman's "gnar" might be another's casual afternoon. Take everybody's description of a slope with a grain of salt, and keep your eyes peeled for conditions and what's "real" for you.

stopping to regroup or rest an option? A good idea? Can you actually help/ take care of other riders in this terrain?

Answer these questions, and do not make a choice simply because somebody might feel left out or you're looking to cash in big on a high-ratio guide day.

More teammates means more time exposed to hazards like serac fall, avalanches, and rockfall. More bodies to manage, more stuff to go wrong in consequential terrain. Consider if this is manageable and wise.

BOOTING VERSUS TOP-DOWN

Riding consequential terrain from the top down immediately introduces uncertainty to your day. Do not underestimate this. It's worth mentioning again: In no-fall terrain, if it's possible, strongly consider booting what you're about to ride. You need as much information about snow conditions and terrain as possible.

Trams and lifts open up riding opportunities and immediately bias us (for obvious reasons, booting is laborious and time-consuming!) toward going top-down. Ask yourself, though: What are the consequences of an unexpected patch of ice or shallow, buried rocks during your descent? Make the best, smartest choice for your team—do your homework if you're not booting.

Established on the Slope

Getting safely onto the slope is your first challenge. If you booted your objective, you will have had plenty of time to eyeball a less-exposed, more comfortable transition spot. Consider digging platforms when you arrive, and watch your overhead hazard.

For top-down descents, though, we need to get onto the slope. Can we ease onto it then transition and prepare to ski? Do we need to lower teammates or guests first? Rappel? Terrain and team will dictate our answers to these questions.

Before any transition in tricky terrain, consider your briefing with the team. (Again, we'll use "team" to indicate guests and/or your riding buddies.) Get as clear an understanding of what's going to happen and when, before everyone is perched in a couloir or atop a face. This applies to teams, guided groups, all of us.

If you're guiding, you might want to be below people to help them and protect from a lost ski or pack. Once skiing, you might want people to slide in below the group so there's less chance of a slip and fall that takes out the whole line of you. If you're downclimbing, lowering, or rapping in, let people know if they'll need to get skis on by themselves, and coach them how to do it more safely and securely. (We'll introduce lowers and rappels here, then revisit them from a more technical perspective in the following chapter.)

Often, particularly when guiding, we feel rushed at a transition. Other skiers, cold, or just mad pow disease get us feeling like we need to go faster. Maybe—but carefully consider what you're risking. A rushed decision on snow safety? A dropped ski or pack? Are you sure you're in the right entrance/gully?

Take the time to set your team up for its safest, best chance at success. Assess the terrain, keeping in mind your teammates' strengths (and weaknesses) and how best to manage everything. Let's look at some common situations and investigate each.

RIDING FROM TOP

Often we can transition safely and slide into the feature we're about to ski. "Forever Young" on Rogers Pass comes to mind as a big line, but one that offers a flat, safe transition at the entrance. "Forever" has an easier, five-star run nearby, so it's a great team-guiding itinerary because you can offer a lower-commitment line instead of the steeper confines of the gully. The adventurous skiers who decide to ride it have a safe, comfortable transition at the top.

Regroup, discuss, and make a careful decision. Is everyone psyched? Anybody quiet and nervous in the back? Check in with them and get their unvarnished opinion. You don't want to find out 100 meters into the feature that they're nerved out by the exposure! Make sure everybody is on the same page about regrouping, snow conditions, and tactics. Who goes first? Short pitches at the start? Give people an "out" if they're unsure about the day. And now's the time to employ some of those decision-making tactics—a pre-mortem, etc.

LOWERS

Occasionally we'll need the rope to get established on a slope. Passing a (stable!) cornice or near-vertical headwall might require a lower. Lowers can be faster, as they allow a more experienced teammate to manage the transition and teammates to leave their skis on.

Obviously you'll need a secure anchor. We use rock gear whenever possible, as it's more predictable and easier to assess than snow or ice. You probably have a preferred method between a Munter hitch or belay device for the lower itself—but either way, give a smooth, controlled lower with clear instructions on how to unclip, what comes next, etc. Body/hip belays work on less-than-vertical terrain too, but know your limits and practice before applying them. And no matter what system you use, how will you get down?

Often for lowers, we prep a landing zone for guests so they are more secure once on the slope. Two guides working together can expedite this process. If the snow is firm and the slope genuinely steep, having a platform on which a skier can relax, unclip the rope, and scope the line will go a long ways toward reducing the chances of a fall. Even if you have to go in first to dig a platform, then come out, it might be worth the time and effort.

Consider how you'll get down to your team after the lower. Down-climbing (with or without boot crampons) is an option. Side-slipping with an ice ax or in *baton ramasse* might

The belayer takes a braced stance, using his skis for security and sitting in a dug-out "seat." Using a hip belay, he lowers the skier until he feels comfortable and secure. MATT KENNEDY

work too. Lowering your team and then rappelling can definitely reduce your fall hazard, if you can fashion a secure anchor. Assess the situation carefully.

Keep in mind that a lower involves the rope moving over snow, ice, and/or rock. Many times that's not a big deal, but loose rock or icicles present a real hazard to the person being lowered or anyone below; a sharp edge (on rock) is another hazard to consider. When in doubt about a lower, it's probably safer to rappel.

Make the transition from lower to standing on board or skis as easy as possible. In lieu of tying in, you might use a large, HMS-style locking carabiner to clip guests to the rope. Teammates simply unlock and unclip the carabiner after getting established and secure on the slope below. A large locker facilitates ease of use with gloves, and it's plenty strong for the application.

RAPPELLING IN

Rappelling is another viable means to get the team into a feature. In higher-traffic areas like the Alps, we'll find more fixed anchors. Throughout North America and on more remote terrain, be ready to improvise your own. Some riders sling long, rectangular rocks or even short sections of lumber. Improvised snow anchors require expertise and a real sense of snow quality. In general, the harder the snow, the stronger the anchor. More on this later.

Leaving gear gets expensive, and tying off every tree or V-thread with material amounts to litter in the landscape, so get strategic and master your naked threads or slung horns. Avoid wrapping your rope around trees—repeatedly retrieving the rope damages the bark and eventually kills the tree. Do your best to limit or eliminate "tat," especially in wilderness areas. Likewise, clean it up when you find it.

When lowering or rapping, we need to decide if we're leaving skis on or off. Ideally, we leave them on, as it saves us the risk and time of getting into them on the slope below. If we can get away with skis on, we face uphill (this applies for lowering, as in the previous photo) and slide backward, controlling our rappel carefully. Extending our rappel and using a third-hand backup is a great idea, though less practiced on snow than it is on rock. However we choose to rig our rap systems, remember we're often using skinny ropes, so take your time and be careful.

Rappelers should stash poles in any secure manner they choose. "Shouldering" poles, as you would an ice ax, works, as does sliding poles horizontally between the small of the back and the backpack. Clipping pole straps to a carabiner on your waist can work, but it invites getting poles tangled with the

Arm-Wrapping

On a slope that feels too steep to ski, but not so steep you need a full-blown rappel or lower, you can "arm wrap." It's a quick-and-easy, low-friction means to descend a slope quickly but with some security. You rig the rope as you would for a rappel, or even fix the rope single-strand. The descending skier then stands perpendicular to the fall line. He holds the rope with his uphill hand and then wraps the rope several times around his arm. The rope exits the wraps and goes around the back (over the skier's backpack) and then wraps the downhill arm several times, before exiting through his (gloved!) hand.

The wraps around the arms and pack provide enough friction to control the speed of descent, provided you're using an appropriate rope. The skinnier and "slicker" (think: Dyneema) the rope, the less friction a skier will generate. Experiment with different ropes and wraps *before* trying this out on a big, 70-degree slope!

A 30-meter rappel midway down one of the "road runs" above La Grave. Vallone shoulders his poles and chooses to leave skis on. He's familiar with the terrain, so he forgoes a third-hand backup on his rappel, but he has knotted the ends of his strands. Note that he shoulders his poles so they point into space rather than into the chimney/rock feature. I shouldered mine more vertically and on my left side, toward the rock, which ended up complicating my life. Do like Joe does! Rig yourself for a smooth, relaxed rappel! ROB COPPOLILLO

feet while you're rapping, so be careful if you adopt this approach.

If you are strapping skis onto the pack, make sure they are secure and that you have a stable stance (for you and the skis!) when transitioning. A more experienced teammate can rap in first and shovel platforms if necessary. Not digging a platform will save you a few minutes, but if a teammate drops a ski, it will cost you much more in lost time—balance speed versus security.

First person in may need to "landscape" a bit by stomping off or digging out the lip of a (stable!) cornice, knocking down icicles, or sluffing out snow. You should know if there are teams below you and either avoid dropping in on them or wait to remove any hazards. Once the whole group has rapped into the top of a gully is not the time to wonder about wind slabs or notice a line of daggers hanging above you or see a team 200 meters below in the choke.

If your team will transition from boots to skis/splitboard once on the slope, coach each person to plunge poles into the snow, carefully remove his pack, and loop the shoulder straps over the poles; this guards against dropping the pack. Then he can lay the pack down so the split or skis are accessible and then remove them. If on skis, he plunges one into the snow vertically then takes the other and slides its tail into the slope; the ski is now flat, facing out and into space, so he can work on stepping into it. If he's using a leash, he can affix it to a boot buckle before stepping into the ski; now he's got a little insurance against dropping it. This should become his downhill ski. Now he slides the tail out of the snow and stomps it into the slope so it's a stable platform on which to put on the other ski.

Note: As of this writing, B & D Ski Gear makes a stretchy, extendable ski leash that's perfect for this application. It looks a little goofy, like an old-school phone cord, but it allows you to clip a ski to your boot/lower leg from several feet away, giving you the option to pre-clip the ski to yourself on steep terrain before stepping into it.

The splitboard requires a bit more care, but a rider can stomp out a wider platform (even while on rappel, put a BHK below the device for security while stomping) before performing a similar transition as above. A split rider should also consider building her board before rapping in.

The B & D ski leash, made in Jackson, Wyoming, allows you to clip the ski to your boot, even before it's off your pack. In firm snow on steep slopes, it might save you a dropped ski. If you clip the leash on before the skis come off the pack, you can rerig the leash once your skis are on your feet securely. ROB COPPOLILLO

The last teammate into the gully decides if/how the anchor needs backing up, then raps in. Once off rappel, she can hand a rope end to a teammate and transition to ski while he coils the rope in whatever fashion seems best for the ensuing descent.

READY TO SEND!

Phew, wow, OK; we are finally on the slope and ready to send! Wait, not so fast.

Maybe you're guiding, maybe one of your team doesn't share your unshakeable confidence; whatever the case, you need a method for assessing the slope and instilling some confidence. After all, a mistake in this terrain can easily end in death.

What follows is the Joey Method. After twenty seasons guiding, most of those in the Alps, apprenticing with Doug Coombs and Euros like Per Pelle Lang, Vallone has arrived at a progression that helps build confidence and gather information. Joey's description (lightly edited) starts with you and your teammate(s) or guest(s) transitioned and ready to ski.

No Matter What

Just a friendly reminder. Steep skiing is sexy, rewarding, challenging, and many other things . . . but it's also free-soloing. Falls are often fatal. Don't downplay the risks, and if you're working in this terrain, don't misrepresent the situation to guests.

Easing onto a Slope: Joey's Method

by Joe Vallone

1. Lift the skis up and down off the snow, sidestepping in place with small steps. This releases and engages your edges in place. We can feel the snow texture, edge grip, and relative degree of the slope. This simple movement sets you up for what to expect in stance and how much angulation is required for a solid steep-skiing stance.

His initial movements are merely lifting the skis up and down, sensing the snow, how much ski-penetration he has. He's just getting a "feel" for how the snow is, how to maintain his control and balance on a steep pitch. This is in "Trifide 2," a couloir just off the tram at Le Meije, above La Grave—just shy of 50 degrees with bad fall potential below. ROB COPPOLILLO

2. Sidestep down the slope a meter or so. Slow, engaged steps. Now we are moving down the fall line. Use your poles and feel the position that will be required to start and finish the first turn. Remember, even though we are standing sideways, let's keep our upper body facing the fall line as if we were still in the correct steep-skiing position. It is out of balance and counterproductive to be facing the direction of the tips of our skis when we do this. Remember that good skiing requires almost always keeping the upper body in the fall line, shoulders facing down the fall line.

Now Joey sidesteps downhill just a few centimeters. No commitment yet, just gathering info and feeling how steep the slope is and how much edge pressure and angulation he'll need to maintain control. ROB COPPOLILLO

3. Now we release the edges and allow a small side-slip. A little bit of energy and then engage the edges again. Feel the edging required to shut down the skis and come to a complete stop. Again, the upper body is squared to the fall line in an aggressive stance, as if we are about to make that first turn. Slide and stop, no turns yet. At this point we have moved down the slope a few meters or more and have gained quite a bit of information.

Reset and now prepare to side-slip and travel a bit farther downslope. He'll feel how much momentum he gains and how to shut it down. Notice his head is always facing downhill and his downhill pole plant is lined up with his heelpiece. Eventually he'll make a turn around that downhill pole. ROB COPPOLILLO

Now he's sliding downhill. Note how little he has traveled downhill on the slope at this point, from initially just standing to a couple side steps to now actually sliding. His uphill pole folds forward while his downhill pole lifts and prepares to plant again. ROB COPPOLILLO

Stop, reset, and prepare to get a little more dynamic. In this variation, Joey will take a small hop downslope. This gives him a more active sense of the slope, its steepness, and how it feels to come around in a turn and set his edges. Remember, once you're starting, it's not a jump turn but just a small hop downslope that eases you into more dynamic motion and builds confidence for your first turn. ROB COPPOLILLO

4. Now we will anticipate turning, but almost repeat the last step. If this is truly engaged steep skiing, we will most likely be applying a pedal hop or some form of a stem into the turn, along with a folding pole plant. Stem with the uphill ski and move it back into starting position a few times in place. Feel that movement out a few times, as it is how we will initiate that first turn before committing the tips of the skis into and across the fall line for that first turn.

Joey lifts his downhill ski. His weight transfers momentarily to his uphill leg, just as you would when performing a pedal-hop turn. He doesn't lean uphill or backward; rather, he keeps his shoulders square, faces downhill, and takes a small hop. ROB COPPOLILLO

Mid-hop, but notice his uphill ski maintains shovel-contact with the slope and his uphill pole folds forward, while his downhill pole is already reaching for the next pole plant. ROB COPPOLILLO

Now repeat that stem, allowing the downhill ski to release as well, but shut it down and return to the stopping position. Stem and slide then return into a hockey stop without making that first turn. We are building up to that and still feeling the snow texture and slope angle out. Remember, upper body squared to the fall line; pack and weight behind

Landing, with the uphill pole folded forward, downhill pole about to plant for the next "turn." ROB COPPOLILLO

you and out of the fall line. This is critical. Good position and poles ready to attack. I can't emphasize enough how important the upper body position, along with the poles and hands, is in this critical stage of the turn.

5. The pole plant is the most underrated part of a skier's ability, and it separates good skiers from great skiers. You can only turn as fast as you can pole plant. With that in mind, think of how fast mogul skiers turn, then watch how their hands coordinate with their feet and how quiet their upper bodies are. If your downhill hand is not reaching for that next turn, or it's lazy and moving more than it should, it will take you that much longer and more movement to prepare that next turn. So think of where your hands are while doing these steps. Is your next pole plant prepared and ready? You won't be able to initiate that next turn until it is.

6. OK, here it is; let's go for that first turn. Imagine that your feet are on a rail and where that downhill pole is placed is where we will stem and pivot around. *We will not move across the fall line.* I can't emphasize that enough.

Ready for a real turn. He has planted the downhill pole, lets the skis come around, shoulders forward, in an aggressive stance.
ROB COPPOLILLO

Committed and pivoting around the downhill pole
ROB COPPOLILLO

That is unnecessary momentum, and the turn we are about to initiate is one that we want to shut down and not accelerate out of. Feet will stop down the fall line just below that downhill pole's pivot point.

Our upper body is open to the slope and our arms are not across the body or the fall line. We want to end up in the same position, ready for the next turn but stopping at the end of the turn. Poles are now in the opposite, but mirrored, position of the previous turn. Downhill pole reaching for the next turn, don't forget to open up the wrist and show that new pole to the next turn. We are finishing this turn with the next pole plant ready, in position and prepared to initiate. This is how we will move into dynamically linked turns.

Depending on the steepness of the slope, this turn might move you a few meters down the slope, but remember, this is not a jump turn. We are not doing jump turns or "Blizzard of Ahhs"–style, Scott Schmidt turns.

Joey comes around the downhill pole; all the while, his skis' shovels are in light contact with the slope. ROB COPPOLILLO

Landing in an aggressive, "attacking" stance. The downhill pole already planted and ready for the next turn. Compare the sequence of photos and notice how little Joey traveled across the fall line and how his momentum has moved him down the fall line, albeit only a few meters in the whole progression. He's ready for another turn. ROB COPPOLILLO

And that's how you do it. Joey Vallone, relaxed and happy, showing me around his home mountain and playground, Le Meije. Thanks, Joey!
ROB COPPOLILLO

Techniques and equipment have evolved—we all skied like that back then, and Schmidt was an all-star!

Now, though, we want to keep the tips of the skis as close to the snow as possible. Stem with the uphill leg to initiate, then let the tips of the skis pass through the fall line. The lower body pivots through, while the upper body stays open and engaged to the fall line. The upper body hardly rotates even though the skis crossed the fall line making a 180. The upper body stayed mostly in the same position, minus the repositioning of the arms and poles as we finished the turn. That uphill pole should fold, and let's finish this turn with our weight on our downhill ski.

If it is really steep, folks have a tendency to keep their weight back and sit on the snow, or use their uphill hand to grab the slope. This is really bad; the last thing we want to do is sit on the slope. Weight forward and on our feet and edges. Let gravity pull you and your edges into the slope to control your momentum. Remember, try not to jump or to leave the snow, and try not to go too far down the fall line. The more you jump, the more you will twist and rotate and throw unnecessary energy and momentum into the fall line that will be more difficult to arrest—especially if you are wearing a heavy pack. A few of these should give you the confidence to start linking turns or, if you are really feeling it, carving up the giant open face if conditions allow.

Go big with your buddies, but let's not fool ourselves—we are playing with fire. We need to remember we can only do so much for a less-experienced friend or paying guest in terrain like this.

In the following chapter we introduce some technical solutions to problems encountered on skis and boards. Many of these "fixes" apply to steep terrain, but they can be applied any time we need to up security.

CHAPTER 8

Technical Solutions

Terrain before the rope and the rope before despair.

—Marc Chauvin

It's not technology that limits us. We're the limitation. Our technology is an expression of our intelligence and creativity, so the limitations of our technology are a reflection of our own limitations. We can't fundamentally advance technology until we fundamentally advance ourselves.

—Christian Cantrell

As my mentor and great friend Marc Chauvin says in *The Mountain Guide Manual*, "Terrain before the rope and the rope before despair." The wisdom!

Any time we feel the urge to deploy the rope, we need to ask ourselves: Is there a simpler way to fix the problem? Could we avoid the situation altogether? Could we use terrain to mitigate the hazard or manage the team without breaking out the rope? All of us enjoy the fun and freedom of ski touring, so interrupting the flow with the use of more complex technical systems should be undertaken only when necessary.

Another wise friend of mine once remarked, "As soon as the rope comes out, you just kissed a half hour goodbye." It's a good reminder to focus on the more subtle terrain solution whenever possible.

No matter how expert our use of the landscape, though, eventually we need the rope. On some days it's part of the fun—embrace it, execute your techniques efficiently, and revel in your Mountain Jedi skills! We already introduced lowers and rappels in the context of steep skiing. Now we'll delve a bit more into their actual execution then graduate to a bit more on anchors and belayed skiing.

The Rope

The rope before despair, but . . . which rope?

The endless debate—dynamic or low-stretch, skinny or fat, and exactly how long? You will find no definitive answers for much of your skiing and riding, just more- and less-appropriate choices. Between the time

As beautiful a place as you'll ever ski, the Vallée Blanche between Chamonix, France, and Courmayeur, Italy, high on Mont Blanc. In spring, the cracks are covered and the skiing a bit more relaxed—but you'll still want to have your technical tools in the pack. MATT KENNEDY

of submitting this manuscript and its publication, I can think of at least one rope in development that might be a significant step forward in terms of cut resistance. Others must be out there too, pushing the boundaries of weight, durability, and moisture resistance. My point? Do your research based on your objectives and current information, and make the best choice possible—by the time you read this, some of this advice might already be obsolete.

Ski guides are using everything from super-skinny, low-stretch cords to single-rated rock-climbing ropes, depending on objectives. When choosing a rope, we might ask, "What's the likelihood we'll actually need it? Will the rope only act as an emergency backup, or will it be more actively employed to lead, lower, or rappel? Will we be in a rocky environment? Shall we take two 30-meter ropes or just one 60-meter?

Consider your objective carefully. For midwinter touring in Canada, where the snowpack is usually deep and the glaciers a bit less spooky than Alaska or Asia, your rope might stay in the pack all day. If, however, you'll need to cross a bergschrund, scramble on rock, or even short-rope guests, suddenly you're asking your rope to accomplish far different tasks. These demands on the rope dictate what type and length you'll take.

Rock

Any rock on your day's itinerary needs to be taken seriously. All of us love to save weight by packing the skinniest, lightest cord possible, but if we expect our rope to interact with rock, we need to err on the side of caution and take a thicker cord. This, I concede, is an inexact strategy; rope characteristics like cut-resistance, for example, depend on many variables. That said, all other variables constant, a larger, heavier rope *probably* endures abrasion and edges better than a skinny one.

Note that I am being maddeningly wishy-washy. In speaking with rope designers and researching this topic, I was overwhelmed by the complexity in determining something as seemingly simple as cut-resistance. No one variable (sheath percentage, rope diameter, etc.) guarantees more cut-resistance, especially in ever-changing conditions. So I hesitate to make definitive recommendations here. I suggest making the best, most commonsense decision possible. In the example of rock, take more of a rock-climbing rope than you would a ski-touring rope—slightly thicker, certainly dynamic if you're leading on it—and accept the weight penalty.

Crevasse Rescue

I threw out the example of ski touring, when the rope will most likely stay in the pack—you're carrying it just in case somebody goes in a hole. I grew up in Colorado, so I'm probably more chicken of crevasses than I need to be, but if I'm skiing above cracks, I take a rescue rope (even if the locals aren't carrying theirs!). My choice in a crack-rescue rope is my skinniest low-stretch cord, because I don't expect to use it for anything but hauling. No leading, probably no glacier travel, and certainly no rock.

Rescue ropes can be anything from Edelrid's 6-millimeter "Rap Line II" to Petzl's superlight "RAD Line" to Sterling's "V-TX." They're all skinny, light, and plenty strong enough, making them less cumbersome while stashed in my pack.

A quick search and you will find Petzl's RAD Line, with the impressive weight of only 22 grams/meter. Whoa; you should buy one! But wait—for any of the above ropes, do your homework. There is no free lunch, so while the RAD Line is mind-blowingly light, it will also be trickier to use with a rope clamp, like Petzl's Micro Traxion, than a single strand of twin-rated dynamic rope (as would the Edelrid Rap Line and the Sterling V-TX). The RAD Line works, as Petzl's own testing proves, but it requires care and precision—a sloppy pull or two with a Micro Traxion and you can destroy the sheath. This will not be a relaxing occurrence during a rescue. A 60-meter RAD Line is also, as of this writing, $460. Worth it? Up to you.

You can also get away with a single strand of twin rope, like Blue Water's popular 7.7-millimeter "Ice Floss." It's way less expensive, more durable, slightly

These Germans . . . They're Smart!

In working with Edelrid over the years, I've learned a few things. First, these folks are *smart*; second, true to form, these Germans play by the rules.

Edelrid manufactures the Rap Line II, a mere "tag line" at first glance, but if you dig into the details, it's amazing how much thought they put into it. The Rap Line II indeed functions as a tag line. You can rig it to pull your dynamic rope when climbing. This is where the obvious attributes end, though.

Let's imagine your dynamic rope gets stuck, so now you've got your tag line but need to retrieve your lead rope, which is snarled above. Normally you'd be in a pickle, because you can't safely lead rock on a tag line. Your choices would be solo up, call for a rescue, or lead on a static cord. Ack! The Rap Line II, however, functions as a dynamic twin rope when you double it—it will hold two UIAA leader falls when it's double-stranded. Equipped with a Rap Line II, you can double it, climb up, and retrieve your thicker, dynamic rope. Awesome.

For backcountry riders, this offers some versatility; namely, you could have a lead-capable cord in your pack that's almost as light as a pure rescue cord. Imagine a long glacier approach with a beautiful couloir that

less finicky with rope clamps, and you can double it to lead a pitch or two—but far heavier than the RAD Line (it's 38 g/m; almost double!) and stretchier for hauling. Can you live with this? Again, decide based on your objectives.

Bottom line: For a crack-rescue rope, lots of riders choose ropes and tag lines outside their intended usages. If you do this, know the rope you are using very well—what it will and won't do. And if you go the super-skinny, superlight route, practice in snow and ice before you are in the field. You need to know how your rope is going to respond with prusiks, rope clamps, and the like. Practice!

Rock Rescue

Yes, it happens: A rider gets cliffed out and ends up needing to rap or get hauled off a rock ledge. Patrollers at resorts like Telluride know this and prepare accordingly; their rescue practice involves saving people on chairlifts and rocky outcrops!

Once rock rescue or other complicated rope techniques are required, you need to consider abrasion resistance. How will the rope behave running over rock? You probably climb a bit too, so perhaps you've noticed how these super-sexy, mega-skinny twin ropes behave on sharp limestone

may or may not end in an icy or rocky headwall—you just don't know the exact conditions. You want the option to lead the steep headwall, possibly even placing gear, if it's tricky. Most likely, though, the rope will live in your pack all day. Carrying the additional weight (31g/m for the Rap Line II versus 22g/m for the Petzl RAD Line) gives you some lead potential without the severe weight penalty of carrying a fully dynamic rope.

These Germans, in addition to being smart, are careful too. The technical notice for the rope does not recommend leading on the rope, only that the rope is capable of withstanding two lead falls when used as a twin. They don't recommend using the Rap Line II as a leading rope except in very limited circumstances.

But we all know skimo freaks live to break the rules! So, the Rap Line wasn't designed for this usage and the Germans won't recommend it for a day like this; fair enough. Having seen numerous skiers using the rope this way, though, I think it's better to address issues like these rather than pretend they're not happening.

I bring this up to illustrate the rabbit hole we often go down when selecting a rope. Lots of choices, lots to consider. Choose carefully and from a position of knowledge—don't just wing it!

or gneiss. A bounce on rappel and you could core-shot your rope, no problem. If you know you'll be using your rope on rock, treat it like a rock-climbing day. Protect your rope as much as you can. If there's very little chance you'll need the rope, maybe you can get away with a skinnier static. If you end up using it, just do so with more care and caution. Be realistic and smart with your choices.

Booting–Leading–Skiing

Often our itineraries mix some glacier travel with a steep headwall or bergschrund, then more glacier travel, and finally a fantastic ski descent. These days deliver great satisfaction because of all the skill and multifaceted decision making. Choosing a rope for this kind of day requires some thought.

If you know you'll be leading with any significant chance of a fall, the odds strongly push you toward a skinny dynamic rope, and perhaps a single twin rope long enough you can double it for clipping into protection pieces. You will see and read of banzai climbers occasionally leading on a single twin on huge alpine objectives. They're doing this knowing that the rope is not designed for this purpose, but their movement skill and the demands of fast-and-light climbing require it (think: experienced alpinists on 8,000-meter peaks). If you choose this option, do it consciously and know you are pushing the rope beyond its capacities.

You will also encounter ambitious skimo athletes leading on a low-stretch rope. Is it recommended? Mostly, no. If you elect to do this, ask yourself: "How will I belay?" "How do I account for no dynamic capacity in the rope?" "What terrain might allow for leading on a low-stretch cord?"

If you don't know the answers to these questions off the top of your head, I strongly suggest you avoid leading on a low-stretch rope. You need to know how to manage the rope's inability to dissipate energy. More homework, hire a guide, ask your mentor—but don't just grab your RAD Line and start leading on it because somebody else is doing it. You are asking to get hurt or killed.

Balance the pros and cons of each rope and realistically consider how much glacier travel you'll do versus the difficulty of the lead pitches—and then make the best choice possible.

Glacier Travel

Let's distinguish glacier travel from crevasse rescue. If we need to rope up, we're acknowledging that a crevasse fall is a possibility. At this point, we're using the rope to manage a possible to likely crevasse fall rather than just having a rope at hand for an unlikely

Hybrid Systems

My good friend Dylan Taylor, a Chamonix-based IFMGA guide, gave me some helpful feedback on this chapter, including the beta on how he's using specialty cords like the Edelrid, Sterling, and Petzl low-stretch models.

For a Vallée Blanche ski run, Taylor and other guides often use a hybrid system with ropes. While the skiing in the Vallée Blanche is pretty casual, getting out of the top station of the tram is not for many people. Involving a relatively short, but very steep, downclimb of a snow arête, many guides short-rope guests down the narrow shoulder to gain access to a flat, secure transition spot. If it's firm, they may even put the whole team in boot crampons for the steep section.

For such a short segment of the day, Taylor will take 5 to 7 meters of single rope for the arête then a 40- to 50-meter RAD Line for crevasse rescue/remainder of the day. Overall it saves significant weight and space in the pack. Thanks for the wisdom, Dylan!

fall. Early season, unknown conditions, a thin snowpack, or low visibility all increase the likelihood of a crevasse fall and should therefore have you thinking about deploying the rope for glacier travel.

What rope are you taking, both in terms of length and type? I encourage you to visit the chapter on glacier travel and rescue in *The Mountain Guide Manual* or grab a book like Andy Selters's *Glacier Travel and Crevasse Rescue*. Alpinists and skiers debate rope type, endlessly and for good reason: The data can be somewhat confusing.

When it comes to rope type, both dynamic and low-stretch cords can be effective. Testing performed by ENSA in 2012 returned results that at first glance can be confounding. Looking at just the data, peak forces are indeed higher with a low-stretch cord, but then forces drop off after the initial load. A dynamic rope dissipates some of the initial energy in the system (resulting in lower peak force), but then there is a secondary "bounce" or "load," which surprised some "belayers." (I'll use the term "belayer" here for the person on top arresting the fall, whether on skis or on foot.)

The bottom line in their testing is that climbers/skiers catch falls with both rope types in different situations. With no slack in the system and no "surprise," belayers were more effective at arresting falls on low-stretch cords. A situation like this would involve two partners staying vigilant and keeping slack out of the rope.

When belayers had slack in the system (which happens too often), they had an easier time arresting falls with the dynamic ropes. It's easy to imagine traveling with a rope team and letting a meter or two of slack build up—low vis, a corner in the track, a moment's inattention; all could result in a situation such as this.

Whichever type of rope you decide is best for you and your team, the size of your team dictates rope length(s) to a large degree. A two-person team will most likely have knots in their system in hopes they jam in the lip of the crevasse and arrest a partner's fall (more on this in a moment). This makes direct-hauling more complicated, so most two-person teams elect to employ a drop-loop system. This means a much longer rope, and a 60-meter becomes the reasonable choice.

A larger team can get away with a shorter rope, as after a fall, teammates can come forward to the arresting climber and free up cord to haul the victim (and they probably won't have knots in the rope). This might sound like gobbledygook; if it does, study up and develop the tools you need for both drop-loop and direct-haul rescues. You should know both systems, why and how to effect them, and the pros and cons of each.

Knots

In the ENSA tests, with more than 1.5 meters of snow on the glacier, braking knots arrested a crevasse fall in every test. Especially in a team of two, with only a single person on top to arrest a fall, having knots in your rope greatly increases security.

Most American practitioners opt for an alpine butterfly in a dynamic cord (approximately 8 millimeters and greater in diameter). As more and more of us use super-skinnies, that alpine butterfly knot looks kinda puny. One solution ties a figure eight on a bight, and then wraps the bight around the knot and threads through it to bulk it up. Other solutions exist, but recognize that as you tie "bigger" knots, you use more rope per knot, which lessens the distance between you and your partner. Eyeball your spacing to make sure you've not inadvertently stacked yourselves too close.

In more ENSA testing, with only 30 centimeters of snow on the glacier, none of the knots held. They simply have nothing to "slice" or "penetrate" and therefore just slide on glacial ice and into the hole. Knots on a thin snowpack or dry glacier are probably of little help. That said, cracks are also more visible, so hopefully you can avoid them more effectively. With little snow cover, be especially vigilant of

The Escaper

French brand Beal manufactures an interesting tool for climbers and ski mountaineers, the "Escaper." The Escaper allows you to retrieve a rope fixed to an anchor, allowing you to rappel the full length of the rope rather than doubling it over for retrieval, as we normally do. This doubles your potential rappel length without having to carry a second cord.

Thoroughly tested, the Escaper is indeed safe (at first glance, it looks a little spooky, but testing has proven its security) and increases flexibility if you find yourself needing to do a longer rappel than expected.

The Escaper offers you the ability to do a 60-meter rappel on a single, 60-meter rope rather than lugging two 60-meter ropes along for the day; you can see the obvious appeal to backcountry riders. And in the ski discipline, our rappels are often on a smooth(ish) snow surface, so the likelihood of snagging the Escaper (a significant problem in the alpine) is minimal.

If you elect to use an Escaper, make sure you practice with it before going into the field. You've heard that line before, eh? The Escaper works as advertised, but with friction in your system (e.g., a rope running through snow), it requires more work to release—and might not release at all.

Experiment with it to see if it works for you.

remaining bridges and seasonal snow. Ask yourself if you can manage the hazard another way—avoidance, traveling elsewhere, etc.

Snow Anchors

Any anchor should be unquestionably strong; otherwise it's not really an anchor! All of us have had to use a less-than-inspiring anchor, whether rappelling or belaying. Try to avoid this as much as possible. Snow anchors require extra vigilance and mastery.

Joe Vallone, our steep-ski guru, reminds us, "Snow is a tricky and very dynamic medium to assess. Unless you have experience building rock anchors, have rock gear, and good quality rock close, you often only have the snow and the skis you're standing on to work with. Or maybe you are lucky and there is some solid ice close and you are proficient with ice screws; otherwise you need to know how to work with the snow you have."

The easy rule of thumb is harder snow is stronger snow. Luckily for many of us, we get to ski soft snow many days a year too, so really we need to perfect our anchor building in a variety of snow conditions and begin developing our sense of what snow works for what type of anchor.

If snow hardness is trending toward 1F, you're getting good conditions for building a snow anchor. If it's light, dry, or, worse—faceted—snow, you'll need to dig deeper, entrain more snow, or "work-harden" what you've got. Work hardening involves stomping unconsolidated snow (with skis hopefully; otherwise you just posthole endlessly) or packing it with your shovel until it begins to bond with surrounding grains. This will eventually harden the snow into a workable medium. It's time-consuming, though, so reconsider whether you need to be there or if you can improvise another solution.

You will find endless descriptions of anchors, including the acronym

Anonymous Improvisation

A mountain guide who shall remain anonymous reports having urinated on a snow anchor on Mount Huntington in Alaska. This person and their partner had faceted, weak snow to work with and hoped the added liquid would saturate the facets and then freeze them into a more solid layer. The rope team lived to tell the tale, so apparently it worked.

I did not ask for photos. (You're welcome.)

Often in the mountains, unexpected solutions present themselves. Improvise, innovate, and . . . urinate if you have to.

Trenched ski anchor. The blue sling (aramid material) is a double-length (120cm) girth-hitched to the skis. This refrozen spring snow is hard enough (pencil) that a double-length allows enough snow downslope to provide security. Add a longer sling in softer snow, and consider work-hardening the snow if it's wet or unconsolidated. If you're girth-hitching sling material, note that the orientation of the hitch on the skis can rotate the skis when loaded. Try to account for this when rigging so there's no rotational force on skis, just directly downslope. At the master point, a bit of excavation prevents the carabiner from being pulled into the snow when loaded.
ROB COPPOLILLO

"T-H-I-N-X," which represents different configurations of skis in the shape of the corresponding letters. I see mostly the "T" and "I" versions in actual practice.

A T-slot, as most of you know, involves laying any long item like a ski or skis, two ski poles, or an ice ax in a trench and then a sling or cord attached to the object extending downhill to a master point. The buried object forms the long top of the "T," while the sling leaves the object in the middle and extends downhill. This is a T-slot, or "trenched," anchor. Trenching a ski, ax, or poles is relatively fast and generally secure—as long as the snow is hard enough and you know what you're doing.

"Every T-slot is different," explains Vallone. "Often they are much easier to build in the spring, when the snowpack has more moisture and the snow is more consolidated. We don't need to dig as deep. In hard snow, you can get good purchase from skis that are set well in the snow or dig into consolidated snow that has better holding strength. The con, though, is that if a belayed skier falls, for example, he'll have less friction on the snow surface and accelerate much faster down the slope. This will put more forces on your belay and anchor."

In winter snow, when it is light and dry, anyone who falls will most likely just plop in the soft snow, assuming the slope angle is not too crazy."

Ski poles beside skis for comparison. Despite being markedly shorter and with smaller surface area, two poles clove-hitched with a sling can be very secure. In this refrozen, springtime snow (pencil hardness), they didn't budge when buried 30cm deep. By no means definitive nor standardized, bounce-testing anchors like these with body weight helps give you feedback on what holds and what doesn't. Get several partners together on a rope and see how much an anchor like this will take. ROB COPPOLILLO

Bottom line: There is rarely a definitive answer to solve a mountain problem. So many ways to skin the cat. But in the end, if we are questioning anything, then overkill and a little more time to build something bombproof is the more conservative way to approach the problem. Except, of course, when time is of the essence, and the more time we take, the more we increase the hazard. There is always a balancing act of trying to find the perfect amount of efficiency with the perfect amount of security, but sometimes we have to sacrifice one for the other. With time, hopefully, these decisions will become more obvious and can be applied without overthinking.

Belayed Skiing

As mountain guides, part of our job is to introduce climbers and skiers to terrain they might not otherwise be ready to manage. That might mean from a technical or a movement perspective, but either way, mitigating

Joe Vallone, opening the traverse into the "Pan de Redeau," above La Grave. With questions about conditions and stability, an efficient use of the rope increases security and allows safer gathering of information.
ROB COPPOLILLO

hazard for another person is integral to mountain guiding. Recreationists often find themselves in a team of mixed abilities, so some of these "guide-specific" techniques can be useful, with a clear caveat: *Master the techniques before using them*. Practice, experiment, and add them to your toolbox slowly, then consider helping teammates with them.

Skiing on a rope is less than ideal . . . I said that, right? I should have said most of the time! Occasionally we push ourselves onto a steep feature or a slope with significant fall hazard or consequences, and a belay comes as a welcome safety addition to our day. This is, of course, if we execute the technique appropriately. All these techniques require practice and repetition, so find a day when the conditions aren't so appealing and, rather than riding manky snow, practice some newer tools.

Belayed skiing in particular can be a time-consuming, annoying affair for both belayer and skier, or a useful addition to your tour. First thing—you must have a solid anchor. Asking your buddy to experiment with pedal-hop turns on a 50-degree slope requires that you actually offer real security. If your anchor can't withstand her taking a slip and fall, you're asking for it.

Start with a good anchor, then consider extending it via a longer sling—a 120-centimeter sewn sling (preferably Dyneema for its low weight, smaller size, and better resistance to water) at a minimum. A 240-centimeter sling offers more options in terms of extending your anchor, slinging a horn, and precisely locating your master point, but it starts to add bulk to your gear.

Trenching skis, poles, or an ice ax relies on the downhill snow for security, so you attempt to leave that snow undisturbed—unless you're intentionally work-hardening it. Extending your anchor means extending the amount of snow (and therefore holding power) downhill of your slot. Knowing how much you need requires deep experience with building and testing anchors.

In very firm conditions, like wind-hammered snow at a ridgeline, you might get away with simply putting one or both skis vertically into P-hard slab. Make sure your skis, ax, or picket is securely driven in consistently hard snow. If the slab is only 30 centimeters thick and your ski tails end up in faceted, F-hard snow, you do not have a reliable anchor.

For merely arresting a slip, particularly in softer snow down the slope, a vertically driven ski might be adequate. How do you know for sure? Practice and personal experience. In these situations, you might be able to throw a shorter sling (or bight of the rope) around the skis. If you're using a single ski, face the base/edges downhill and wrap the ski with a skin to

A slotted ice ax in firm, consistent spring snow, extended with a sewn sling. In a braced stance, backed up with the trenched ax, the belayer can confidently lower his teammate. MATT KENNEDY

Vertically driven skis as an "I" anchor. Pencil-hard, refrozen snow provides a secure medium. Skis without brakes should be bound together with two ski straps to prevent shifting. In hard snow, skis driven to their heelpieces should provide excellent holding power. A basketed sling provides a quick master point. ROB COPPOLILLO

protect your anchor material from the edges.

Once you have skis, an ax, or even a picket securely anchored, you decide how you'll belay your skier. With a belay device directly off the anchor? Off your harness, once you're anchored? Eyeball the terrain and evaluate your belaying method, the length of the pitch, and how you'll transition after you run out of rope.

The Plaquette

If you're about to belay a teammate, we assume you have an anchor built, strong enough to handle the forces of a falling skier. How many kilonewtons (kN) is that? Ha! Herein lies much of the uncertainty with snow anchors and these systems. Snow surface, slope steepness, the rope you're using, your belay method, and even what clothing

Other Applications

In addition to belaying a skier on extremely steep terrain, belayed skiing can be helpful in other situations too. Getting on to a slope to test the snow, during a high-consequence ski cut, or sneaking around a wind slab or sketchy entrance are all examples of when an efficiently executed ski-belay might be a great idea. Don't just think of it as a technique to protect against a fall on steep terrain. Break out an effective belay any time a smaller sluff or wind slab might be a threat or a partner wants to investigate tricky skiing above consequential terrain.

the skier is wearing will all affect the forces required to stop a slide or fall.

With this tricky equation, you've got to decide what tool will pay out rope with as little friction as possible, while also progressively arresting a sliding skier's fall.

Catching a skier means gradually slowing and then arresting the rope. Imagine immediately locking off your belay on a relatively flexy ski anchor or with a T-slot built in softer snow—you're stressing the anchor by introducing higher peak forces from an abrupt fall rather than limiting peak forces by gradually catching the skier. You should try to give a bit of a dynamic catch, closer to a sport belay in the rock gym. In the gym we do it to give our partner a more comfortable catch; in ski-belaying we mainly do it to protect our anchor and give our skier a chance to recover and continue.

Imagine putting a Munter (Italian) hitch on your T-slot's master point. Your skier will make turns downslope, pulling out rope in dynamic bursts as she turns. The Munter works well for lowering, but for paying out slack on an unweighted rope, it gets challenging for the belayer to "keep up." For these reasons, the Munter isn't appropriate for a ski-belay.

A better solution will be hanging a belay device like a Black Diamond ATC or Petzl Reverso on the anchor. You would do this in "regular" (non-guide) mode. Remember, you're not top-belaying a follower as you do multi-pitch rock climbing; you're letting rope slip through the device with the option of stopping a fall. If you're using a skinny rope with a smaller diameter than the ATC or Reverso can accommodate, you need to consider another tool like Edelrid's "MicroJul" or equivalent rigged in non-assisted braking mode. Black Diamond also makes a smaller "alpine" version of its ATC. Find an appropriate tool, test it, and stick with it. Do your research.

With the plaquette hanging on the anchor and both the load and brake strands hanging parallel, the rope can rapidly feed through the device with very little friction. (If we were rock climbing, this would be an inappropriate/ineffective belay!) You should be holding the brake strand loosely while watching your skier. If she wobbles in a turn, you can move your brake hand uphill and above the device into the braking position. With some practice

DELIBERATE PRACTICE:
To practice this, find a non-consequential slope, short enough that your skier can take a (relatively) benign slide to the bottom if you blow the belay or your anchor fails. A smooth, gradual runout is essential. You're looking for a slope that if the whole system explodes, you and your teammate will get a laugh out of it—rather than a trip to the hospital.

Forgiving terrain to demo a lower. Softer snow reduces the need for a true lower, but a dug-out hole for the rope, a bucket seat, and plunged ski tails make for a secure execution. MATT KENNEDY

and knowing your rope and device, you'll be able to gradually arrest the fall or even just control/slow the skier so she can regain her edges. This will require some subtle technique and trial and error.

Once you begin to get the hang of it, practice both directly belaying off your anchor and then incorporating yourself into the anchor (more on this in a sec) by belaying with a plaquette off your body. Remember, when anchoring yourself, try to line up the anchor, your body, and the expected direction of pull. Pay special attention to how you feed rope quickly but then gradually catch a sliding rider.

Either of these techniques require a stacked, clean rope. Help yourself with this endeavor by digging a quick hole into which you can neatly stack your rope. Close the system by either tying into the end of the rope or at least knotting it. You cannot risk dropping your skier if you somehow lose control of the rope!

Old School

Wait, but what about the tried-and-true hip belay?! Certainly for a controlled lower on less-than-vertical terrain, a hip belay can work, but if you're going to belay a skier, you need to make sure the rope will feed smoothly, without jerking your skier uphill/backward. You can hip belay with low enough friction to be effective, but it requires a bit more finesse than using a plaquette. My perception is that most guides prefer the plaquette, but you should know how to apply an effective hip belay too.

Stack the rope carefully, beside you on the same side as your braking hand. As your rider moves downhill, your brake hand is out to your side so that the rope is generating little to no friction. You'll quickly see this provides so little friction, it doesn't pull back/uphill on the rider.

You need to have eagle eyes on your rider, though, as she slays her first 55-degree pitch. The moment you see her wobble, you go from allowing rope to feed to increasing friction and progressively braking. This is your "soft catch."

To begin slowing/catching your skier, move your hand forward and then across your body. Now the rope is running from the stack downhill/forward to your hand then back and around your entire body and downhill to your skier. You need to be 100 percent sure the rope around your waist can't slide down, under your butt, and sneak below your legs; this would result in losing control of the belay.

Digging a bucket seat helps secure you on the slope, but it also guards against the rope slipping from your low back to under your butt. You can also clip the strand going to the skier through a non-locking carabiner on your harness's belay loop.

With the rope running around your waist and down to the rider, you should have enough holding power to slow her fall and then stop it completely if you need to. Keep in mind

With the brake hand out to the side, it provides little friction—perfect for feeding rope quickly. MATT KENNEDY

If the skier slips or wobbles, the brake hand moves into position, slowing and/or arresting the skier's fall. MATT KENNEDY

your holding power will depend upon the rope diameter, the skier's weight, the snow hardness, slope angle, and how "rad" they're getting. Sounds tricky and full of uncertainty? You're right; err on the side of caution.

Reinforcing the Anchor with . . . Yourself

I touched on, and some of the images displayed, incorporating the belayer into the anchor. You might do this because the terrain is mellow enough that you can take the skier's weight yourself and just want a backup, or, with no other options, you're not satisfied with belaying directly off an anchor. Either way, we should know how to incorporate ourselves into our anchor.

Now we are playing with fire—I'm not aware of any systematic testing for these types of anchors/belays, and you could make a good argument for just avoiding these techniques altogether. Problem is, people see this stuff online or see an experienced guide like Vallone performing these techniques . . . and then it's out there.

If any of this seems too sketchy, for you it probably is. No stress; just don't incorporate the following techniques into your repertoire. If, though, you'll commit to experimenting and perfecting a couple of these more aggressive belay/anchor tools, then read on.

"You have to stay so far inside your comfort zone. If you are at your limit, it is the wrong time to try these things," warns Vallone.

Having exceptional movement skill frees up your attention and bandwidth for noticing terrain solutions and executing some of these more technical solutions. To even consider most of these techniques, you need to have been assessing snow quality throughout your mission, as well as keeping a close eye on your guests and teammates. When it comes time to use yourself as an anchor, you should be well practiced and have an intimate knowledge of the conditions in which you're riding. Otherwise there's simply too much uncertainty in your process and too high a chance of a system failure. (We're thinking in bets here, remember? Ask yourself: "What are the chances of a problem here?" If you don't have a confident answer, you're flirting with disaster.)

We start with the bucket seat as a belay stance. This is no different than taking a braced stance on rock—sitting behind a horn or boulder, bracing one's feet against it, then belaying off the harness or with a hip belay. In snow, we dig a quick bucket seat, deep enough that we are down in it. To bolster our bucket seat, we drive one or both of our ski tails vertically into the snow. For this to provide real holding power, we need to have a sense of snow hardness and how much we can trust it.

Now we can elect to belay off our harness or around our body, depending on the situation—whether we're headed into a lower or belayed skiing, how steep the slope is, how much our skier weighs, etc.

If we find ourselves in our bucket seat, unhappy with how much holding power we feel we have, our next step might be to pop off one ski and then drive it vertically into the snow

With a deep bucket in which to sit and one ski tail plunged up to the heelpiece and the other braced across the slope, the belayer gives his teammate a reassuring belay just before the choke in "The Silver Sneak," a couloir on Buffalo Mountain, Colorado. MATT KENNEDY

right in front of our body. We face the base uphill and into our body. This will take some experimentation, aligning the ski such that it makes firm contact vertically along our body and actually increases the strength of our stance.

The ski should be positioned so that our other ski—the one attached to our boot at the end of our leg—is driven into the snow, with its leg in an almost locked-out position. This allows us to distribute the pull of a sliding skier against both skis: the one we're leaning into and the ski on our leg. This should be a stronger, more stable, more secure position than leaving both skis on and driving our tails into the snow.

In any of these variations, we want to be aware of our ski edges and space our legs such that we protect the rope. If our skier does happen to take a slide, we want to make sure we don't run a loaded rope along our ski edge. At a minimum we'll probably destroy the rope; at worst . . . well, let's not even consider it.

Again, as you can see, we're now conjuring the Dark Arts of ski guiding. Many will argue these should be left in the realm of black magic and forbidden spells. They might be right. For any of you, though, who have seen these techniques, take a methodical and humble approach to mastering them before applying them in serious terrain. Always ask, "What if this doesn't work?"

Rigging the Rider

We've previewed some scenarios in which ski-belaying and lowering might be appropriate and also taken a look at specific tools to execute these maneuvers, mainly from the guide's or belayer's perspective. Now let's set our skier up for a comfortable belay or lower. Myriad variations exist on this theme, and many of the functional systems involve an improvised cow's tail on the harness.

Let's keep it simple at first. Our skier will descend a slope, making flawless steep turns on the slope, then

Twin Tips . . . the Enemy

You will rarely see a mountain guide working in steep terrain with much early rise in the tail, let alone a true "twin-tip." We use the tail of our skis as a solid anchor at various times; if it's too curved or upturned, it's nearly impossible to use as a plunged anchor. Favored guide skis like the Dynastar Mythic or Blizzard ZeroG have almost no early rise, making them a bit less forgiving for some skiers, but vastly more useful as an anchor.

The guide installs a sling at the back of the skier's harness for a belayed ski. He could then clove-hitch the rope to the skier's belay loop to start with a lower before having the skier drop the clove hitch from his harness and go into skiing.

MATT KENNEDY

pull off and detach from the rope. Pretty straightforward. However, if we tie our rider in at the front of her harness, not only will the rope potentially hang in front of her, it will also spin her around in the event she blows it. There's no way she's recovering from that.

The haul loop on the back of the harness isn't the worst place to connect the skier, but it will force the skier to unclip the locker without being able to see it. It somewhat limits the skier's ability to rotate left or right.

To remedy these issues, take a shoulder-length or preferably double-length sling and loop it around the back of her harness. Now you have a sling threaded around the back of her harness and you're holding both loops. Tie them off to create a double-loop master point, or cow's tail. To that, you will clip a large, HMS screwgate or double-action carabiner. Using a "triple-action" locker will be trickier to unclip after she's skied her pitch—a hassle you don't want to impose on your teammate.

It's worth talking over exactly what will happen and in what order for your skier. Let her know you'll give her a relatively loose belay to allow her to ski well, and how you'll communicate when she's almost out of rope (or agree where that is ahead of time), and then what you want to happen when she stops. Ideally she makes her turns then pulls off into a protected, stable spot; reaches behind her to slide the cow's tail around to her front; unclips the carabiner from her cow's tail; and

The guide rigs the skier for a lower into belayed skiing. He does this by attaching a doubled sling to the back of the harness, then clipping a large, locking carabiner to it. The rope disappearing behind the skier's waist goes to this locker. Then he clove hitches the rope to a locking or non-locking carabiner on the skier's belay loop (pictured here). The guide lowers the skier on the clove, then, when the skier feels comfortable to begin skiing, he drops the clove hitch off his belay loop (following image). MATT KENNEDY

you pull the rope/carabiner up to you. Easy, comfortable, and doable with gloves. Repeat!

What if . . . ?

What if you want to lower into a belayed ski or vice versa? We've probably all seen a rocky, unskiable headwall that transitions into super-steep, but skiable, terrain. In this case, you'd want to lower your skier, then allow him to start linking turns.

To accomplish this most securely, we can simply rerig the skier's attachment a bit. Start by building the cow's tail at the back of the harness, as we did above. Clip the end of the rope to it with a large screwgate (or twist-lock, double-action) carabiner. An overhand-on-a-bight is fine in this application. Now travel about 1 meter up the rope, put a clove hitch on the rope, and clip this to the skier's belay loop on his harness. You can even use a non-locking carabiner here, as it's not the skier's primary connection to the rope and will facilitate easy unclipping when the time comes.

The progression will go like this: Perform a thorough briefing as to what will happen so your teammate knows what to expect. Start by lowering your skier with him facing uphill, toward you. No doubt, this will feel awkward/scary to the skier, especially in "real" terrain. Have him stash his poles securely so he can use his hands to steady himself or guide himself around rocks if need be. You lower him in a controlled fashion, with the weight on the carabiner on his belay loop.

Once he passes the unskiable terrain, he can transition into a stable position with skis across the fall line. You gradually let him get his feet set; he can also stomp around a bit, seeing how much edge-pen he has, what it will take to stay in control, etc. Now he can unclip the clove hitch from the carabiner on his waist (we use a clove hitch here so the connection disappears and there's no knot to actively untie). With his hands free and still on belay, he gets his poles ready to ski . . . and goes for it.

Doing your homework ahead of time will let you gauge what length rope will serve you best. Trying to ski-belay an entire, 500-meter slope will be time-consuming and involve numerous mid-slope transitions, so really consider what you're doing and your teammate's/guest's ability level.

After being lowered, the skier sets his skis, gets comfortable, and drops the clove hitch from his harness. Now you can see the primary attachment to the skier—the doubled sling attached to the rear of the skier's harness.

MATT KENNEDY

The Awkward Need to Pull the Plug and Other Unexpected Reasons for a Mid-slope Transition

by Dylan Taylor (and stolen from Tony Lamiche)

What happens if you're skiing a face with diminishing snow depth? Or diminishing snow depth with glacial ice beneath? Or the slope you're skiing becomes unskiable? Plenty of skiers have gotten into trouble this way in Chamonix because it's easy for people to approach steep skiing from top-down routing. Col du Plan, Cosmiques Couloir, Couloir du Capucin, the shoulder of the Capucin, the Brenva, and Hannibal are all places I could imagine the awkward need to pull the plug.

Or maybe you're just transitioning to rappelling and need to get into boot crampons.

Here's a quick method for transitioning mid-slope on very steep terrain:

1. Place an ice screw or plunge your ice ax and attach yourself.
2. Take your uphill leg out of its ski. Let's say it's your left. Secure the ski (plunge the tail into the slope or mount on your pack).
3. Put your *right* crampon on your left foot. This makes it easy to do up the buckle. Try it!
4. Kick a secure step with your crampon.
5. Remove the right ski and secure the ski. Now put your *left* crampon on this boot.
6. Manage your rappel rigging or climb the slope of shame until you are out of danger of falling to your early demise.

Oh, and don't credit me; I stole this from Tony Lamiche!

Mid-slope Transitions

For providing additional security through a short section, the transition from belayed skiing to merely skiing is pretty straightforward. The belayed skier unclips after setting his edges and maybe even deploying his ice ax and plunging it. He might even clip into an anchor if you're heading into a rappel. Whatever the case, you pull the rope back to you and then rappel, downclimb, ski, or whatever you need to do.

If you need to provide another pitch of belayed skiing, arrive at your teammate, fashion the anchor system of your choice, and repeat. The terrain, if it's truly no-fall, will present a real hazard. Your less-confident skier may need to hang out and protect himself for the duration of your descent and rerigging. You need to manage your fall hazard too. Is this reasonable? Doable? Worth it? Balance your safety and enjoyment with the day's objective. For most of us, getting seriously injured or smoked in the field just isn't worth it.

Conclusion

Steep skiing involves pushing our limits, so hopefully some of the techniques described will help you and your team do it more safely. Keep in mind, though, that many a long, fun, fulfilling ski career has been made on skiing hero-snow on safer days. Just because the rad crew in the films are skiing steeps doesn't mean you and I have to. If you're going to, make humility and skill your foundations and incorporate some guiding techniques to keep you safer.

Steep skiing typically means no avalanche hazard whatsoever. Even a small sluff in steep terrain can provoke a fall. You must be highly confident in your snowpack assessment and have weeks of relevant observations under your belt to pull off a steep descent.

Up until now we haven't taken the deep dive into snowpack and assessing it. The following chapter builds upon your Level 1 knowledge and hopefully puts into context some structural indices and snowpack tests and how they complement our observations.

A quick review might help you before you turn the page. AIARE, the Canadian Avalanche Association, the Kiwis, and our National Avalanche Center all have online resources reviewing typical Level 1 content. In a perfect world, if you need to refresh, you should take an AIARE 1 or 2 if you're ready. Find a dialed instructor in your area and let her know you're reviewing and hoping to digest some new skills and information too.

CHAPTER 9

Snowpack

Being wrong is acceptable, but staying wrong is totally unacceptable.

—Jack D. Schwager

If I am fool, it is, at least, a doubting one; and I envy no one the certainty of his self-approved wisdom.

—Lord Byron

There is no greater evidence of superior intelligence than to be surprised at nothing.

—Josh Billings

We talk about it, photograph it, read about it, imagine what it will be like, and finally slide on it—the snowpack is the medium in which we play. Endless gigs of video have been posted evaluating and testing the snowpack. We've all read thousands of pages on how to describe, catalog, and study the snowpack. Any ski book catering to advanced practitioners has to dive into the snow at some point.

I initially shied away from a chapter on snowpack observations, tests, and maybe even a bit of snow science. First, I am by no means an expert; second, there are far more detailed resources out there. From *The Avalanche Handbook* to watching archived videos at the Gallatin Avalanche Center to taking a professional-level course, we should all strive to improve our application and understanding of snow knowledge. Get yourself a graduate degree in the snow and snowpack tests.

That said, there was a time when it seemed like every other avalanche accident involved a team that slid right into an involvement, only to say later, "Well, we dug a pit!" Avalanche educators will attest, a significant percentage of students show up in the courses expecting to learn that one magic test that will give them all the info they need, with just a few moments of digging. Some newer practitioners give near-mystical importance to their favorite test, as if a hole in the snow trumps every other observation on the day.

I've tried to put "digging" in its proper context with motivated, well-meaning students, but it's a tough sell.

Look closely: Across the meadow is a shooting crack nearly 30 meters long—that says a lot! No digging, no stopping, and you get a relevant ob if you're listening and watching. Vail Pass, Colorado. ROB COPPOLILLO

We're down in the snow, doing science, with a lens and fancy terms and everything. It just looks important and serious!

So, before we even pull out the shovel, we should review a few observations that, while less sexy than digging, are every bit as valuable and important as snowpack tests. After discussing field obs, I'll take a whack at some more detailed, "science-y" snowpack bits—namely, snowpack tests and snowpack structure.

Simple, No-Dig Observations

I call these observations "simple" solely because they don't require a shovel, often don't require a formal stop, and rely only on our paying attention and making a note or two in our fieldbooks. Imagine if I ordered a magic tool from some exotic Swiss avalanche site, a gadget that would return high-quality snowpack data twenty times during your tour. *Twenty "results" on a single tour, miraculous,* I might think! These simple obs do exactly that; they're every bit as valuable, accurate, and important as a fancy snowpack test—and far faster to perform. Do them frequently, and take them seriously.

Visual

The AIARE "Ride Safely" checklist in the fieldbook screams "STAY AWARE." It's the only phrase on the whole page that's all caps. Was it a typo on Murph's part? Colin Zacharias got carried away with his espresso maker again? No—it's a critical mindset we must employ during any high-risk activity.

We leave the hut or trailhead with a trip plan, the forecast's danger rating, a list of avy problems, a terrain mindset—but our job is not done. We've forecast conditions in the field

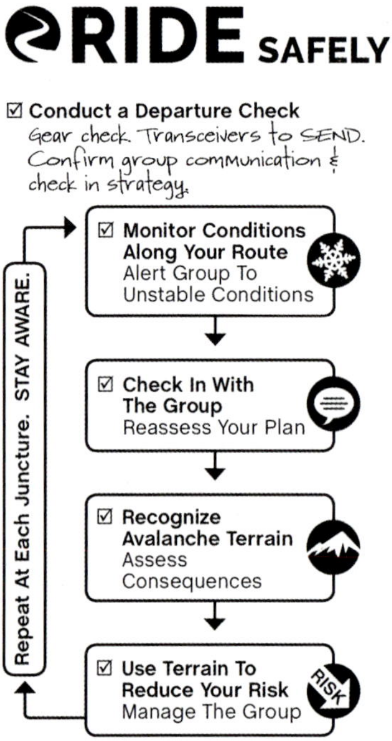

The AIARE Ride Safely checklist
COURTESY AIARE

as best we can; now it's time to localize the forecast to each slope we ski, as well as update our information as we travel. Observations help us first verify the forecast then update it as conditions change. Indeed, after the STAY AWARE prompt, the checklist flows directly into "Monitor Conditions Along Your Route." Simple obs like these keep the day moving, maintain that "panoramic awareness" on ever-changing conditions, and fill in blank spots in your knowledge.

AVALANCHES

You might say, "Duh, avalanches. Who wouldn't recognize avalanches as a sign of unstable snow?" But stories abound of skiers touring right past debris and skiing an adjacent, nearly identical path to the one that just ripped.

Note any avalanche you see and share it with your team. Savvy practitioners will record avalanche obs according to SWAG or OGRS standards, but you don't necessarily have to; keep it simple: elevation, aspect, what type of avalanche, what triggered it. If it's a path in your usual touring zone, make note of it and commit it to memory. You're gathering info for future seasons too. Take notes in your fieldbook so you don't forget the details.

WHUMPFING AND CRACKING

A whumpf and/or a crack is an avalanche that almost happened. Maybe the slope wasn't steep enough or the slab not quite right, but whumpfing and cracking means your body weight is a sufficient trigger and you have unstable snow ready to slide. Put all that on a steep slope and you may get an avalanche. Make note of where you observed either of these phenomena; when you have a bit more time, investigate the layer or slab you're affecting, if it's not obvious.

A whumpf is literally the sound of air escaping when one layer of snow collapses into another layer, usually through a large-grained, persistent layer. Bam! A whumpf is a test you perform just by sliding onto an area of snow. Fast, instructive, and it gives you solid information. Note it!

A crack, on the other hand, indicates a slab of snow cohesive enough to transmit a fracture over some

Now that's an avalanche. A 1.5-kilometer crown, in "Upper Cheap Scotch," outside Sorcerer Lodge. This was the beginning of a deep-slab cycle in the Selkirks. Two days later, a size 4.5 would be recorded at an operation nearby. Of note: Avalanche Canada had warned of a potential deep-persistent problem later in the season in December. A crust capping a layer of depth hoar had developed, and the wise crew at Avalanche Canada identified a snowpack structure with the potential for deep-slab issues later in the year. We were just (un)lucky enough to be there when it turned on. ROB COPPOLILLO

distance. A fracture is crack propagation; it's how a crack crosses a slope. Where are you seeing the cracks? On rollovers? Wind-exposed areas? How fast do they shoot from the tips of your splitboard? How far?

Note all this and extrapolate that information to your tour: Did you expect to see this? Will you be on terrain in which the same type of cracking could turn into a size 2 or greater avalanche? Terrain where even a small slab could knock you into a terrain trap? Share this data; then, as a team, update your information and decision making accordingly.

RED FLAGS

Often we teach "red flag values" in recreational avy courses. Parameters

CAUSE: Hazard from warming or rain			
PROBLEM	**SIGNS OF UNSTABLE CONDITIONS**	**OBSERVATIONS AND TESTS**	**CONSIDERATIONS**
Wet Loose Avalanche 	• Fan shaped avalanches with lumpy and chunky debris. • Rain on snow, especially on dry snow. • Pinwheels or roller balls.	• Wet snow surface from sun, heat or rain. • Air temperature at or above 0°C (32F.) • Timing is critical: danger can increase quickly (minutes to hours.)	• No freeze for multiple nights worsens condition. However, nighttime freeze can stabilize. • Avalanches may start from rocks or vegetation. • Can occur on all aspects on cloudy days/nights. • Conditions may also include increased hazard from cornice fall, rockfall or icefall. • Difficult to escape from loose wet or wet slab avalanches. Avoid terrain when wet conditions begin to penetrate into the snowpack.
Wet slab avalanche 	• Observe recent wet slab avalanches with debris that has channels/ridges, high water content. May entrain rocks and vegetation. • Prolonged warming trend or rain, especially the first melt cycle on dry snow.	• Avalanches may have rocks or dirt in debris. • Deep foot penetration through wet surface snow. • Snow profiles show slab is at 0°C (32F) and/or weak layer below is wetted.	• Loose wet conditions may lead to wet slabs. • Shallow snow areas become unstable first and may slide to ground. • Nearby glide cracks may be widening during rapid warming or rain event. • Consequences of an avalanche in steep, confined or cliffy terrain increase as surface wetness penetrates deeper into the snowpack.

Guidance and information on wet problems from the AIARE "Avalanche Observations and Reference" pages COURTESY AIARE

like 30 centimeters of snow in the last 24 hours, snow plus wind, and rapid warming all qualify as red flags. Hopefully we left the hut or trailhead with a very clear idea of what red flags we might see or what observations might represent them. A note of "pinwheels out of steep terrain" would be a concrete symptom of warming snow—and one of your red flags on a day with potential for wet avalanches.

As an advanced practitioner or mountain guide, you should have a very good idea of these red flags. If not, revisit your Level 1 material.

Attaching these red flags to decisions can be a solid strategy to make sure you don't miss something in the field and/or succumb to a heuristic or bias. For example, on a day with wind and snow in the forecast, but the timing of the storm is in question, writing "snow plus wind" as a red flag would be a good anchor to keep you watching for building wind slabs. Later, when the skiing is going off and the snow piling up, a quick glance in your fieldbook will remind you that you agreed to dial it back with "snow plus wind."

Different avalanches will have different red flags associated with them. The AIARE fieldbook features a "cheat sheet" of the most common "signs," "symptoms," or red flags associated with each of the nine avalanche types. If we're skiing couloirs in the spring and worried about loose wet avalanches, for example, we need to look out for pinwheels, "roller balls," and/or rain.

Identify and note in writing some of these red-flag parameters before leaving the trailhead so you'll be watching for them. Remember to keep your mind open to unexpected obs, but attaching some red-flag limits to your day will help you adjust your terrain selections as you tour.

Quick Pits

I'll throw these under "no dig" options because, as most of you know, they require no real digging and you can perform them in seconds. Obviously they're mostly applicable to upper-snowpack problems like new and wind-affected snow.

SKI POLE

You can gather dozens of ski-pole obs in a day. Simply flip your pole over and drive the grip end into the snow steadily, feeling it as it plunges through the layers. As you do this, sense how much resistance you feel, if the pole "pops" through certain layers, and if you feel similar (or different) snowpack structure as you move across the terrain.

This observation becomes more useful the more you use it. Comparing how the upper 60 to 70 centimeters of snow changes from the trailhead to a col gives you a clue about snow totals, where certain layers start and end (in terms of elevation), and how things are changing around you. Especially if you have a layer of concern, you can informally track it as you move along, literally without even stopping to "make an ob."

THE PROBE

Don't discount how valuable your probe pole can be outside of its usual duty as a rescue tool. With some practice and by using the centimeter grading along the shaft, you can begin to accurately identify numerous layers. The probe helps do this more precisely and more deeply than the ski pole, but it usually requires a quick stop to retrieve and deploy it.

Guides routinely employ the probe during rest breaks just to get a sense of snow height and to identify any layers they might be tracking. Often, with a large-grained layer with an obvious resistance change, you can get accustomed to "feeling" the layer as your probe moves through it and noting the depth. This gives you a very good sense of where a layer might be and if it's shallower or deeper at different locations.

Professionals often assign a date to layers of concern. (The layer is dated based on the day it's buried, not

DELIBERATE PRACTICE:
When you have an obvious layer in the snowpack, called out by the forecast or one you've identified (and dated?), spend a morning trying to use your probe to locate it in as many places as you can. Compare your findings with buddies and your local forecasters for feedback. You might also dig once or twice to verify you're sensing the right layer(s). Now you can track that layer's depth and approximate hardness throughout the terrain, without needing your shovel, and without spending too much time on it.

formed.) On a trip to Sunrise Lodge, we had a "Jan 17" and a "Jan 31" surface-hoar layer. Throughout the week my Canadian colleague and I would exchange information, saying, "I dug and found the Jan 17 layer 80 down at valley bottom," where he might've found it far deeper in another location. As the weather gods would have it, it was so cold that week (-30°C every morning; I wore heated socks!), the upper snowpack eventually faceted down to the Jan 31 layer, removing any hazard from that one.

QUICK PITS

These require a few quick digs with the hands or maybe "cutting" a block with the ski pole, but they take mere seconds and are great for investigating surface snow.

Imagine that 35 centimeters of new snow fell overnight after a typical Rockies-bluebird dry spell. Your first thought is buried near-surface facets and how well the snow is bonding the old snow surface. As your tireless teammates set track ahead of you, you can stop, step out of the skintrack, and

Eventually the "slab" atop our Jan 31 layer faceted into sugar, and we removed that layer from our list of concerns. The layers were most pronounced below tree line, so in the alpine a few ski cuts easily sluffed out 50 centimeters of facets by week's end. Sunrise Lodge, British Columbia.

ROB COPPOLILLO

quickly dig a micro-profile with your hand. It should be easy to see the old snow–new snow interface. Your digging should reveal some information in and of itself.

If you want to do a quick test, take your ski pole and saw out a 30 × 30-centimeter column—no stress; it will be ugly compared to your beautifully crafted compression tests—then tap the back of it with your hand. Does it pop out easily, in one cohesive slab? Dissolve into powder? Storm snow stay bonded to the old snow surface? Now you're collecting real-time data on what the storm snow is doing. Note how the results change over the uptrack, and record any significant changes. You can do this six or eight times on a single climb, amassing a ton of data over a morning.

THE SKINTRACK TEST

You can gather another interesting observation by merely stepping above the skintrack and traveling parallel to it, on a traversing section. As you go along, simply nudge the snow below a bit, seeing if it easily slides off and into the skintrack below or stays put. Again, it's an informal test, but you'll quickly be able to see how "slabby" the new snow is and how easily it slides off the old snow.

Many of these quick and informal tests rely on a large sample size to really get good information. Doing them three times won't yield much insight into what's going on beneath your skis, but a morning spent doing this and you will have an intimate sense of how the snow varies and changes throughout your drainage. Get a dozen or more of these obs before lunch time.

SKI-CUTTING

The guides and forecasters just gave a collective groan—ski-cutting: the sketchiest, most over-applied field tool known to humankind.

They might have a point. I frequently hear people recount heroic tales of ski-cutting and occasionally read of practitioners caught in an avalanche while doing the same. Ski-cutting is generally a bad idea for most of us. "Why?" you protest. Think of it: We are actively trying to trigger an avalanche when ski-cutting. We've gone from avalanche avoidance to avalanche hunting. Sounds like a bad idea.

The only reason I include ski-cutting here is to at least offer some guidance on how to do it, if you choose. Ski-cutting works for nonpersistent surface instabilities like storm slabs, softer (1F) wind slabs, and loose-dry and loose-wet problems. Remember from the "Avalanche and Observations" page in the AIARE book: Persistent slabs tend to be unpredictable and fail in "surprising" ways. You can't be ski-cutting a slab that fails way bigger than expected. No sane person ski-cuts on persistent slabs or deeper, persistent problems. If you could pull out a larger, more destructive avalanche, should you be there in the first place?

First, make sure your partners have eyes on you and are in a truly safe spot.

A Red Flag, but Never a Green

Often we try to frame snowpack tests for students as possibly a red flag, but never a green. What do we mean by this?

Basically, after seeing accidents in which practitioners let a single "stable" snowpack test overrule other signs of instability, instructors needed a metaphor to put pit tests in the proper context. I'm hammering this theme here, and Dr. Birkeland's sidebar below will echo the sentiment.

Imagine you've observed cracking under your skis, heard two audible whumpfs, and the morning forecast warned of reactive wind slabs on the aspects available to you, giving the day a "Considerable" rating. Sounds like a touchy day (or much of winter in Colorado).

You and your team, though, just can't resist the temptation of an open bowl of fresh pow—40 centimeters have fallen over the last two days! During your guide meeting, you'd agreed not to mess with the run, but once in the field, you tour over there "just to have a look." That turns into, "Well, let's just bang out an ETC to see what's going on." Lo and behold, you get an ECTX. (If these terms don't make sense, rewind, revisit your Level 1 avalanche course, read up, and seek some professional instruction.)

All of a sudden you and your team have reason to believe the bowl holds stable snow, right? Now hang on! You've had cracking, whumpfing, and an avalanche forecast warning you of considerable danger on your aspect—human-triggered avalanches are likely. That's three very strong indications of likely triggering an avalanche, but suddenly a single ECT trumps all of that?

We know from the literature that spatial variability makes determining a slope's stability from a 30 × 30-centimeter, or 30 × 90-centimeter, column an impossibility. That's like shining a tiny headlamp on the corner of a huge painting in the dark and asking what the rest of the painting looks like.

Now flip the example on its head: moderate danger (human-triggered avalanches possible), no cracking or whumpfing observed. You tour over to the bowl, which you agreed in your guide meeting was a reasonable objective on the day. It's an open run. Everything you've seen (and not seen!) and read leads you to believe it's good to go. You've given yourself the green light to ski the slope—and then you perform an ECT near the start zone: ECTP 22. You just got your red flag. Maybe you missed something, maybe something changed, but one thing seems likely: There's unstable snow that wants to fracture across the slope. Red flag! Ski your other option, and discuss what you missed later in the debrief.

If you allow a snowpack test to only close a run, as your "red flag," it can only short-circuit a bad decision, never enable one. In the first example, the team might've used a test to green-light a run, despite everything else indicating it should be closed. This will eventually catch up with them.

Students perfect their execution of the ECT during an AIARE 2 outside Nelson, British Columbia.
ROB COPPOLILLO

As we move beyond hard-and-fast rules and into expert/master territory, snowpack tests can add valuable data to our process. We can eventually move beyond the "rules" of red and green flags, but we should stay vigilant not to over-prioritize snowpack tests or give them more weight than an avalanche observation or loud whumpf under our skis.

Snowpack tests are simply data points. For less-experienced practitioners, we frame them as red-flag tools, but as we acquire years and years of experience, we can begin to incorporate them as data points like any other. More on this below. For now, remember that it requires mastery and discipline to apply snowpack tests correctly, outside of our biases and apart from our gut desires to ski a slope.

Second, you must travel from a safe spot to a safe spot, where you are no longer exposed to the hazard. Third, you must carry sufficient speed to be off the slope by the time it could gain any momentum—for this reason, ski-cutting applies to short sections of terrain. Ski-cutting a 125-meter slope is impossible. Fourth, you can't fall. Last, avoid ski-cutting above consequential terrain. We're all capable of blowing it, so even a size 1 in consequential terrain could be . . . uh, consequential.

Communication

Backstopping all this information collection is communication within the team and even between teams. I've mentioned the Ride Safely checklist a few times throughout the book. If you're not using it, you probably already have your own version of the process. Integral to your process is alerting the team to unstable conditions. You heard a whumpf on the uptrack? Your teammates must know this—where, when, how large and loud?

Many of us enjoy the solitude and quiet of backcountry touring, and radios disturb this. The upside, though, is the significant risk-management advantage they offer. Getting an avalanche ob from the next drainage over is critical information; the annoying crackle of the radio is outweighed by the importance of knowing there's avalanche activity in your zone.

Figure out what works for your team, and incorporate it into your process.

Digging: Snowpack Tests

Note that I buried snowpack tests at the end of the snowpack chapter. It's

Before pushing into the alpine and highly exposed terrain, the guide gathers one more datum with an ECT. Burnie Glacier Chalet, British Columbia.
PETE COPPOLILLO

a conscious choice. I certainly don't mean to diminish the value of snowpack tests and test pits but, rather, to make sure other observational and decision-making strategies don't take a back seat to them. The previous section probably felt a bit remedial for you. Apologies, but I'm just trying to reestablish "no-dig" obs as equal to snowpack tests in terms of relevance and decision making.

Decades of accident analyses have revealed skiers, riders, and climbers dying not from misidentifying grain types or weak layers in pits. So, while I'm not trying to dissuade anyone from digging, I am trying to give pits and snowpack tests the same weight as no-dig obs. No more, no less. And remember Atkins's analysis of accident data: Ninety percent of accidents involved human factors, not unfamiliarity with snow science or snowpack tests.

The reality is, many backcountry riders make unwise decisions despite having ample information rather than not enough. Many of them have the forecast, other observations, and usually some avalanche education. Often, too, "pit data" is used to justify a poor decision rather than manage hazard. In effect, skiers sometimes succumb to confirmation bias, actively seeking out information to merely do what they want (ski a run), at the expense of disconfirming data like whumpfing and cracking, other avalanches, and the forecast's key message.

Recall Gawande's thoughts on ignorance versus ineptitude. Our problem these days often becomes how to apply relevant information to make better decisions rather than poor decision making because of a lack of information. Ineptitude comes from not applying information correctly—ignorance a product of

Fracture Character and Shear Quality

Just a heads up: I'll use the term "fracture character" below, but I could just as easily have used "shear quality." We classify fracture character with the codes SP (sudden planar), SC (sudden collapse), RP (resistant planar), PC (progressive compression), and BRK (break). Shear quality, on the other hand, we classify as Q1, Q2, or Q3, based on the appearance and how "clean" the fracture appears on our column. Both systems work, and both systems get us to the same place.

There's a false debate between the two methods. Don't waste your time; either means of classification works. Note that I used "and" instead of "versus" between the two terms in the sidebar title. Use one or both systems in your practice; the pros do it, and so should we.

Spatial Variability and Fracture Character

Chances are you're familiar with the term "spatial variability." It simply means the snowpack isn't uniform over the terrain. Wind, topography, different precipitation rates, exposure to sun—all these phenomena affect our snow both as it falls and once it's on the ground.

By now, robust data proves that the snowpack can change in as little as a few meters, especially in shallower, continental snowpacks like the Canadian and American Rockies. Wind and relatively little precipitation (when compared to coastal zones) make spatial variability even more marked in a continental snowpack, but even maritime snow can vary greatly.

Point is, when we start thinking about snowpack tests, we need to keep in mind that a single column, even a large one, on a slope tells us very little on its own. Indeed, graduate-level research by Cam Campbell suggests this. A small slope of variable underlying terrain returned wildly different Rutschblock scores over just 10s of meters. If we look at score as determined by number of loading steps or taps, then snowpack tests like the ECT, CT, RB, and DTT appear (at first glance) too variable to be useful.

But hang on a sec. What varies less on a slope is fracture character. Campbell intentionally selected a variable slope in his research, and

little to no information (or incorrect information).

Lastly, if you take only two points away from this "science-y" snowpack discussion: Fracture character matters at least as much or more than number of taps, and pay attention to snowpack structure. I'll elaborate on these points in a sec.

The Tests

You should learn these tests from a pro. Videos, books, and partners on the hill might give you a good intro, but snowpack tests need to be done well to return good data. Just like using a buggy computer or a glitchy stopwatch, the data you get is only as good as the collection tool—and then we have to incorporate it into our decision-making process. You wouldn't use an inaccurate ruler for carpentry, so don't use a sloppy snowpack test for your touring.

I strongly urge you to download both the SWAG and the OGRS as PDFs and store them on your

naturally his tests generated varying loading steps/taps. This shows that poor site selection in a snow pit can yield terribly variable results in terms of loading steps (in the case of an RB) or taps (in a CT, ECT, etc.).

Before you lose hope, though, there's a viable strategy to manage all this. First, site selection matters. Do your best to select a safer slope that's more representative of where you'll ski. If you're unsure, perform more than one test and/or recognize that your snowpack taps/steps may be all over the map.

Second, remember the prior point: *Fracture character matters at least as much as, if not more than, taps.* When practitioners and forecasters perform tests across a slope, fracture character varies less across the terrain. Remember this! *Our taps might vary on a slope—but what varies less is fracture character.* Use this to your advantage. A sudden-planar result during hard taps for a CT should alarm you more than a resistant-planar result during easy taps.

Pay attention to how the fracture propagates and/or "looks" after it fails. Did it cross the column quickly and leave a clean, "laser-cut" block? Did the overlying slab "drop" quickly onto the lower column? Slide out into your pit? If the answer to these questions is yes, you should count that as a stronger sign of unstable snow and, most important, snow with the potential to propagate across the slope after fracturing under a skier's weight. Heads up!

phone. You'll then have definitive resources for how to execute and apply snowpack tests. For SWAG visit the American Avalanche Association (americanavalancheassociation.org/swag/); for OGRS visit the Canadian Avalanche Association (avalanche association.ca/).

If you haven't performed any of these tests yet, I'd recommend hiring an experienced instructor or a practitioner who's adept to teach you. She can spend a day in the field with you, reviewing execution, application, and integration to your process. You'll probably pick up some tricks to speed up your pit work too.

A variety of tests exist, and some are more suited than others for specific avalanche types. I won't go into specifics on how to perform the tests. If you're unclear on how to execute a PST, for example, get into a high-quality AIARE 2 with an experienced instructor. Let her know before you arrive at the course that you'd like

Determining Variability on a Slope

Turns out we are not particularly adept at identifying shallower and deeper areas in a start zone or on a slope. Sure, in Lake Louise, where the wind strips a shallow ridgeline down to bare rock, it can be pretty easy in places, but a few meters downslope and where you think you'll find deep snow, you often find 40 centimeters of P-hard windboard . . . and then rock.

Spatial variability introduces uncertainty into any snowpack test. Are you in a representative spot? Is your result valid just 10 meters away? Revisit how the experts urged us to manage uncertainty—by applying a margin of safety that allows for an error. Dial back your terrain choice, gather more information, or just avoid the slope altogether; these are all effective strategies. Don't let spatial variability surprise you.

to learn the ECT, PST, CT, and DT snowpack tests.

I'll mention a few pros and cons for each test and how professionals apply them in the field and to which problems.

DELIBERATE PRACTICE: At the top of a relatively safe slope, challenge yourself to identify deeper and shallower areas by reading snowpack clues and looking at how you think the snow sits on the ground. Once you've verbalized it, pull out your probe and go see how accurate you are. Knowing where thin and weak snow rests is an important tool in managing terrain. Get good at it.

THE RUTSCHBLOCK (RB)

Nobody does the Rutschblock anymore, you say! Well, you are mostly right, but let's discuss this thing a bit.

Yes, it's slow to perform; yes, it's a lot of digging. Consider, though, that the RB (2 × 1.5 meters; 30,000 square centimeters) is a way larger sample size than a compression test (30 × 30 centimeters; 900 square centimeters). It's also a fantastic teaching tool—the visual of a rider sliding onto the block then initiating a fracture (and potentially sliding into the pit; heads up!) will give students an unforgettable representation of triggering and propagation. Pro tip: All the digging required also warms up six students during a cold course.

With a larger team or on a course, don't discount how cool an RB result can be. If you've got the human power to dig one, why not?

Pros:

- Visually instructive, great for students
- Larger sample
- Fun to do and watch (Watching your buddy slide into the pit is worth videoing; tag me if you post one.)
- Great for testing weak layers 20 to 140 centimeters deep, depending on snowpack structure
- Tests deeper layers in soft snow, if edge-pen is sufficient (For example, the RB will effectively test a layer 180 centimeters deep if a rider's edge-pen is 60 centimeters.)

Cons:

- Slow and laborious, especially for small teams
- Not an appropriate test for layers within the depth of a rider's edge penetration (e.g., a layer 50 centimeters deep if a rider penetrates 50 centimeters into the snowpack upon standing on the block)

Suited for:

- Avalanche courses
- Large teams
- Layers at least 20 centimeters deeper than edge-pen
- Persistent and deep-persistent weak layers (more than 120 centimeters deep)

THE COMPRESSION TEST (CT)

The familiar and popular compression test is probably the most overutilized test out there. Before the ECT and PST came along, we used the CT to predict propagation propensity via fracture character. Old habits die hard, however, and too often we see less-experienced practitioners using a compression test for . . . well, just about everything.

The compression test identifies weak layers and gives a good indication of failure initiation; that is, can you initiate a failure in a weak layer? What it does not do is measure propagation directly—i.e., will the crack keep cracking? (Remember, well-meaning but misinformed skiers also ascribe near-mythical importance to the number of taps required to initiate a fracture.)

Let's try to put the CT into its proper context. Imagine a weakness in the snow that failed every time a skier turned, but the crack didn't continue across the slope (propagation). This happens all the time; a highly reactive weak layer fails under the weight of a skier, but the crack doesn't continue. In a compression test, you would probably see easy results, but then you'd need to interpret/qualify the fracture character to get a suggestion of whether the crack will propagate. It's this last step that often confuses decision making and interpretation with the CT. The CT is not your best test for determining propagation.

The newer ECT and PST tests measure propagation potential. This is why the columns in those tests are larger, to allow for a crack to propagate (if it does). With the compression

Site Selection

Digging in the right place matters. I'll try to differentiate between two goals for digging; the distinction is a bit subtle, so bear with me.

Less-experienced backcountry riders, many experts would argue, should use their snowpack tests only as "red flags." I alluded to this above, and Dr. Birkeland's sidebar below highlights the use of the ECT in this very manner. You've read the forecast carefully, collected observations, held a guide meeting, open/closed terrain on the day, and, once in the field, paid attention to changing conditions. At last you're at the top of an "open" run that seems safe. You've made your decision and then you perform your ECT. Stable result, no stress; it aligns with everything you've seen. Unstable, though—boom, you have your red flag.

Applied in this manner, your site selection boils down to digging where you plan to ski. You've already decided to ski it. You've already accepted the risk of being on the slope, so all your other decision making should have led you to the conclusion that it's safe. Now, one person gets onto the slope and performs a snowpack test, and the team uses it as a red-flag tool. In a larger team, perhaps two people get on the slope, but you should avoid having too many people exposed to the hazard at once.

test, we're not measuring propagation, we're inferring it from fracture character. For another couple moments of digging, we can opt for the ECT—or, for a few minutes more, the PST—and remove much of this interpretation.

This is not to say the CT is useless. Anything but—it is a fast, accurate test for identifying weak layers in the upper snowpack. The priority here should be knowing what the CT is good for—and not good for.

Pros:

- Fast to execute.
- Simple.
- Very effective at identifying weak layers between 20 and 100 centimeters down.
- Fast, sudden, clean fractures ("pops" and "drops") can direct practitioners to perform an ECT or PST to measure propagation potential.
- Widely known.

Guides, patrollers, academics, and snow-safety specialists use snowpack tests in a different capacity, though. Perhaps an operation hasn't skied north aspects in several days or has just opened new terrain. They need to gather observations and begin piecing together the snowpack on a relatively unknown aspect or zone. They're filling in a blank spot in their knowledge.

Used in this capacity, site selection becomes critical in gathering quality information. We're trying to dig in places that are representative of start zones or terrain we'd eventually like to ski. Digging in the "wrong" place would be akin to studying the wrong disease if we're trying to come up with a vaccine.

When gathering data on a specific aspect or problem, we want to be as precise as possible when selecting a spot to dig: similar aspect and elevation, similar zone, similar snowpack. We avoid areas that are unusually affected by wind or vegetation. We're trying to dig somewhere as similar to the snowpack in our "blind spot" as possible—all the while reducing or eliminating our exposure to the avalanche hazard while digging.

Keep this distinction in mind: Are you digging to gather information, or are you digging to perform one last fail-safe test that your slope is safe to ski? If you're gathering obs, do so as safely as you can and in as representative a spot as you can find.

Cons:

- Does not measure propagation.
- Won't test layers deeper than approximately 1 meter, depending on snowpack structure.
- Assigning fracture character can be difficult for less-experienced practitioners.
- Often mis- or over-applied by inexperienced practitioners.
- Number of taps often over-prioritized or misunderstood.

Suited for:

- Storm slabs, wind slabs, persistent slabs down to approximately 1 meter.
- Identifying weak layers.

THE EXTENDED COLUMN TEST (ECT)

One of the most popular snowpack tests since its debut, the ECT boasts the advantage of directly measuring propagation. This is a vast improvement over using fracture character to

How We Moved beyond Taps

We used to slavishly count the number of our taps during snowpack tests, thinking the number would give us a reliable indication of "touchiness," "reactivity," or "ease of initiation." Problem is, these loosey-goosey terms sometimes were only weakly correlated with skier-triggered avalanching.

Over the years, researchers like Dr. Alec van Herwijnen, Dr. Bruce Jamieson, and others realized that what does correlate more strongly with avalanching is the character of the fracture initiated in small-column tests like the CT. Later, after researchers developed the ECT and PST, we were finally measuring propagation on the column. Note that we do not record fracture character with either the PST or the ECT. We're no longer correlating character; we're simply testing whether a fracture will cross a block. (You can, of course, still record fracture character in an ECT or PST, but SWAG and OGRS guidelines do not call for it.)

predict propagation propensity, but the test still has its limitations.

First off, with the ECT and any test, craftsmanship matters. A thin, devious weak layer of 1- to 2-millimeter surface hoar is easily missed in a pit (just ask any student on a Pro 2 avalanche course). Seeing a fracture in such a thin layer is easier with smooth, laser-cut pit walls, so taking the time to craft your pit well will prove valuable. That said, learning how to perform the ECT is totally doable in an afternoon.

We use the same loading steps (ten taps from the wrist, ten from the elbow, ten from the shoulder) as we do with the CT or DT, and we record the number of taps if we get a result. We do not record fracture character, though you certainly can—it's not going to hurt your process or the test, as long as you keep in mind what matters is whether a crack crosses the whole 90-centimeter column on one step, or one more tap. What matters is whether the crack crosses the block and how quickly it did so.

Again, a crack that requires four or five taps to get it across the entire 90 centimeters shows little propensity to propagate. In field terms, this means you might get snow to crack under your skis (failure), but it won't continue cracking across the slope (propagation).

The ECT performs very well, returning few false results, and it directly measures propagation—the very thing we're worried about in terms of avalanching. Once practiced, riders can bang out a quality ECT in several minutes, especially if they're working together.

The ECT has some limitations with weak layers deeper than about 1 meter. With very soft snow (think much of interior British Columbia and Alberta), the ECT becomes less effective from about 70 centimeters and deeper, according to Jamieson's research and experience. It turns out that soft snow doesn't transmit our tapping very well, so deeper than about 70 centimeters in fist-hard snow, you may start seeing false stables (results indicating stable snow, when in fact it is not). With harder snow (think wind layers), the ECT returns valid results down to 1 meter or deeper. If you find yourself trying to test a layer 85 centimeters down in softer snow, consider this and add tests, or consider another test like the PST or DT.

Pros:

- Returns reliable information on propagation potential
- Quick to perform once you practice
- Less interpretation than a CT
- Relatively simple to perform correctly
- Great visual with a fast, clean result
- Relatively low rate of "false stable" and "false unstable" results (i.e., it's accurate!)
- Representative results even on low-angle slopes (safer to perform)

Cons:

- Bit more time to execute than a CT
- Won't test layers deeper than approximately 1 meter, depending on snowpack structure
- Like most snowpack tests, less effective with wet-avalanche types

Suited for:

- Wind slabs, storm slabs, persistent problems
- Use as a "red flag" test before skiing a slope
- Tracking layers over time (i.e., is the layer still propagating, bonding, or worsening?)

THE PROPAGATION SAW TEST (PST)

The PST has taken a bit more time to filter into practice with US recreational practitioners, but if we're using snowpack tests as part of our decision making, it should be in everyone's toolbox. Developed in Canada and Switzerland independently and concurrently, the PST is the only test that directly measures propagation propensity.

I'll call this the most "expert" or "difficult" test in our arsenal for two reasons. First, competent execution of the PST requires correctly identifying the weak layer you'd like to test; second, disturbing that layer consistently

The ECT in Context

by Dr. Karl Birkeland

Dr. Karl Birkeland
COURTESY KARL BIRKELAND

It is essential to maintain our awareness of avalanches when traveling in the backcountry. We tend to get distracted by good weather, high-quality skiing, gear problems, or any number of other factors, thereby taking our focus away from the snowpack. Finding a way to bring our attention back to the snow in a positive way is key to cutting through the distractions we may be facing on our day out. A perfect way to do that is to stop, put your shovel in the snow, and do a quick snowpack test.

Snowpack tests don't have to take a long time. If your targeted weak layer is in the top 50 or 70 centimeters of the snowpack, and you are skilled and practiced, you can easily get in and out of your pit in less than 5 minutes. In the process, you will get extremely valuable information about the snowpack that might well save your life. An unfortunate part of my career is that I've done investigations for many avalanche fatalities. Most times my partners and I have done a quick snowpack test, gotten obviously unstable results, shaken our heads, and wondered if the outcome would have been different if the victim had only taken a few quick minutes to do a test.

If you are going to do a test, how do you decide which one? I—and most professionals I know—choose the Extended Column Test (ECT). The ECT is great because you get a sense of the force required to initiate a crack as well as the propensity for that crack to propagate. It's good because you don't need to know the exact location of the weak layer, which you need for a Propagation Saw Test (PST). Further, you don't need to assess shear quality or fracture character, which are indirect indices of crack propagation propensity, like you do with a Compression Test (CT). Finally, the interpretation of the results is relatively straightforward. If you get an ECT that propagates (ECTP), *regardless of the number of hits it takes to get it to go*, you should strongly consider turning around unless you have some really good reasons for believing the snowpack is stable.

If you are going to do a snowpack test, where should you do it? You should try to do it in a place that has a similar aspect, elevation, and wind exposure as the slope you are planning on skiing, but your test slope should be gentle enough that it will not slide (generally less than 30 degrees and not connected to any steeper terrain) or small enough to not be dangerous. Make sure not to do your test in a deep, wind-loaded drift (such as near the top of a ridge), as those areas are less likely to produce representative results than a shallower area. Ideally, you should target a slope that is more similar to the mid-slope areas of avalanche starting zones.

While one *unstable* test result can be enough to turn us around, we never make a decision to ski a slope based on a single (or even a couple) *stable* test results. Years of research on spatial variability have shown us that it's possible to get stable test results on unstable slopes. *Only use your snowpack test to turn you around; never use it to justify skiing a slope you might otherwise avoid.*

In addition to the critically important snowpack information you'll get from your snowpack test, you may get something else that is just as valuable. Doing the test will help you to slow down, cut through the distractions of the day, think about the snowpack, and connect and discuss the conditions with your partner(s). The importance of refocusing your attention on the snowpack and avalanche conditions cannot be overstated. The simple process of stopping and putting your shovel in the snow might help you to discover an instability you overlooked, and also might allow you to have discussions with your partner you may not otherwise have had. Either one or both of those things might well save your life.

Dr. Karl Birkeland is the director of the National Avalanche Center in Bozeman, Montana. He and Ron Simenhois developed the Extended Column Test. Karl also founded the Gallatin National Forest Avalanche Center in 1990 and cofounded the National Avalanche Center in 1999. He holds a PhD in physical geography, doing snow and avalanche research; has been a pro-patroller and avalanche forecaster; and skis a ton worldwide.

Slope Angle and Snowpack Tests

I begged you not to expose yourself to avalanche hazard while digging a pit. I also urged you to dig on a slope similar to the one you'll ride. Aren't those conflicting goals? Maybe, but often we can find a smaller slope to work on, or even a much lower-angled section of terrain nearby.

Now, make sure the "low-angled" terrain isn't connected to steeper terrain above. Can't see? Make darn sure you're reading the map correctly, and don't just hope. But if you're sure of your position, doing snowpack tests on low-angled terrain might be fine. Early research suggests the ECT and PST in particular return consistent results whether on 38-degree or 20-degree terrain. (Research currently under way is revisiting this topic; stay tuned.) Use that knowledge to keep you and your team safe. There is very little reason to get out into "real" terrain to dig. Find safe, representative terrain, and do your digging there.

and accurately with the back of a snow saw requires some refined technique.

If you've done a fair amount of digging, especially in a highly layered snowpack, you know how difficult it can be to identify thin weak layers, not to mention correctly match those layers to dates and/or layers of concern highlighted in the avalanche forecast. For these reasons, using the PST as a data-collection tool presents more challenge than the ECT or CT.

This is not to put anyone off the test—far from it. We need to dedicate ourselves to perfecting it. We should continue to improve our layer ID and practice, because the PST works very well and is also our best tool for testing deeper layers.

I'd be remiss if I didn't connect some dots here: All things considered, deeper layers result in larger, more destructive avalanches. Stubborn, low-probability events like deep-slab avalanches are tricky to forecast and manage. If we're recreating in a snowpack with a deeper instability, the PST is our best means to track and test that layer. Low-probability, high-consequence events are among our most difficult decisions to manage, in any realm. Any tool that gathers hard data for these decisions should be employed. (Our other reasonable and totally effective tool for "managing" deep instabilities? Total avoidance of the terrain in which it's found—i.e., no exposure.)

As mentioned above, the ECT begins to struggle below about 1 meter. If you're blessed to live in a deeper snowpack, there will come the day when you have an angry layer 140 centimeters down, one worth watching. Is this layer still triggerable with a large load (think of Colorado's 10-inches-of-water storm winter of 2019–20) or with a warm-up? You hucking your meat off a cliff?! Has the layer healed completely? The best way to answer these questions is through observations, reading the forecast—and the PST.

This quality of the PST—namely, its ability to accurately test deeper layers—does not mean it's inappropriate for shallower layers. The PST works just fine on shallower layers and can actually be a good tool to test softer slabs. A 50-centimeter storm slab that's only 4F is often difficult to test with a CT or ECT, as the tapping destroys the slab too easily. A PST in that same snow, however, can often return valid results. Play with it.

If we are testing layers deeper than 1 meter, though, we craft the PST block as long upslope as the layer we are testing is deep. So, for a hypothetical 140-centimeter-deep layer, we need to dig the PST 140 centimeters upslope. Time-consuming, yes, but with some practice you'll also see that you're excavating far less snow downslope of the test. Digging out the long side of the PST takes less time than digging out the same width across the slope would. Is it easy and quick? No, but it's less time than you might think, especially if you have a longer saw or can cut with cord (see sidebar).

A 70-centimeter- or even 1-meter-long "snow sword" can be of great help if you can't cut with a thin cord. ROB COPPOLILLO

Once you're ready to run your saw through the weak layer, remember it's 20 centimeters/second. The blunt, long edge of the saw should not be more than 2 millimeters in width. You should cross a 1-meter column in 5 seconds—try to hit this number. And as you know, if the crack shoots off the front of your saw in the first one-half of the column and crosses the entire column, that indicates strong propagation potential. (Note, again, how the crack crosses the column: Stubbornly? Quickly? Suddenly?)

One subtle variation on the PST is its ability to test multiple layers. Imagine two layers at 75 centimeters and 110 centimeters down; you've dug out the PST, so you may as well test both the deeper and shallower layer if you can. You can dig your column 110 centimeters upslope (because you'll test the 110-centimeter layer), then run your saw through the deeper layer first. Often the column will slide off into your pit; if it does this, you obviously can't test the shallower layer. But if the layer doesn't fail, or it fractures but the column doesn't slide, you can record the result and then test the shallower layer just like you did the deeper one. Record it as you would normally.

A little trick: If you have a snow saw that's stiffer than usual, use it for the PST. Superlight saws often flex quite a bit, making it difficult to keep the saw consistently in the weak layer across the block. If you get wonky results, see if perhaps your saw is flexing out of the weak layer on the far side of the column from your hand. This often affects (and invalidates) your result.

Pros:

- Directly measures propagation (great!) on shallow and deep layers
- Accurately tests deeper layers
- Visually cool
- Tests multiple layers with some luck
- Easier to see a subtle fracture, as you're down in the pit and looking directly at the layer

Cons:

- Slower to excavate
- Need to ID the weak layer to test it effectively
- Requires some technique with the saw

Suited for:

- Variety of layers, both shallow and deep
- Monitoring a deep layer over time (i.e., do you see results changing?)
- Testing deep and persistent weak layers
- Complementing ECT results if uncertain

THE DEEP-TAP TEST (DT)

Another option for testing deeper layers is the deep-tap test (DT). The DT is nothing more than a compression test with the top of the column sawed off, allowing our taps to reach a layer deeper than they normally would.

Cutting with Cord

Without P-hard layers in your snowpack, it's often possible to cut your pit walls with cord rather than a saw. Stiffer, 3-millimeter cord, with a knot every 35 centimeters or so, cuts quickly and gives you beautiful pit walls.

For an ECT, for example, dig out a rough, ugly hole 30 centimeters deeper than the layer you'd like to test, approximately 100 centimeters across. Take two probes and position them slightly wider than the hole you just dug. You now have two probes approximately 110 centimeters apart. Loop the cord around both probes and then saw the cord back and forth. Gently, with your shovel, clean the snow downhill of the cut you just made. Bam! You just created your front wall.

Now move your probes uphill 30 centimeters and make the same cut again, approximately 110 centimeters apart. You just isolated the back of your column. With a saw, cut off the ends of the column so that it's 90 centimeters wide. Gorgeous, laser-cut walls and sides, and you're ready to test.

In a snowpack with crusts and harder wind layers, you might need to just buck up and cut them with a snow saw/sword. No stress; do your best. Experiment with different tests and cord. Soon you'll have a quick and efficient approach for whatever test you're doing. And you always know why and what test you're doing *before* you dig, right? Good!

You can excavate the DT as deep as you like. Often practitioners do a CT on the upper 100 centimeters of snow then chop the top of the column off down to 15 centimeters above your deeper layer of concern. You can do this only if your deeper layer didn't fracture with the initial test. Now you perform your DT exactly as you would a CT—same loading steps, record the fracture character, etc.

The DT allows us to identify weaker, deeper layers if we're going to do a PST and need to ID a subtle layer, or if we're just poking around and curious about deeper instabilities. Again, the DT is not measuring propagation, but it does ID layers and allow us to observe fracture character.

In shallower snowpacks like the Rockies, the DT can be tricky if you cut the back of the column all the way into basal weak layers (depth hoar). Your whole column almost invariably "fails" at the base. For this reason, try to end your back-cut in firmer

Pit Craft

On the days when the skiing is no good, your partners bail, or you don't have the mojo for a big tour, get out and practice your pits. Be strategic about how you craft them, and know what tests you'll perform before you dig into the snow.

For example, an ECTX leaves you with a column wide enough to get two CTs done. Take advantage of this. You'd rather end the day with an ECTX and two CTs than just an ECT. Consider doing a DT on one of those columns, too, if you have any layers of interest.

Time your pits and see how quickly you can do a beautiful one. Don't sacrifice craftsmanship for speed—nail it all.

Compare your results with others' and the forecasters. If you're getting significantly different results, it might be spatial variability, but don't fail to consider pilot error—we can all improve, and we all mank up a test now and then. And remember: *Sudden results trump number of taps.* Don't sweat the number as much as the character/quality!

One way to force yourself to improve craftsmanship? Video your tests and post them online. The peanut gallery will be happy to critique your pit-craft; just ignore the kooks, and don't take anything personally.

snow rather than F-hard basal facets. If you're touring with 3 meters of snow on the ground, then hot damn, you are one lucky soul—and you should have firmer snow available.

Pros:

- Tests deeper layers than the CT
- Relatively fast to excavate
- Far faster than a PST
- Allows for multiple tests with one 30 × 30 column

Colin Zacharias talks snowpack tests and craftsmanship.
ROB COPPOLILLO

Cons:

- Does not measure propagation
- Can be tricky in continental snow-packs with more faceting

Integrating Snowpack Test Results

With some practice and intention, you'll soon have great pit data to incorporate into your decision making. Your time in the pit will lead to more questions rather than fewer—good! Pursue workshops, find a mentor, and consider taking a professional-level avalanche course.

In the meantime, what to do with all this new data? First, make sure it's balanced against the context of your field observations and forecast. Digging a tiny hole on a slope somewhere does not trump recording an observed avalanche or an avalanche warning from your forecast center. Embark upon snowpack tests with an attitude of "Why am I wrong?" rather than to confirm your decision. Actively ask yourself, "What have I missed?" when you start digging.

Bottom line: The forecasters know more than most of us about weather, avalanches, weak layers, and snow-pack tests—listen to them! Don't let a couple snowpack tests overrule your local bulletin.

COMPARE AND VALIDATE

Take your new information and competence into the field and compare it to what you are seeing. Widespread whumpfing and cracking should be easily verified with a few snowpack tests. Once you start accurately verifying what you're seeing, try to identify in your guide meeting what tests will be effective in the field that day: What problems are you facing? Where? How

Tools of the Trade

Once you are locked and loaded for snowpack tests, pause to evaluate your tools. A snow saw is great, but do you have a cutting cord too? Cutting your columns with a long section of 3-millimeter cord, with knots tied every 35 centimeters or so, can give you beautiful pit walls. A longer "snow sword"—a snow saw as much as 1 meter long—also works well in a snowpack cursed with thick wind slabs and/or sun crusts.

Over time you'll have a good idea about what works and what doesn't work for cutting. In the Columbias, cutting deep, uniform ECTs with a cord works great. On Colorado's Front Range, not so much. Experiment with your tools and see what you need on what kind of days, and with what problems.

might they behave in snowpack tests? Answer these questions in the meeting, then see if your predictions and tests were valid.

TRENDS

Snowpacks tests are especially useful for gauging trends. A single snowpack test every two weeks should be used as Dr. Birkeland recommends—a red flag and nothing more. Now imagine if you're lucky and get to tour eight times over three weeks. If you perform one or two quality snowpack tests each of those days, in similar terrain and with an eye toward the same layers, you will have amassed enough information to observe a trend.

Particularly with deeper, more stubborn layers, snowpack data can

Deep-Slab Cycles

I've mentioned in a few places the tricky, unpredictable, and usually lethal beast: the deep-persistent slab. Researchers are still decoding this problem, looking for similarities between cycles, but these are confounding problems. Deep slabs often don't respond to explosives; rarer still do they trigger under the weight of a skier. We usually "get away with it," which is part of the problem with recreationists—you might see dozens of people skiing slopes forecast to have a deeper problem. After a few days of watching everyone else get turns, you think, *It has to be safe! Look at all those jokers getting the goods!*

It appears as though a few things suggest a deep-slab cycle. First, a dormant but identifiable weak layer persists deep enough in the snowpack that it will produce a size 3 or greater. Often the first big warm-up of the season reawakens this layer. Deep-slab avalanches within the region might also predict other deep-slab avalanches farther away. We discount wind slabs 50 kilometers away, opting to identify them on the drainage- or slope-scale. There is some anecdotal evidence accumulating that suggests we pay attention to deep-slab avalanches, even if they are farther away than we usually take note of with other avalanche types.

This will be an area of hot research over the coming decades, but in the meantime, remember: Deep-slab avalanches are rarely survivable, and they are highly unpredictable. With so much uncertainty surrounding them, the best option is usually to avoid the terrain in which they are forecast.

DELIBERATE PRACTICE:
Verbalize
As you begin to apply snowpack tests in the field, before you dig, verbalize a few things with teammates. First, why are you digging? Second, what do you expect to see? Third, what test(s) will you do and, most important, why? Lastly, be ruthless with your process and results. If you're routinely surprised by the snowpack, what are you missing?

be very useful. Natural and human-triggered avalanching may have all but stopped, and along with it whumpfing and cracking. For a buried surface-hoar layer, though, it probably hasn't gone away—it's just "dormant" and hard to trigger. Snowpack tests (particularly DTs and PSTs in the case of a deep-slab problem, to stick with our example) may provide useful information when very little else helps. Share and compare your trends with others and your forecast center. If your forecasters have any spare time, they might even throw you a bone in the form of some feedback.

USE YOUR PITS TO MAINTAIN AWARENESS

The AIARE Ride Safely checklist urges you to stay aware. Easy to say, sure, so challenge yourself to identify in your morning meeting *specifically* how you'll do it. When using a snowpack test, make sure it matches the day's avalanche problem, and then do it. Attach a specific snowpack test to a forecast problem. If the forecast has wind slabs on the list, commit to quick pits, observations, and perhaps an ECT in a representative spot. What results do you expect? What results will nudge you onto lower-angled, less-exposed slopes?

PERFECT THE PIT . . . BUT THEN ASK, *DO I NEED TO DIG?*

Digging pits has a certain sexiness to it. It makes us look like we know what we're doing and gives us (for better or worse, often worse!) a result we can point to as proof of what's going on around us. Ask yourself, though: *Do I really need to dig?* If you've experienced widespread whumpfing and read of several reported skier-triggered avalanches in your zone the day before, do you really need to dig to make a decision about terrain? Now, you may dig to verify the forecast and investigate what the layers look like and how they behave, but if these other observations are conveying clear information, wouldn't another run on a low-angled, untracked meadow be more fun than digging in a hole?

If you're guiding, you already know the answer to the above question. Clients don't like to stand and watch someone shovel. Frost-nipped toes and noses don't help the tip at the end of the day. And you should have a very, very good idea of the snowpack before leaving the trailhead. Will you even need to dig?

AND THAT SECOND CRITICAL POINT? (SNOWPACK STRUCTURE!)

I mentioned above that there were two critical points to remember when incorporating snowpack data into our decision making. First, fracture character matters more when predicting skier-triggered avalanching; second, snowpack structure is an invaluable tool in identifying unstable snow. Huh?

Snowpack structure is fancy-speak for how our snowpack is built. One huge, cohesive, firm layer or a poop-sandwich of facets, crusts, buried surface hoar, and wind layers? We get a rudimentary sense of structure by probing with our ski pole or probe pole. Do we feel just a couple layers, all relatively uniform, or does our probe hit a crust then pop through low-resistance snow, only to hit another hard layer?

To get a better sense of structure, we need to dig. Once we dig, we can identify certain "indices" or characteristics of the snowpack to see if it's inherently strong or weak. How hard are the layers? What grain types make up the layers? Are they persistent grain types? How large are these grains? Just by digging into the snow, we begin to gather info on structure. Did we make easy progress down to 1 meter, or did we find a hard layer that required chopping through? And below that? Did sugar-snow pour out into our pit? By digging, we "ask" these questions and get answers.

Add a bit more time to fashion a clean pit wall and then identify layers and grains, and you'll glean even more data, amassing those "lemons," or "yellow flags," that can help you determine how strong or weak your snowpack is.

So what? you ask. In the AIARE fieldbook, back in the snowpack observations pages that start on page 44, you'll see a sentence that draws on research from Drs. Jamieson and Joerg Schweizer. It reads, "When identifying weak layers 'focus on soft coarse-grained layers, especially when just above or just below a harder fine-grained layer, and between 20 and 85cm below the snow surface.'"

This sentence functions as shorthand for lemons, or yellow flags. It warns us of snowpack structure associated with weak snow and avalanching. Soft, coarse-grained layers are usually facets or surface hoar. There's your

Common weak layer characteristics:

- Weak layer is softer (less than 1F resistance)
- Weak layer has angular, sugary grains (SH, DH, FC)
- Weak layer grains are large (>1mm)
- Layer above or below has finer grains (>0.5mm)
- Layer above or below is a step firmer
- Weak layer is found less than 1m deep

When identifying weak layers "*focus on soft coarse-grained layers, especially when just above or just below a harder fine grained layer, and between 20 and 85cm below the snow surface.*"
B. Jamieson, J. Schweizer. Dec. 2015.

The AIARE prompt for "structural indices" associated with a weak snowpack
COURTESY AIARE

weak snow. If they're above or below a harder, fine-grained layer (a slab or crust), there's your layering between weak and strong snow. And if these layers are found between 20 and 85 centimeters in depth, it's easily triggerable by a skier's weight. Boom! Those yellow flags add up to a snowpack prone to avalanching.

Above this sentence, the AIARE fieldbook provides more specific yellow flags for snowpack structure. Keep this checklist handy if/when you're going to dig. Two, three, four yellow flags and they become your red flag. You're dealing with an unstable snowpack.

In a new zone or a zone without an avalanche bulletin, establishing structure is your baseline. Get a sense of how layered the snowpack is and what yellow flags are present, and you're a long way toward building awareness of what snowpack you're dealing with. And remember to balance this information with equally important observations like whumpfing, cracking, and of course avalanching!

In a zone where you have more information, like your home area with a local forecast center, monitoring snowpack structure helps you track trends and address uncertainty. Often in a large forecast zone, the bulletin will need to address huge variability over hundreds of miles. Colorado's Front Range zone, for example, goes from the Wyoming border to well south of Denver, more than 125 miles. The forecasters may warn of buried facets, for example, or any weak layer on which they've observed avalanche activity. Accounting for variability over such a huge area, they'll warn of finding similar structure on a slope. They simply can't be sure the same weak layer on Cameron Pass is present on Pikes Peak. If you dig down and find those facets, they might warn, you are playing with fire. They've given you a specific, identifiable weak layer for you to identify in your pit.

As a mountain guide, going into the field without knowledge of that layer and an idea of how to find it would be negligent. As an educated, elite recreationist, it would be poor planning and set you up for missing a critical observation in the field. Either way, you're using snowpack structure to inform your decision making. It's identifiable in a pit, verifiable in the field in minutes, a concrete datum attached to the danger rating.

Snowpack structure trumps almost every other observation we can make. If you have snowpack structure that reveals strong-over-weak snow, you are set up for avalanches. This is as important as the danger rating or snowpack tests or field obs. When uncertain about avalanching and unstable snow, defer to snowpack structure, structural indices (as listed in the AIARE fieldbook), and lemons, or yellow flags. Whatever you call them, pay attention to snowpack structure, especially if you're short on other observations or data to use.

Obs, Digging, and Panoramic Awareness

By now you're either psyched to go apply some snowpack tests or you're fried on the whole matter and your shovel looks like the enemy. I urge you to take the middle path and simply put your non-digging field observations, quick pits, and snowpack tests into a thorough process that balances them in the context of better decision making.

We strive to create that panoramic awareness from those tiny facets in our snow pit to distant overhead hazard to weather phenomena to the subtle dynamics of our team. Snow information is simply one piece of the puzzle, made up of our observations and digging.

Pay attention to fracture character and structural indices, but remember that an observed avalanche is an instant red flag and gives you a tremendous amount of information too. Put it all together as part of your repeatable process. It all matters, and you should be taking it all in.

Conclusion

The most important thing is this: to sacrifice what you are now for what you can become tomorrow.

—Shannon Alder

One of the dominant suggestions for success throughout this book is to nurture an attitude of skepticism over optimism. . . . Skepticism, when applied inwardly as introspection, is nothing more than humility.

—Bruce Kay

But I also have to say, for the umpty-umpth time, that life isn't fair. It's just fairer than death, that's all.

—William Goldman, *The Princess Bride*

The End

It's a tough, fun, confounding, dangerous, and rewarding business, this backcountry thing. Make it your work, and it's all that and more. Leaving it to chance or figuring it out "on the fly" doesn't seem like the way. These pages and photos amount to just one way of doing it more safely—an algorithm, a process, a method, or a recipe for skinny folks sliding around on skis and snowboards without hurting themselves. Nothing more. Use it, proclaim it your own, take credit for it with your friends. Improve upon it.

And, hey, disregard what doesn't work for you—but pause a minute before you do.

This book offers hard-won solutions and insights from people way smarter and better than I. I merely had the crafty little idea to steal their work, slap my name on it, and earn a couple years of slacking after the book comes out. Give their words careful consideration.

I've had exceptional mentors and teachers, many of whom helped with this project. This is their book more than mine. And these are successful, wise people, every one of 'em.

Hanging with a few jokers, having a blast, and keeping one another safe. Pretty simple, but pretty tricky too. A good team working together in the "Silver Sneak" on Buffalo Mountain, Colorado.
MATT KENNEDY

The collected knowledge presented here represents the best way I know of to have fun and stay safer in the backcountry.

We work and recreate in an error-prone, complex activity. We're fallible humans. We fall prey to our biases more than we realize. A handful of visionaries have begun to help us upgrade our operating system. Now it's up to us to download, install, and run the system. Use the algorithm. Let me know how it goes. I'm easy to find, and I'm interested.

The Chapters

Looking back, it's interesting, months after writing some of these chapters, to let them settle out in my mind. In a sentence or two, what should readers take from each chapter?

I think of my nephew, Henry, 21 years old at the moment, who has just started his guiding career, on Mount Rainier. He'll be a few courses into his education with the AMGA by the time this book comes out. If I could get him to take one or two things from each chapter, what would they be?

Trip Planning. Do it and do it well. This is the foundation of our repeatable process. Trip planning anchors us in evidence and conditions, before we're standing atop 1,000 meters of untracked goodness. Planning helps us pre-bias and de-bias and identify uncertainty . . . but only if we do it. Leave the party early, wake up before your teammates, spend a little extra time. It's the professional thing to do.

The Up. Keep your angles low, collect observations, leave some gas in the tank. Traveling uphill efficiently and elegantly is more than half the experience. So deliver on it. You'll know you're good when teammates and guests remember your uptrack as well as the fantastic descents. Keep exposure low, and cultivate that panoramic awareness.

The Down. Use terrain, say less, harvest the fruits of your great planning and expert uptrack on the down. Enjoy your descent; you earned it! Everything moves quickly, so error correct early and remember, "Hope is not a viable risk-management strategy." Inspire with your skiing.

The Debrief. It's one of the most productive things you can do, debriefing with smart teammates. Improve a bit every day. It doesn't have to be a lot, but debrief daily. Process before outcome. Never fail to see your near misses. Identify your shortcomings, even when they're hard. Fix them. You'll be a Jedi by . . . well, someday.

The Team. Be selective, take care of your teammates, be generous with their mistakes, and identify your own. A good team is your body armor, your virus protection, your blind-spot monitoring system. Build your team and nurture it. Be willing to have your mind changed: strong opinions, weakly held. Remember that you might be wrong; give praise when it's deserved. Be an awesome teammate. Listen!

Decision Making. Practice. Sound, better decision making will save your hide in everything you do. Assume you're blowing it and look for the reasons. Cultivate skepticism; laugh at your own confidence. Think in bets.

The kid. My nephew, Henry Coppolillo, showing me around Bridger Bowl, Montana, during his first day as a working guide. He was 9. I didn't tip.

REBECCA YARMUTH

Time flies. Henry and me years later on Loft Peak, high above the Burnie Glacier Chalet outside Smithers, British Columbia. This time I was guiding—he didn't tip. PETE COPPOLILLO

Put time into your decision architecture. Just remember, if Kahneman says he's not very good with a Nobel Prize and eight decades under his belt, we probably suck too. Account for that with a margin for error.

Steep Skiing. Buyer beware. Steep skiing requires all the above, plus great movement skills, even better prep, and the acknowledgment that you're asking for it. And guiding steep skiing? Probably a bad idea, but if you're going to do it, be very, very good.

Technical Solutions. Keep it simple when you can; for everything else, slow down. Find a mentor like Marc Chauvin and sponge everything you can from him. Heckle him now and again too. Be good with the rope, and try to use it less than the next guide. Terrain before the rope, and the rope before despair.

Snowpack. Develop a panoramic awareness of everything around you, most of all snow. Listen to your field observations and acknowledge what's going on. Dig when you have to, then be a scientist and craft your pits well. As you assemble your shovel, ask yourself, Why am I wrong? If you ever feel like you're totally nailing it, remind yourself that it borders on impossible. Second-guess your decisions using the snowpack.

Acknowledgments

After all this, I'm going skiing. My bro and I have Sorcerer Lodge reserved for our fiftieth. Oh yeah!

Thanks to everybody who helped make the book happen—mentors, guests, and family alike.

Sincere thanks for everyone's photographic contributions, most of all Matt Kennedy and Mahting Putelis. Thanks for the friendship and being part of the team.

Fred Engel, my writing mentor and critic, I miss you. Thanks for all the hard feedback and great times. I'm still a Golden State fan. You helped every one of your students and made our writing a bit less clunky too.

For the crew who wrote sidebars and offered advice—Karl Birkeland, Colin Zacharias, Sheldon Kerr, Mike Hattrup, Rob Hopkins, Benja Glatz, Alex Do, Ken Wylie,

Matt Kennedy (right) contributed a ton of beautiful images for the book. He's pictured here on the Gran Paradiso on a stormy morning in spring 2018 with his partner, Ali Vagnini (center). Thanks for the good turns and friendship! MATT KENNEDY

Skier, hunter, photographer, founder of Hunt to Eat, my travel partner and good buddy, Mahting Putelis MAHTING PUTELIS

Marc Chauvin, Joe Stock, Bruce Kay, Tom Murphy—many thanks. You helped put some serious cred into the book.

Many friends and mentors—Brian Lazar, Blase Reardon, Dylan Taylor, Wil Rickards, Mikey Arnold, Joe Vallone—assisted with suggestions, clarifications, and ideas. I owe you.

I'm off to start packing for Canada, to teach with Colin, the Snow Yoda. I'll take notes.

Suggested Reading

"Analyzing Cockpit Communications: The Links Between Language, Performance, Error, and Workload," J. Bryan Sexton and Robert L. Hemreich, *Journal of Human Performance in Extreme Environments,* 2000

Autonomy, Mastery, and Purpose: In the Avalanche Patch, Bruce Kay, 2015

Black Box Thinking: Why Most People Never Learn from Their Mistakes–But Some Do, Matthew Syed, Portfolio, 2015

"Can We Rely on Our Intuition?" *Scientific American,* August 2019, https://www.scientificamerican.com/article/can-we-rely-on-our-intuition/

"Crevasse Falls: Do Brake Knots Work?" ENSA testing, 2012. YouTube: https://www.youtube.com/watch?v=IgNR-VZMwHo

Decide and Deliver: 5 Steps to Breakthrough Performance in Your Organization, Marcia W. Blenko, Paul Rogers, Michael C. Mankins, Harvard Business Press, 2010

Dialogue Mapping: Building Shared Understanding of Wicked Problems. Jeffrey Conklin, Wiley Publishing, 2006

"Dilemmas in a General Theory of Planning," Horst W. J. Rittel and Melvin M. Webber, *Policy Sciences,* 1973

Evidence of Heuristic Traps in Avalanche Accidents, McCammon, 2002 ISSW

Free Skiing: How to Adapt to the Mountain, Jimmy Oden, Choucas Productions, 2007

Glacier Travel and Crevasse Rescue, Andy Selters, Mountaineers, 2003

"Group Size and the Trust, Cohesion, and Commitment of Group Members." Shane Soboroff, PhD (Doctor of Philosophy) thesis, University of Iowa, 2012

Horse Soldiers: The Extraordinary Story of a Band of US Soldiers Who Rode to Victory in Afghanistan, Doug Stanton, Scribner, 2010

How We Decide, Jonah Lehrer, Mariner Books, 2009

Human Error, James Reason, Cambridge University Press, 1990

Influence: The Psychology of Persuasion, Robert Cialdini, Harper Business, 2006

"Judgment under Uncertainty: Heuristics and Biases," Amos Tversky and Daniel Kahneman, *Science,* 1974

Mindset: The New Psychology of Success, Carol Dweck, Ballantine Books, 2007

Open to Outcome: A Practical Guide for Facilitating & Teaching Experiential Reflection. Micah Jacobson and Mari Ruddy, Wood 'N' Barnes Publishing, 2004

"Perspective From a Humbled Skier: Lessons Learned from the Pucker Face Avalanche," *The Avalanche Review,* April 2014

Predictably Irrational: The Hidden Forces That Shape Our Decisions, Dan Ariely, Harper, 2009

"Psychological Safety and Learning Behavior in Work Teams," Amy Edmonson, *Administrative Science Quarterly,* 2009

"Risk Management—Guidelines," https://www.iso.org/iso-31000-risk-management.html

"Senator Beck" accident report, https://avalanche.state.co.us/caic/acc/acc_report.php?acc_id=685&accfm=inv

"Snoopy's Near-Miss," Rob Coppolillo, *The Avalanche Review,* December 2017, https://static1.squarespace.com/static/59d2a0f0e9bfdf20d6d654b7/t/5d72c606eb84be303e2435cf/1567802899861/TAR_36-2_low+%281%29.pdf

Sources of Power: How People Make Decisions, Gary Klein, MIT Press, 1999

"Strong Opinions, Weakly Held," Dr. Paul Saffo, 2008, https://www.saffo.com/02008/07/26/strong-opinions-weakly-held/

Talent Is Overrated: What Really Separates World-Class Performers from Everybody Else, Geoff Colvin, Portfolio, 2010

The Avalanche Handbook, Schaerer and McClung, The Mountaineers, 2006

"The Better the Team, the Safer the World: Golden Rules of Group Interaction in High Risk Environments: Evidence Based Suggestions for Improving Performance" Ladenburg and Rüschlikon, Gottlieb Daimler and Karl Benz Foundation, Swiss Re Centre for Global Dialogue, 2004

The Debrief Imperative, William Duke and James Murphy, Fast Pencil Premiere, 2014

"The Effectiveness of Avalanche Airbags," Haegeli, Falk, Procter, Zweifel, Jarry, Logan, Kronholm, Biskupič, Brugger; 2014, https://pdfs.semanticscholar.org/0988/07cf2ad887ef713706b3e5539e34bfd58b07.pdf

The Fearless Organization: Creating Psychological Safety in the Workplace for Learning, Innovation, and Growth, Amy Edmonson, Wiley, 2018

The Field Guide to Understanding "Human Error," Sidney Dekker, CRC Press, 2014

The Invisible Gorilla: How Our Intuitions Deceive Us, Christopher Chabris and Daniel Simons, Harmony, 2011

"The Propagation Saw Test (PST): A Review of Its Development, Applications, and Recent Research," Gauthier and Jamieson, 2012 ISSW, http://arc.lib.montana.edu/snow-science/objects/issw-2012-1047-1053.pdf

"The Role of Deliberate Practice in the Acquisition of Expert Performance," Ericsson, Krampe, Tesch-Römer, *Psychological Review,* 1993

The Success Equation: Untangling Skill and Luck in Business, Sports, and Investing, Michael Mauboussin, Harvard Business Review Press, 2012

Think Twice: Harnessing the Power of Counterintuition, Michael Mauboussin, Harvard Business Review Press, 2012

Thinking in Bets: Making Smarter Decisions When You Don't Have All the Facts, Annie Duke, Portfolio, 2018

"What Google Learned From its Quest to Build the Perfect Team," Charles Duhigg, the *New York Times*, 2016, https://www.nytimes.com/2016/02/28/magazine/what-google-learned-from-its-quest-to-build-the-perfect-team.html?auth=login-email&login=email

Meet Your Guide

Rob Coppolillo was among the first one hundred Americans to earn international certification in mountain guiding through the AMGA. He coauthored *The Mountain Guide Manual* and has published hundreds of magazine articles in *Climbing, Skiing,* and *Elevation Outdoors*. Rob guides throughout North America and Europe, on skis, on rock, and in the high mountains. He lives in Chamonix, France, where he and his wife are raising twin boys, Dominic and Luca.